Thurber's
Anatomy
of
Confusion

THURBER'S
ANATOMY
OF
CONFUSION

Catherine McGehee Kenney

ARCHON BOOKS
1984

Printed in the United States of America

Illustrations are used by permission of Mrs. James Thurber from the following sources:

Let Your Mind Alone © 1937 James Thurber. © 1965 Helen W. Thurber and Rosemary T. Sauers. Published by Harper & Row.

My Life and Hard Times © 1933, 1961 James Thurber. Published by Harper & Row.

Men, Women and Dogs © 1943 James Thurber. © 1971 Helen W. Thurber and Rosemary T. Sauers. Published by Harcourt Brace Jovanovich.

The Beast in Me and Other Animals © 1948 James Thurber. © 1976 Helen W. Thurber and Rosemary T. Sauers. Published by Harcourt Brace Jovanovich.

Lines from "Ash-Wednesday" in *Collected Poems 1909–1962* by T. S. Eliot, copyright 1936 by Harcourt Brace Jovanovich, Inc.; copyright © 1963, 1964 by T. S. Eliot. Reprinted by permission of Harcourt Brace Jovanovich, Inc., and Faber and Faber Publishers.

Lines from "East Coker" in *Four Quartets*, copyright 1943 by T. S. Eliot; renewed 1971 by Esme Valerie Eliot. Reprinted by permission of Harcourt Brace Jovanovich, Inc., and Faber and Faber Publishers.

Lines from "The Second Coming" from *Collected Poems of W. B. Yeats*. Copyright 1924 by Macmillan Publishing Company, renewed 1952 by Bertha Georgie Yeats. Reprinted by permission of Macmillan Publishing Company, Michael B. Yeats, and Macmillan, London, Limited.

Lines from *The Tempest*, by William Shakespeare, used by permission of Penguin Books.

The paper in this book meets the guidelines for permanence and durability of the Committee of Production Guidelines for Book Longevity of the Council on Library Resources.

Library of Congress Cataloguing in Publication Data

Kenney, Catherine McGehee, 1948–
    Thurber's anatomy of confusion.

    Bibliography: p.
    Includes index.
    1. Thurber, James, 1894–1961—Criticism and interpretation. I. Title.
PS3539.H94Z75 1984   818'.5209   84-465
ISBN 0-208-02050-0

This book is dedicated to the memory of Esther Bindursky

Contents

Acknowledgments

One of my colleagues maintains that writers are a strange lot, because writing necessitates closing doors on life. While it is true that writers are strange, and that books get written only when we close the door and settle into solitude, writing also necessitates opening some doors. I would like to thank those people who have opened their doors to me during the writing of this book.

For reading the manuscript and making thoughtful comments and suggestions, I am indebted to Agnes McNeill Donohue; Yohma Gray; John Jacobs; my parents, J. D. and Norma McGehee; James Rocks; and Mary Thale. For technical assistance and advice, I thank Deborah Marks and Miriam Schneider; and for proofreading, Kimberley Hunt.

A special thanks to Mrs. James Thurber, whose help, encouragement, and wit have been invaluable to me. The drawings in this book are used with her kind permission.

Finally, to my husband, who has been here for the beginning, middle, and end of this job, I am grateful for too many things to mention here, but especially for his belief that this book would be. And quite the deepest of bows to my aged Vizsla, Boris, for keeping watch over me through the darkest and loneliest nights of writing.

Mundelein College
Chicago

Preface

A few words about my methodology are in order. Thurber's work is extraordinarily diverse, being comprised of tens of stories, sketches, essays, and fables. In addition, there are five fairy tales, the last three of which barely approximate novellas in length. Any Thurber critic must find a way to discuss so many short and varied works in a coherent fashion. Unlike a critical study of a novelist, for example, an analysis of Thurber's work cannot easily be divided into several chapters, each dealing with a different work.

I have chosen to focus upon those pieces collected in the sixteen anthologies or published as books, since these are the works most readily available to readers, and Thurber's judgment about his best work should be acknowledged. In dealing with these works, I have attempted both a broad survey of Thurber's world and a selective analysis of what I consider characteristic texts. The reader will note that a number of these characteristic texts come up for discussion several times in the book; this is intentional. My discussion of Thurber's world is so structured for two reasons. First, consideration of the same story from several viewpoints will allow the reader to become better acquainted with Thurber's work and to judge the validity of my arguments about his entire canon. A second and more important reason for this method is that such a sequence demonstrates the essential integration of Thurber's diverse subjects, themes, genres, and styles. The reader can, if desired, apply my method and conclusions to other works.

We can think of the work under analysis as a prism: when we first hold it in our hands, it looks transparent, perhaps even ordinary; but upon turning, all the colors of the rainbow appear. Thus, we study "The Secret Life of Walter Mitty" or *The Wonderful O* from different angles, with each turn in our discussion disclosing a new light, a new hue. Yet, when such a prism is returned to its original stasis and shelved, it does not ever become for us the simple, colorless lump it once appeared. We know forever the multifarious fire and brilliance locked within it. We learn, too, that the prism is not just the sum of its facets, but a complex phenomenon defined by the juxtaposition of all colors. If we should take it down again, or examine another work in the same way, we would discover anew all the dazzling colors of the spectrum.

Now, let us unlock some of the fire and light of Thurber's prose.

1 Introduction

Why a serious book about James Thurber? Perhaps this is to be a ponderous volume on a presumably "lighthearted" (and light-weight?) subject—a tedious analysis of a rather plain and common-place national holding, a holding of which everyone, surely, is aware? The reasons for such a book are implied in these very questions, for they focus on two basic assumptions about Thurber: one, that he is so well-known that there is nothing left to be said about him; and two, that he is so inconsequential that he cannot bear much examination. This book is for people who understand why Thurber deserves serious study, but it is also for those who do not.

Two decades have passed since the death of James Thurber—master prose stylist, critic and creature of the human predicament, and imagination *extraordinaire*—but still we have not discovered this national treasure. Let us claim him now, and hear what he has to tell us about language, about humor, about history, about ourselves. A trip through the Thurber carnival is frightening as well as funny, disturbing as well as entertaining—but go we must. Thurber is an authentic American magus, beckoning us to follow him and trans-forming our experience as we go along. In one of his last essays he argued that any time is a time for comedy. My exploration of his "Anatomy of Confusion" is based in my belief that not only is any time a time for Thurber, but that there could be no time when he was more needed than now. Knowing him is a richly rewarding and liberating experience. He is not to be missed.

Thurber is an almost universally recognized name, and every literate person will claim at least a glancing acquaintance with his work. His stories have been widely anthologized and adapted in English, as well as being translated into many foreign languages. Because of the purity of his expression, his texts have even been used by students of English as a second language. And the Thurber myth-ology has become part of American language and culture: we speak of "the Thurber dog," "the Thurber woman," "the war between men and women," of "looking like a Thurber cartoon," and of a "Walter Mitty type." The last phrase holds an assured place in our lexicon, even though many who use it have never read the story from which it came. References to Walter Mitty abound in conversation and publications around the world; the British medical journal, *Lancet,* has even described a presumably widespread pathological condition as "The Walter Mitty Syndrome."[1]

Although Thurber has not been the subject of much serious study, he enjoyed a good measure of critical success in his lifetime. In fact, he could be called a "writer's writer," as evidenced in the reviews of his work. Some of the best comments on Thurber's work are in these reviews by fellow writers, a mixed group ranging from Dorothy Parker to T. S. Eliot.[2] Eliot offered Thurber's own favorite criticism of his work:

> It [Thurber's writing] is a form of humor which is also a way of saying something serious. There is a criticism of life at the bottom of it. It is serious and even sombre. Unlike so much humor, it is not merely a criticism of manners — that is, of the superficial aspect of society at a given moment — but something more profound. His writings and also his illustrations are capable of surviving the immediate environment and time out of which they sprang. To some extent, they will be a document of the age they belong to.[3]

Although Eliot made this comment in 1951, little has been done during the past thirty years to expand our awareness of Thurber's seriousness, craft, or significance. Just a handful of scholarly articles and dissertations have been attempted on his work,[4] and the only critical books about Thurber — Robert Morberger's *James Thurber* for the Twayne series, Richard Tobias's *The Art of James Thurber,* and Charles Holmes's *The Clocks of Columbus* — are introductory studies.[5]

Besides the sparsity of serious commentary, Thurber's work has also been plagued by an abundance of superficial reviewers and readers. Thurber himself often lamented that "the comparatively few who really read me know I'm not just 'zany' or 'whimsical,'"[6] yet even today he could be described as one of the best-known unread writers in the English language. (Many of Thurber's contemporaries are also in this category, led perhaps by Scott Fitzgerald.) Just before his death, Thurber urgently stated his artistic intention to an audience that he preceived as unknowing or misguided: "I try to make as perceptive and helpful comment on the human predicament as I can, in fables, fairy tales, stories, and essays. I am surprised that so few people see the figure of seriousness in the carpet of my humor and comedy."[7] Characteristically, Thurber chose a Jamesian metaphor to describe the body of his literary work, thus implying the serious source of his comedy. This study will attempt to trace this figure of seriousness in the carpet of Thurber's humor, and thus to make Thurber's work at once more understandable, more engaging, and more significant for his readers and potential readers.

Throughout this discussion, I have been using the words "serious" and "humorous" in reference to Thurber. I realize that these two words are often used as antonyms, but this is a habit that obscures rather than clarifies our understanding of comedy. Indeed, one of the chief reasons that a writer like Thurber must wait for critical attention while lesser artists, who are manifestly and lugubriously "serious," have whole forests destroyed in their interest, is that humorists are not considered "serious" writers in this narrow sense and, therefore, they are not regarded as appropriate subjects for scholarship. An examination of Thurber's anatomy should disabuse the reader of such an idea, if a recollection of Chaucer, Shakespeare, Moliere, Congreve, Austen, and Twain does not. Thurber is often funny, but he is usually funny for the same reasons that he is a serious artist — because he probes the foibles and failures of human experience with delicacy and insight.

Thurber himself gave us the vocabulary for analyzing his work. Noting the humorous/serious controversy, he once said that "humor is the other side of tragedy. Humor is a serious thing."[8] Thurber clearly did not understand comedy and tragedy in classical or pure terms, as his 1936 definition of humor for Max Eastman's *Enjoyment of Laughter* demonstrates: "I think humor is the best that lies closest to the familiar, distressing, even tragic. Humor is a kind of emotional chaos told about calmly and quietly in retrospect."[9] This statement indicates not only how far Thurber is from the Bergsonian definition of comedy as a purely intellectual experience, but also how far his humor is from classical definitions of tragedy and comedy. Thurber is marking new territory in the comic tradition, seeing it as a place filled with emotional chaos, hard by the tragic abyss. This is a distinctively modern understanding of the comic.

Perhaps no one has better explained this modern understanding of comedy than Wylie Sypher, who in his essay, "Our New Sense of the Comic," asserts: "The most important discovery in modern criticism is the perception that comedy and tragedy are somehow akin, or that comedy can tell us many things about our situation even tragedy cannot. At the heart of the nineteenth century Dostoevsky discovered this, and Soren Kierkegaard spoke as a modern man when he wrote that the comic and the tragic touch one another at the absolute point of infinity — at the extremes of human experience, that is."[10] Thurber's work deals with the extremes of human experience, where laughter and tears, hope and despair, chaos and order touch in terrible tension.

It is this terrible tension that gives Thurber's art its enduring brilliance, interest, and energy. The clash between chaos and order, which is implied even in his early definition of humor as chaos recollected in tranquility, is the defining image in Thurber's mind and art. Some of his readers have noticed what Thurber called "the occupation of my mind by a sense of confusion that has never left it,"[11] but no one has pursued the meaning of this abiding interest. Wolcott Gibbs, in a particularly appropriate paradox, described Thurber's method better than most by noting Thurber's "sure grasp of confusion."[12] Thurber himself was conscious — and indeed became increasingly conscious — of the significance of confusion in his work. He demonstrated in many ways that the world is in a state of perpetual chaos because we come from the common "womb of confusion,"[13] yet it was not until 1953 that he struck the appropriate title for the complete body of his work, his massive accumulation of pictures of this chaotic world: "The Anatomy of Confusion."[14] This anatomy is really what Thurber had been working on all along, and the paradoxical nature of the phrase captures the clash of order and disorder that is the basis of his art. Thurber's work is the result of a systematic study of chaos, delineating the structure of disorder. His anatomy of confusion draws the chaotic human predicament in great detail, focusing upon some confusions more than others: the war between men and women; the chaos of "organized" society; the confusion in human systems, institutions, and machines. Thurber's specific subjects are, in fact, only elements of that large view of the chaotic human predicament that he characterizes as the anatomy of confusion.[15] By considering the entirety of Thurber's work as his anatomy, we will be able to see the essential integration of all his subjects, forms, and themes. In the absence of a novel, Thurber's anatomy is his long work, providing through its organization a basic unity among diverse works.

I speak of Thurber as a humorist because this is the term he used to describe himself. For Thurber, humor was an attempt to effect order in a chaotic world, and he accomplished this through a careful analysis of experience in a particularly refined English prose. Thurber's conception of the world as a state of chaos is conventional, of course; such an idea is central to both the tragic and comic vision. In the simplest terms, one could say that in a tragedy, people are destroyed in the process of establishing order, while in a comedy they survive the same process. Thurber's humor walks a tightrope between these two classical forms, producing what he regarded as the highest form of human expression, the tragicomedy: "The true balance of life and art, the saving of the human mind as well as of the theatre, lies in what has long been known as tragicomedy, for humor and pathos, tears and laughter are, in the highest expression of the human character and achievement, inseparable."[16] These inseparable but paradoxical pairs are, according to Thurber, the generators of both life and art.

Thurber's tragicomic humor couples the tragic vision—the sense of the inevitability of fate, death, and extinction—with the comic sensibility, or what Langer calls the "life-feeling" of comedy[17]—the indomitable spirit that survives in spite of a chaotic, destructive world. Although this brand of comedy or tragicomedy has been rediscovered by the moderns, it is not new, for modern tragicomedy is closer to Shakespeare, for example, than to post-Restoration conceptions of comedy. *King Lear* is perhaps our quintessential tragedy, but even in its final moments, the tragic hero wrestles with his button. The mixture of terror and banality in this scene only intensifies our sense of Lear's tragedy, just as Walter Mitty's mumbling about puppy biscuits somehow underscores our horror at his wasted life.

Like all great comedy, Thurber's humor recreates the world anew, which is to say, it creates meaning from nonmeaning, order from disorder, life from death. His characters often die, however, and thus share the fate of tragic characters. It is the survival and triumph of the narrator in his stories, and of the poet in his fairy tales, that most closely connects Thurber with the plot of classical comedy. The persistence of this human voice, articulate and measured in a world of chaos and destruction, causes the rejuvenation of the dead world that is so basic to comedy. As I use it here, the term "comic" has two basic characteristics: it deals with the survival of life in a chaotic, destructive world, and it effects an acceptance of that world, terrible as it may seem. Much of Thurber's work edges toward the abyss and the extinction of human life, but as *The Last Flower* (1939) demonstrates, the regenerative powers of life fight endlessly against destruction in his world.

Some of Thurber's work is also close to satire in its angry insistence upon correcting life rather than accepting it. This tendency is particularly evident in his fables and some of the essays. Since Thurber was far from certain that anything could improve the human situation, however, his ambivalence makes him less of a satirist than a humorist with a tragicomic vision of experience. The tension in Thurber's world results in part from his ability to ask the essential questions about human existence—Where are we going? Why are we here? What brought us to this place?—and his inability to formulate final answers. Yet he longs insistently for order, sense, and good. These things are impossible in a world marked by confusion, perplexity, and destruction, but, as one of his last fables concludes, "All men should strive to learn before they die what they are running from, and to, and why?" The striving is what is important, of course, since no final resolution is possible for an endlessly revolving cycle of confusion, and Thurber concludes that "It is better to ask some of the questions than to know all the answers."[18]

Thurber's art, therefore, is not only his attempt to effect order within disorder, but is an expression of the basic ambiguity in the human condition. The anatomy of confusion is the whole field of human experience as seen through the tragicomic lens, a lens that does not distort reality but rather focuses life's inherent contradictions. Perhaps Thurber's tone and meaning could be clarified somewhat by comparing him with other moderns: his work has the heavy ennui and frustration of Chekhov's tragicomic stage, the super-refined sensibility and introspection of James's fiction, the illuminating energy of Shaw's intellectual inversions, and the brittle splendor of Wilde's trivial comedy for serious people.[19] Thurber shares as much with these writers as he does with Mark Twain, the humorist with whom he is most often compared. Both Twain and Thurber understand the brutality of human nature and both long for human decency, but neither holds much hope for change. In the absence of such improvement, the writer offers something to help the sad human animal languishing in confusion and destruction.

Thurber offers laughter—the "only solvent of terror and tension,"[20]—the creative powers of the female, and the salvific voice of the poet as possible ways to end or forestall confusion. Thurber's humor is an indispensable anodyne for our anxious age, and his definition of humor, patterned on Wordsworth's definition of poetry, gives us another clue to the meaning of his art. For Thurber, humor is poetry, the highest expression of the human voice and the most suggestive of all forms. In this sense, Thurber takes an important place in the long history of comic fiction in English. When Fielding defined his novel, *Joseph Andrews,* as a "comic epic-poem in prose,"[21] he was, in effect, defining the English novel, or at least one of its two main branches, with Richardson's domestic melodrama functioning as the other. The more restricted, personal canvas of Thurber's short stories would more suitably be called "a comic lyric-poem in prose," but it is important to remember that, from the first, the comic has had a high and necessary place in the development of "serious" English fiction. Thurber is, therefore, working in two traditions: the major tradition in English fiction and the tradition of American humor. And I would suggest that Thurber's deft use of irony ties him closer to Jane Austen, for example, than to the frontier humorists of nineteenth-century America. At any rate, it is not simply coincidental that so many major novelists in English are also comic, and Thurber's wide reading must have influenced his fiction as much as his Ohio upbringing or his association with *The New Yorker.*

Thurber is all of these things, but he is also and most especially himself. An authentic and original artist, he takes bits of many traditions and makes them his own. Thurber's great accomplishment is that he creates a special, distinctive view of the world that he is able to make comprehensible to others. This idiosyncratic vision is the image he studies again and again in his anatomy of confusion: Man, the irrational animal, talking, thinking, and behaving himself into oblivion. The humorist is always there to pick him up, however, ably drawing his predicament with great wisdom, affection, and comicality.[22]

To begin our travels through Thurber's world, we will survey "The *Corpus Mundi*," that macrocosm of confusion in which all human groups, societies, and systems function or fail to function. This enormous vista contains pictures of societies crumbling, men and women fighting, and machinery breaking down. From a consideration of these external manifestations of confusion, we will move inward to the seat of confusion—"The *Corpus Mentis*," the frail, perplexed human mind. Thurber's anatomy of the *corpus mentis* delineates with great precision the essential cause of confusion in human life. Next we will examine Thurber's "Anatomy of *Homo Loquens*," or his study of man, the talking animal. We shall discover that *Homo loquens* generates much confusion with his perplexing language, but paradoxically, has only language to help him understand and transcend his chaotic existence. Finally, the fifth chapter, "The Anatomist in a World of Time and Death," will attempt to explain why the humorist-anatomist works. All of the parts of Thurber's anatomy are interrelated, but each chapter moves to a more important and less obvious form of confusion. The emphasis of this study is upon the literary achievement of James Thurber, but references will be made to his drawings for purposes of clarification.

By delineating the unique terrain of the Thurber world, it will be possible for us to enjoy more fully the richness and complexity of his art. In his last collection, Thurber wrote that "humor makes its own balances and patterns out of the disorganization of life around it."[23] If we consider Thurber's art in the terms he chose to describe it, perhaps we will be able to recreate the tragicomic humorist's vision, and perceive the pattern it makes in the field of chaos. Studying this supreme balancing act of the anatomist of confusion should also help us understand the role of the artist better. Thurber chose a difficult way, and those who would follow him have a great challenge.

When Thurber titled his retrospective collection in 1945, he called it *The Thurber Carnival*. This is an apt metaphor, for like a carnival, his world is filled with games of chance, distorted mirrors, unusual animals, exhilarating and yet frightening rides through the imagination, and occasional glances at the beautiful carousel—a quieter and gentler image of harmonious movement. Indeed, this term, "The Thurber Carnival," is so descriptive of Thurber's creation that I use it to refer to his entire world, not just the collection that took it as a title. Thurber's world is only faintly reminiscent of the ordinary one, completely involving carnival-goers in a new universe. As new as it is, however, the Thurber carnival becomes immediately, unforgettably ours. It is a state of mind that is fluid enough to admit all comers, most often being a picture of people who have only one thing in common, that they are in one place. It is that remarkable place where seals are in bedrooms and unicorns in gardens and wives on bookcases. And all are there quite naturally. It is the convergence of the various and the vagrant, the frightening and delightful elements of the human scene. Standing a bit removed from all the bedlam is the humorist, James Thurber, anatomizing the confusion.

2 Corpus Mundi
Thurber's Anatomy of the Human Carnival

I write humor the way a surgeon operates, because it is a livelihood, because I have a great urge to do it, because many interesting challenges are set up, and because I have the hope that it may do some good.
                                    —*Selected Letters of James Thurber*

*The wounded surgeon plies the steel
That questions the distempered part;
Beneath the bleeding hands we feel
The sharp compassion of the healer's art
Resolving the enigma of the fever chart.*
                                    T. S. Eliot
                                    Four Quartets

We so often speak of a writer's "world" that the term has lost much of its descriptive power. But some writers do create whole new worlds—worlds that become ours, too, because as writers and readers we share in the unfolding universe of the books we know. Certainly James Thurber has given us such a world, welcoming us to it many times, in many remarkable ways. Coming for the first time upon that part of creation known as "Thurber," we see a place unlike any other, but one that is immediately recognizable. And, because it is the nature of such experience, Thurber's world changes us, makes us see other experiences in a new way. What is it that distinguishes his world?

The world in Thurber's prose and drawings is that part of the universe in which things get remarkably out of hand. It is where tiny, apparently inconsequential misunderstandings grow into monumental confusions—until the nature of reality itself is questioned. It is a world where the language of confusion is spoken, as societies crumble, institutions fail, and people comprehend the sorry scene darkly, if at all. It is a battleground where men and women fight an endless war of nerves, while their dogs howl, quite literally, to the heavens. It is, in fact, the whole decadent field of modern life, or the chaotic *corpus mundi,* which the humorist-anatomist dissects and recreates. As the scalpel of his wit cuts through the many layers of the *corpus mundi,* Thurber points to the origins of our universal disease and dis-ease at once; by focusing on the "little perils of routine living," his work thus reveals a memorable set of images—the anatomy of the *corpus mundi*—describing a malaise at once "cosmic and mundane."[1]

What is the *corpus mundi,* after all, but the massive accumulation of its trivial elements? And what is the anatomist but one who relates all of these disparate elements to each other and to the organism of which they are only parts? Like the biologist, whose field of data is immense and seemingly unconnected, the humorist-anatomist must perceive a pattern in the chaos; divide and classify his subject; and, finally, give each part of his system a proper name. When all of his analysis and synthesis is completed, Thurber's work presents us with a veritable anatomy of confusion, his descriptive atlas of the wide, incongruous human carnival, which is a large and formidable subject indeed.

It is easy enough to miss this pattern in Thurber's work, to fail to see the imprint of his "large subject" on the vast world of his creation. In fact, any student of Thurber is haunted by Chanda Bell's mocking question to the would-be critic: "You have found the figure. . . but have you found the carpet?"[2] The tone of her question implies its own disturbing answer, and even Thurber's best readers have often failed to see the carpet, or the essential integration of his themes, subjects, and methods. Yet, if we consider Thurber's complex work as a whole, we may begin to see the order it creates from disparate, often conflicting elements. This is not to impose a theory or an interpretation on his work, but rather to discern how Thurber's many figures converge in an intricate and highly distinctive design. Through thus examining the paradox of "The Anatomy of Confusion," we may perceive the essential method in the divine madness known as the Thurber carnival.

Let us begin by looking at Thurber's depiction of the enormous vista of the *corpus mundi,* or the macrocosm of confusion, which encompasses all of human society. As the anatomist plies the steel of his art through the distempered parts of our existence, he scans the fever chart of that large and complicated organism called the *corpus mundi,* seeking all the while, as Eliot's lines suggest, some resolution of the eternal human enigma. For Thurber, the human enigma manifests itself in the insufferable battle of the sexes, in the dismal failures of science and technology, and in the imminent demise of civilization. As an introduction to Thurber's anatomy of confusion, we will consider first his dramatization of these external manifestations of confusion by looking at his portrayal of human groups, institutions, and systems. We will see that, although Thurber is not a social writer in the usual sense of the term, his work makes a profound comment about human nature and consequently about human society as well. This chapter will attempt to focus Thurber's world view, to relate this view to his artistic method, and to survey some of the more important works that deal with social or external chaos. Thurber, the master anatomist of confusion, took as his great subject the chaotic nature of human life. His first subject for dissection, therefore, was the *corpus mundi,* or the complicated body of the modern world.

From *My Life and Hard Times* (1933) to *Lanterns & Lances* (1961), we see and delight in magnificently rendered pictures of the bedlam and carnival of human life. These pictures are drawn, not in ponderous tracts for the times nor in thinly veiled propaganda, but in short story, fable, fairy tale, and essay that reveal and instruct gracefully through many layers of meaning. The social commentary in Thurber's work can be divided into two types: the work that studies, in a general way, human beings as members of a group, a class, an institution, or a culture; and the work that deals with more specific abuses and horrors within the macrocosm of confusion. Because of his artistry and intelligence, Thurber is usually able to imply the general in the specific and the universal in the topical.

That Thurber's persistent subject is the confusion of human life can be deduced even from a survey of his titles: *The Owl in the Attic and Other Perplexities, The Seal in the Bedroom, Alarms and Diversions, The Thurber Carnival,* "Aisle Seats in the Mind," "The Pleasure Cruise, and How to Survive It," "What Do You Mean it 'Was' Brillig?," "The Bat Who Got the Hell Out," "The War Between Men and Women," and alas, even "The Collapse of Civilization" itself.

Only in Thurber's world does a seal peer over a strangely amorphous couple in bed, benignly barking as it keeps them company.

Only Thurber sees a *middle-aged* man on the flying trapeze, or foresees human society reduced to mayhem by the omission of a single letter from the alphabet. Only in Thurber's drawings do women seem to have radiating from their heads, neither prosaic hair nor celestial haloes, but rather their own exposed nerve endings, as though they suffer a vitality that cannot be contained. And only here do the noble dogs seem peculiarly able to understand and transcend the troubled scene. Thurber's world is new and, quite literally, fantastic, but it is also remarkably, immediately ours. After reading Thurber or seeing his drawings, as Dorothy Parker so long ago pointed out,[3] our whole existence is altered; if we never have before, we see a Thurber woman (only too often) or a Thurber dog (never often enough); we recognize a "Walter Mitty"; we describe something, perhaps our own sad predicament, as "looking like Thurber cartoon." Even more importantly, after Thurber, we can no longer regard language, reason, history, dignity, or convention in the same way. Our sense of order and control, Thurber shows us, is only fragile self-deception; beneath our cherished conventions lurk thinly disguised savages. Thurber has achieved the ultimate, enduring artistic effect: he has succeeded in creating a new world, a singular, even eccentric vision, which his consummate artistry has rendered understandable and unforgettable. Thurber has become part of our awareness.

The distinguishing characteristic of this special world is a pervasive use of the confusion motif. Images of confusion fill Thurber's fiction and drawings and, in many of the essays, his concept of confusion is stated directly. Such a statement underlies *The Years with Ross* (1959), one of Thurber's last books, which recalls *New Yorker* editor Harold Ross and Thurber's years with the magazine. As Thurber remembers him, Ross always dreamed of the "perfect system," of a "miracle man" to organize the bedlam. To Thurber, Ross himself was ironically the prototypical confused man: "H. W. Ross, being neither artist nor poet, was not equipped to bring 'grace and measure' out of the chaos of man on earth . . . . [He was] a mixed-up modern man driven by the well-known compulsion to build with one hand and tear down with the other."[4] Here, then, is an explanation of the existence of so many images of confusion in Thurber's work: to Thurber, life on earth is a state of chaos, a scene in which mixed-up human beings attempt unsuccessfully to bring order to a perpetually revolving cycle of confusion. Although this vision of the human predicament is far from unusual, Thurber defines his artistic purpose—that of bringing order out of chaos—more boldly and more insistently than most writers. And, more than most, his world is particularly well described as an anatomy of confusion.

In a revealing statement written for *I Believe* in 1939, Thurber reflects sardonically on human society, which he characterizes as "This sorrowful and sinister scene, these menacing and meaningless animals. . . . Every man is occasionally visited by the suspicion that the planet on which he is riding is not really going anywhere; that the Force which controls its measured eccentricities hasn't got anything special in mind." This dilemma is partially the result, Thurber explains, of the reliance upon flawed religious, political, philosophic, and scientific systems to bring order out of chaos, and partially the result of humanity's own fallen nature. Added to these faults are the limitations of the environment, which Thurber describes frighteningly and accurately as a "misfit globe," a place that is "just barely habitable. Its minimum temperatures are too low and its maximum temperatures are too high. Its day is not long enough and its night is too long. The disposition of its water and its earth is distinctly unfortunate. . . . These factors encourage depression, fear, war, and lack of vitality." Human beings match their destructive habitat by the erratic and confused social groups they form: "The survival of almost any species of social animal, no matter how low, has been shown to be dependent on Group Co-operation, which is itself a product of instinct. Man's cooperative processes are jumpy, incomplete, and temporary because they are the product of reasoning and are thus divorced from the sanity which informs all natural laws."[5] There is perhaps no better explanation of the wildly chaotic scenes in Thurber's cartoons than that they record "cooperative processes" that are "jumpy, incomplete, and temporary." They freeze a moment in the confusion, and in so doing, imply a whole erratic universe.[6]

I quote so much from this little-known essay because not only does it show Thurber's early preoccupation with men and women as social animals, but it also includes several revealing statements about his perception of the human predicament. In his essays, and in works like *The Last Flower* and the fables, there is what is best described as an anthropological tone and attitude: he is concerned with the elements and development of human society, with conventions and traditions exposed, codified, and explained, with the rituals of human life and the necessities for human survival. Sometimes he pushes society out to the edge of the cliff, where civilization itself collapses. Or, he sees human beings, like lemmings, drown themselves in a sea of confusion. The human predicament as perceived by James Thurber is a large, all-encompassing macrocosm of chaos in which "we mumble along in our multiple confusion."[7] Because of this dominant sense of disorder in life, his writing tends to have not only a serious but also a melancholy and sometimes frightening tinge.

Thurber is regarded chiefly as a humorist, however, and most of his best work, though often not distinctly "humor," produces what E. B. White called "the inaudible, the enduring laugh."[8] Understanding Thurber's definitions of humor and art makes it possible to relate his subject matter, method, and characteristic effect—that special blend of laughter and melancholy—to each other. If Thurber's great work is the anatomy of confusion, his definition of humor as emotional chaos recollected in tranquility describes his methodology in assembling this anatomy. We must remember that Thurber thought that the best humor was that which "lies closest to the familiar, to that part of the familiar which is humiliating, distressing, even tragic. . . . [and is based in] that hysterical laugh that people sometimes get in the face of the Awful."[9] Exemplifying our essential confusion, the tragic and the humorous lie disturbingly close to each other—they are, in fact, intermingled in human experience. An ambiguous combination of laughter and tears in the face of "the Awful"—that is, in our recognition of the terrible limitations of human experience—thus results from the confusion in which the entire universe revolves. It is the characteristic human response. Paradoxically, humor is not only an instrument of our awful knowledge, but is additionally our best means of dealing with it. Humor is a tool not only of awareness, but of survival as well, for laughter is "the only solvent of [the] terror and tension" resulting from our bitter knowledge of the human predicament—our contemplation of the perplexing expanse between birth and death that cries for meaning. Given our legacy of confusion, only "the recurring sound of congruous laughter,"[10] which effects a unity of humor and pathos or a paradoxical order within the confusion, makes experience bearable. Thurber's kaleidoscopic view of the human spectacle thus appropriately takes as its chief mode a kind of tragicomedy which,

Two thousand people were in full flight.

while presenting a stark picture of the frightening, confusing, and decadent scene, also allows the release of laughter as a mechanism for survival. It is this coupling of savage disillusionment and realistic hope that gives enduring value and richness to Thurber's best treatments of the human predicament, in *The Last Flower, Fables for Our Time,* the fairy tales, and the fine short stories of the thirties and forties.

It is interesting that Thurber has thus demonstrated two of the important conclusions of Constance Rourke's classic, *American Humor* (1931), which was written just as he was beginning to publish. Rourke's study is retrospective and therefore she does not even mention Thurber, but based on the thrust of American humor before 1930, she concludes that although "recognition is essential for the play of a profound comedy," it is equally necessary that comedy also somehow effect a "reconcilement with life."[11] Most of Thurber's humor does both very well.

The awareness that we experience throughout Thurber's work is of that large chaos in which human beings attempt to form groups, institutions, and systems in hopes of somehow organizing and ordering life. In the following sections of this chapter, we will look at representative pieces from each of his periods and genres, to the end of understanding better the main parts of the *corpus mundi* delineated in Thurber's anatomy: social groups and institutions generally; science and technology more specifically; and the institution of marriage, most particularly of all. The beasts, real and unreal, of the Thurber carnival will be noted also, as they blink at the human madness parading before them and make their own profound comment on it.

The Macrocosm of Confusion

Thurber's quasi-autobiographical masterpiece, *My Life and Hard Times* (1933), is a characteristic example of his fictional rendering of group chaos. There is a double irony in the book's title, which is superficially a play on the trite "life and times of—" phrase. The collection, which contains fictionalized reminiscences of Thurber's boyhood, is a set of pictures of his early life, placed contrapuntally against the implicit backdrop of the real hard times America was experiencing in 1933. The title also alludes to the troubled society pictured in Dickens's *Hard Times*. Thurber, of course, disavows rather loudly any interest in social issues in the book's preface, and he notably draws scenes of domestic, painfully personal life throughout the book. How, then, is *My Life and Hard Times* indicative of Thurber's social criticism or world view?

In the magnificent "Preface to a Life," Thurber uses heavy irony to establish a humorous tone and to reveal that he not only is keenly aware of, but is very interested in, the general mayhem in the world outside himself. This passage also gracefully describes Thurber's technique in dealing with his particular experience:

> He [the author] talks largely about small matters and smally about great affairs. His ears are shut to the ominous rumblings of the dynasties of the world moving to a cloudier chaos than ever before. . . . and the confused flow of his relations with six or eight persons and two or three buildings is of greater importance than what goes on in the nation or in the universe. He knows vaguely that the nation is not much good any more; he has read that the universe is growing steadily colder, but he does not believe that any of the three is in half as bad a shape as he is.[12]

Thus, the Preface, while protesting too much that this book is just a "personal" reminiscence, humorously makes the connection between universal chaos and individual confusion. In fact, Thurber admits here that his "type of writing is not a joyous form of self-expression but the manifestation of a twitchiness at once cosmic and mundane." He is not, after all, describing himself in a true memoir, but has created in the narrator "Thurber" a prototypical confused modern man who senses both the growing chaos outside and his own impending doom. So that we will not hope for respite or redemption, we are then told that even if a man could organize his own life, as a member of the class "humanity," he shares a common destiny with his fellow finite creatures: "the claw of the sea-puss gets us all in the end."[13]

Some of the stories in *My Life* provide vivid images of group confusion that adumbrate Thurber's more direct social criticism, which was to develop at the end of the thirties. "The Day the Dam Broke" is one of Thurber's best pieces, for in it he shows, with great economy and humor, how easily order and reason are overthrown by mass psychology, which is to say, by human nature. The story is based on Thurber's memories of the afternoon of "The Great Run" in 1913, when all of placid Columbus, Ohio, was reduced to bedlam. The anatomist of confusion, watching the chaos from the distance of time and space, quietly assures us that the most remarkable thing about this event was not that the dam did not break, but that there was no dam:

> The fact that we were all as safe as kittens under a cook-stove did not, however, assuage in the least the fine despair and the grotesque desperation which seized upon the residents of the East Side when the cry spread like a grass fire that the dam had given way. Some of the most dignified, staid, cynical, and clear-thinking men in town abandoned their wives, stenographers, homes, and offices, and ran east. There are few alarms in the world more terrifying than "The dam has broken!" There are few persons capable of stopping to reason when that clarion cry strikes upon their ears, even persons who live in towns no nearer than five hundred miles to a dam.

No one knew exactly what started the run, but the great and the small citizens of Columbus ran in wild disarray until the police could break up the riot. Thurber, anatomizing the confusion, distances himself and the reader from the chaotic scene under study through a grossly understated, almost droll recounting of the tale. He draws a particularly vivid analogy to dramatize his action of recollecting such chaos in quiet and calm:

> All the time, the sun shone quietly and there was nowhere any sign of oncoming waters. A visitor in an airplane, looking down on the straggling, agitated masses of people below, would have been hard put to divine a reason for the phenomenon. It must have inspired, in such an observer, a peculiar kind of terror, like the sight of the *Marie Celeste* abandoned at sea, its galley fires peacefully burning, its tranquil decks bright in the sunlight.[14]

In one of his last pieces, Thurber states didactically the conviction about human nature that is implied throughout *My Life:* "We are assured...that the normal is a matter of mass behavior, but the normal can never be synonymous with the average, the majority."[15] The irrationality of the masses, as well as the tenuous hold any human being has on order, is Thurber's perennial subject.

Although much of *My Life* takes place inside the Thurber household (even inside little Thurber's mind), the family is but a smaller version of the society revolving madly around it. In "The Night the Bed Fell," after a series of family portraits that presents a startling array of eccentrics, Thurber describes the night of "general banging and confusion" that resulted from the family's thinking that a bed had fallen on father. Father, however, was really sleeping peacefully in the attic all the while.[16] The Thurbers are people, it is safe to assume, who would run from a nonexistent dam if only they were let outside. Yet they are not particularly distinguished in their confusion, for we learn that outside their zany abode there is no immunity to the human disease, as Thurber remembers comfortingly that "everybody we knew or lived near had some kind of attacks."[17] Thurber's habitual skepticism about human behavior must be placed into its historical context for full impact: in these "memoirs" he is recalling the bully world of Teddy Roosevelt and its successor, the world that could envision a "war to end all wars," just as Americans were being told that they had "nothing to fear but fear itself." Thurber, of course, could think of a few other things.

In "University Days" and "Draft Board Nights" the anatomist of confusion turns from the family group to society at large. The inanity of college requirements (Ohio State military drills practiced Civil War tactics during the First World War) and the bureaucratic bedlam of the draft system have never been better rendered. "University Days" pictures Ohio State students pointlessly marching around the campus because of the essential confusion in both the university and the world.

> We drilled with old Springfield rifles and studied the tactics of the Civil War even though the World War was going on at the time....It was good training for the kind of warfare that was waged at Shiloh but it had no connection with what was going on in Europe. Some people used to think there was German money behind it, but they didn't dare say so or they would have been thrown in jail as

German spies. It was a period of muddy thought and marked, I believe, the decline of higher education in the Middle West.[18]

In "Draft Board Nights," Thurber remembers being drafted through some systematic error each week during the war, even though every time he went for the physical examination, he failed because of poor eyesight. Desiring a little variety (going through as an examinee gets boring), he just moves across the line and becomes an examiner. Nobody, amidst the magnificent confusion of the draft system, notices.[19] In the madness of the Thurber carnival, it is just that easy to turn into someone or something else. Thurber must have meant for "University Days" and "Draft Board Nights" to be so identified with each other. In fact, the whole of *My Life and Hard Times* is an orchestration of Thurber's basic theme that in the person, in the group, in the institution, in the entire *corpus mundi,* confusion reigns.

"The Greatest Man in the World" similarly deflates our sense of order, tradition, and reason. A sardonic short story which was written a few years after *My Life* but set in the dreadful present, it tells the story of Jack "Pal" Smurch. This fantastically awful and wonderfully named main character is raised to the apex of national adulation through "hosannas of hysterical praise" following his solo round-the-world flight. When the story was written in 1935, Thurber was very close, literally and figuratively, to a special part of American history and to one of its idols, Charles Lindberg. In "The Greatest Man in the World," Thurber debunks—dare we say "besmurches"?—a particular aspect of history as well as the nature of history itself.

The ultimate irony of this highly ironic story is that its hero's failings, which include illiteracy, vulgarity, and membership in a family of felons, are beautiful when compared with the rampant barbarism of the press corps and the government of the United States. Since these centers of power cannot risk letting the people recognize Smurch for what he is, thereby discovering the futility of hero worship, the President has The Greatest Man in the World thrown from a window high above the excited throngs. This "tragic accident" is then sadly reported in all the papers, which, in fact, habitually misuse the word "tragedy." These "news" reports are followed by a funeral described as "the most elaborate, the finest, the solemnest" in our history.[20] Thurber's story implies that our traditions, heroes, myths, even our "history," are based in profound misconception and confusion—and all of this before managed news events became common knowledge.

An equally bleak vision of history is echoed in *The Last Flower* (1939), which presents Thurber's view of human nature in all its ambiguity. Although sometimes misconstrued as a children's book, *The Last Flower* is a profound parable in words and pictures about the cyclic nature of history and the inevitable clash of the destructive and creative forces in human life. It is neither conventional fiction nor simple cartooning, and thus heralds Thurber's experimentation with new forms. *The Last Flower* begins in a wasteland, for World War XII has finally "brought about the collapse of civilization" and the destruction of the world. Thurber's drawings show buildings blown apart and wasted landscapes of dead trees and grass. After the last war, the parable tells us, human culture declined, as "books, paintings, and music disappeared from the earth" and people just sat around, doing nothing.[21] Like the setting of Thurber's fairy tales, which were to follow in the forties and fifties, the wasteland pictured in *The Last Flower* is a condensed, timeless version of decadent human society as it is portrayed in much modern fiction.

In this bleak world there is no love until a girl finds the last flower, which she gives to a young man. They nurture the flower together and it grows into a field of flowers. As the landscape becomes fertile again, creative sexuality and love are reborn and civilization is rebuilt. Then, to our horror, soldiers return to the world. For emphasis, Thurber includes five pages of drawings of armies, unaccompanied by words, which seem to drown out every other reality. Thurber wrote *The Last Flower* in 1939 and, timeless as the parable's content may be, it was also a timely response to the world outside. When soldiers reappear in the now-fertile landscape, the cycle of destruction begins again. The sardonic storyteller says that "Liberators, under the guidance of God, set fire to the discontent." (The accompanying drawing depicts two demagogues gesticulating before a mass of faceless, sheepish humanity.) And so war returns, too. "This time the destruction was so complete. . .that nothing at all was in the world except one man and one woman and one flower."

The tenuous balance of disillusionment and hope in this book is typical of Thurber's ambivalent and tragicomic view of the human spectacle. We assume from the parable that yet another cycle of destruction will eventually grow out of the lonely trio left at the end, but they are also the only source of humanity's small happiness and hope. The profound paradox dramatized in *The Last Flower* is that out of creation, destruction results, and destruction makes possible future creation. This is the basic paradox of life itself, as sure and undeniable as the seasons of the year or the movement from birth to death. *The Last Flower* presents a frightening, disturbing picture, but even laughter—"the only solvent of terror and tension"—is the result of seeing life as it really is.

The Last Flower not only signals the end of the first decade of Thurber's career, but is prime evidence of a widening in his forms and technique. Until the end of the thirties, Thurber had written primarily conventional fiction and essays. We will now consider works from the next decade that make significant social comments while being examples of his two new forms, the fable and the fairy tale, and the collection *Men, Women, and Dogs* (1942), the best treatment of society in Thurber's drawings.

Fables for Our Time (1940) is a collection of short, Aesopian fables. In the fable form Thurber is able to moralize effectively and humorously because he establishes aesthetic distance by using an ancient form and by displacing human qualities in animals. A special Thurber touch in these stunning fables is to deny, in their morals, the clichéd truisms of Aesopian legend. As one would expect, Thurber's *Fables* abound in images of general confusion, war, and death. In "The Hen and the Heavens," for example, a little hen cries, "The heavens are falling!" echoing Aesop's hen, but in Thurber's world the heavens actually do fall.[22] So much for comforting the smug human reader.

Even more pointed satire is evident in "The Birds and the Foxes," in which the foxes "liberate" (kill) members of a peaceful sanctuary of orioles after they have "civilized" (eaten) all the geese and ducks in the surrounding territory. The parodic moral is direct: "Government of the orioles, by foxes, and for the foxes, must perish from the earth." A similar tale is called "The Rabbits Who Caused All The Trouble," in which arrogant wolves imprison and eat a colony of unwitting rabbits. Speaking in bureaucratic gobbledygook, the wolves say that no investigation of the slaughter will be necessary, for "since they [the rabbits] had been eaten, the affair was a purely internal matter." The reader laughs here, recognizing in the double-talk a common smug amorality, but it is a laughter of discomfiture. The bleak moral advises, "Run, don't walk, to the nearest desert island."[23]

Equally unsettling is the shock of recognition experienced in "The Owl Who Was God," a fable that recalls Thurber's criticism of the masses in *My Life and Hard Times* and "The Greatest Man in the World." Here an owl is mistaken for God by gullible animals who hear in his "To wit" and "To woo" statements of profundity. In a mass of confusion, the entire group walks into the path of an oncoming truck (which they can see, except for the daylight-blinded owl):

> "There's danger ahead," said the secretary bird. "To wit?" said the owl. The secretary bird told him. "Aren't you afraid?" he asked. "Who?" said the owl calmly, for he could not see the truck. "He's God!" cried all the creatures again, and they were still crying "He's God!" when the truck hit them and ran them down. Some of the animals were merely injured, but most of them, including the owl, were killed.
>
> Moral: *You can fool too many of the people too much of the time.*[24]

The Fables are similar in tone and subjects to a Thurber sketch called "Interview with a Lemming," which was published in 1942 in *My World — and Welcome to It.* During the "Interview," a wise lemming says, "I have made a life-long study of the self-styled higher animal. . . . and a singularly dreary, dolorous, and distasteful store of information it is."[25] This lemming is really the anatomist Thurber, displaced in another character in order to engage in a dialogue. Thurber's fables surely dramatize a "dolorous and distasteful store of information" about *Homo sapiens,* which they reveal in compressed, stark images that flash for a moment and illuminate the whole world of experience. In fact, the world revealed in Thurber's fables might make the reader echo Huckleberry Finn's summation of the decadence he has seen along the shore: "It was enough to make a body ashamed of the human race." Again and again, *The Fables* demonstrate Thurber's consistent thesis that there is no refuge, no respite for "human beings born of war" in the last stages of a crumbling civilization.[26]

Men, Women, and Dogs (1942), the finest collection of Thurber drawings, also reveals the cloudy chaos of human life. The drawings are difficult to discuss because, with Dorothy Parker, I fear that "a Thurber must be seen to be believed — there is no use trying to tell the plot of it." In fact, many Thurber drawings seem to be graphic representations, in terse, spare images, of dreams and the dream-world. A great number produce laughter and linger in memory, but like dreams, defy casual or definitive interpretation. I will try, however, to summarize how these inimitable images reveal the macro-cosm of confusion.

There is an element of horror in many Thurber drawings and those in which people appear evoke almost universally a deep sense of disillusionment. Thurber people are ugly. His women are terrible; his men, no better. In contemplating a Thurber cartoon, we experience a feeling of life's facade breaking before our eyes, as the savageness and disorder of human nature erupt through thin layers of respectability and calm. The drawings are not really depressing, however, because they offer relief in laughter. Indeed, an audible laugh is more common in confronting a Thurber cartoon than in reading his more subtle, polished prose.

A Thurber cartoon is an indispensable anodyne for our anxieties, and our anxious age is particularly besieged by the trivial and the ordinary. In *Men, Women, and Dogs* we see horrendous confusion arising out of remarkably commonplace scenes: in a drawing of a middle-aged group playing table tennis, a woman suddenly disrobes and needlessly asks, "Do you people mind if I take off some of these hot clothes?"; in a respectable restaurant, a man strangles his companion as the waiter admonishes, "Here! Here! There's a place for that, sir!"; and in a hospital room, a doctor impetuously accosts his patient with, "You're not my patient, you're my meat, Mrs. Quist!" At a Thurber cocktail party, filled with his pathetic people, we overhear this introduction: "This is Miss Jones, Doctor. . . . She's been through hell recently," and we see a plump, middle-aged nude woman play the piano while two men whisper, "I'd feel a great deal easier if her husband hadn't gone to bed."[27] (How her husband's embarrassed presence would have helped, we never know.) There is no reason to bother asking how these things happened, what brought about this bedlam. Thurber pictures it all as though there is nothing else possible for a group of human beings, as though it is in our eccentricity that we are ordinary.

What is to be done with the lady on the bookcase, a live, but shelved, former wife who peers down on her equally dowdy replacement and a horrified visitor? Or about "the room where my husband lost his mind," with its spare, primitive furnishings and tiny, esoteric drawings on the walls? Or for the respectable couple that desperately hopes — when confronted with a man standing on the back of a woman, who is at the same time balancing a lamp on her head — that "there may be some very simple explanation"?[28] In each of these frames Thurber has managed to freeze a moment of perfectly normal madness; he has captured a telling image of chaos for his anatomy of confusion. In depicting human beings committing eccentric, frightening, inexplicable, even savage acts as though nothing were odd about their behavior or themselves, Thurber exposes the commonality of absurdity and the rule of disorder. The making of his anatomy, of course, requires just such generalization.

Having seen the consistency with which Thurber renders the chaotic *corpus mundi* in story, fable, and drawing, we must turn to the final form he used in constructing his anatomy — the fairy tale. His third tale, *The White Deer* (1945), is a masterpiece of Thurberian confusion in which he displaces the modern world in a fairy tale for adults.[29] Like *The Fables,* the fairy tales achieve artistic distance by employing an old form which, in Thurber's deft hands, indirectly comments on his world. Like all of his tales, *The White Deer* opens in a sterile period, a wasteland. The story concerns a white deer, turned into a lovely young girl by sorcery, who promises to marry the son of King Clode (either Gallow, Thag, or Jorn), who can succeed in the perilous task appointed him. A wood's wizard, the disguised brother of the princess who was once a deer, plays with time, illusion, and reality so that all three sons arrive at the castle at the same hour. The one who wins the lady's hand is the one who is willing to love her after she proclaims herself to be a deer turned into a lady. Only young Prince Jorn, the poet, can accept this reality, and their marriage ends the book.[30]

Into this conventional fairy tale, Thurber interweaves images of a decadent society that constantly, but unobtrusively, remind the reader of his world. The story begins in infertility, following the senseless slaughter of all the animals of the Magical Forest by Jorn's aggressive, violent brothers. Like the world of *The Last Flower,* human beings here have destroyed their own habitat and have nothing left to do but sit around in bitter indolence. There is no escape or mitigation for these unhappy inhabitants of a twentieth-century Magical Forest. King Clode, in attempting to understand and rule his kingdom, is surrounded by a gallery of woefully, maddeningly incompetent specialists who only compound his confusion. These mixed-up advisors are not able to bring order or understanding to the confusion of Clode's domain. That is left for the poet, with some help from his friends.

The tale has three truth-tellers: the white deer (really the Princess Rosanore), who tells the truth about her lineage; Prince Jorn, who asserts that even in "this false flux of fact and form," he knows "what's true is true"; and Tocko, the nearly blind Royal Clockmaker, who was fired from his job as Royal Astronomer when his "constant reports that everything was going out alarmed King Clode." The trouble is that the Magical Forest is filled with human beings, and so everything is going out. The wise Tocko spends his time in exile, writing prophesies such as "After this brief light, the unending dark" on sundials. Thurber's role as artist must be identified with both Prince Jorn, the poet, who makes sense out of the nonsensical forest, and with the aging, blinded Tocko, whose long experience as an observer of the erratic universe lets him foresee the impending doom. Like Tocko, anyone who clearly perceives the face of "the Awful" may be banished from the centers of power, leaving the masses to be deceived as they bumble along in mass confusion.

Thurber does not only generally criticize human society in *The White Deer,* however. In narratives about the quests of each brother, we see allegorical characters and situations representing specific modern abuses and banalities. Prince Thag, for example, rides through a surrealistic landscape, including a trip through the Valley of Euphoria where men cry *"Carpe Diem"* to him in an attempt to slow him on his journey. He continues, only to find that The Blue Boar, one of his society's great legendary beasts, is an easy conquest, since it is asleep when he reaches it. Our pretentions about honor, work, and courage are exposed when Thag's victory is thus trivialized. Similarly, Prince Gallow goes through what could be called the frightening jungle of slogan and advertising: "The Trees were hung with signs and legends. . . . 'Lost Babes Found.' 'Giants Killed While You Wait.' '7 League Boots Now 6.98.' 'Let Us Awaken Your Sleeping Beauty.' 'We Put You In An Urn, Men Put You on a Pedestal.' 'Consult Panting and Young.' 'Seek Grailo, Even Better Than the True Grail.'" This picture of the "Forest of Willbe" dramatizes the destructive vacuity of our lives, coupling as it does the banalities of mass culture with the macabre images of nightmare. This feeling of the emptiness of modern life adumbrates the quester's final realization that both his enemy and his quest are quite meaningless. Gallow fights through the seductive Forest of Willbe in order to win the sword of the Seven-Headed Dragon of Dragore, only to find that this great figure, too, is but a combination of crass carnival attraction and decadent cultural myth: "'Look brother,' said the man. 'Twelve emeralds get you seven balls. You throw the balls at the Seven-Headed Dragon of Dragore in that striped tent yonder — the greatest mechanical wonder of the age, meaningless but marvelous.'"[31] This is an unrelieved glimpse at the Wizard of Oz. That last phrase, "the greatest mechanical wonder of the age, meaningless but marvelous," suggests perfectly the heap of rubbish that industrialized nations accumulate. Today, it calls up images not only of the now rather quaint Rube Goldberg contraptions and the ingenious lamps made from fire extinguishers, but also the ever-widening television screens glowing from coast to coast and the ever-arising golden neon arches, beckoning us into endless McDonaldlands. In the Seven-Headed Dragon of Dragore, Thurber deftly links the inadequacy of all manner of cultural and religious myths with the failure of that god almost universally adored in the twentieth century: the machine. In fact, a general disillusionment with the rituals, systems, products, and pretensions of modern society is at the base of *The White Deer*.

Like Thurber's short stories, fables, and drawings, *The White Deer* dramatizes the macrocosm of confusion, and in this tale, general confusion is tied to the destructiveness of the specialist. The Magical Forest is an inept world generated by the specialist and the technician, where the machine and the mechanical are material exemplars of our essentially confused state. This link brings us to a consideration of the criticism of science, technology, and other "systemless systems" implied throughout Thurber's work.

Exemplars of Confusion:
Systemless Systems and Grisly Gadgets

As we have seen, Thurber portrays a whole world revolving in perpetual chaos. Most of his stories and essays depict the cloudy chaos of the *corpus mundi,* a world in general confusion. The anatomist is especially drawn to a part of this world—science and technology—perhaps because its failures follow an implicit promise to simplify life, order reality, and explain existence. An essential paradox of Thurber's mind and art is that, like a scientist, he carefully delineates a chaotic world, while also indicting the failures and abuses of science itself. Similarly, even though a writer of great complexity, intelligence, and depth, Thurber ironically refuses to trust human reason. In the midst of raising metaphysical questions, he fundamentally distrusts philosophy, just as he assembles an anatomy while criticizing science, or at least some striking perversions of it.

Some of Thurber's readers would argue that his distrust of reason places him in the long tradition of anti-intellectualism in America, but Thurber's own learning, his cultivated aesthetic sense, and his penetrating analysis of the human condition reveal a rich, if lightly borne, intellectualism. I rather think that, as anatomist of confusion, Thurber must study the most signal and influential failures in human history's attempts at ordering life and transcending confusion: this is the pathology upon which the art and science of anatomy depend. Thurber's work was done before such criticism of science and technology became fashionable, while most Americans believed in irrevocable progress through scientific and technological advance, and the nation generally suffered from this disease. In his rejection of science, therefore, Thurber stands squarely against his culture, even though writers ranging from Hawthorne to Benchley preceded him in this antagonistic position.[32]

Thurber's resounding denial of the ability of science to establish order in the chaotic human situation is especially significant because science is usually considered precise and exact. Modern people tend to characterize the scientist as an objective reporter who discerns the clear, the factual, and the absolute. Even though the genuine scientist would agree that we never arrive at the complete or final truth, the masses are usually confident that science at least approaches answers

The Filing-card System

in a careful, orderly fashion. In fact, science is often defined loosely as "an organized body of knowledge." When Thurber overturns this conventional notion and accuses the scientists themselves of instigating and fostering confusion, he not only discovers a great subject for laughter, but makes a serious criticism of the modern world as well. He questions one of the premises of modern life by mocking its almost reverential acceptance of scientific theory and its belief in technological progress. Like our misplaced faith in decadent social institutions, axioms, and conventions, Thurber shows that science offers yet another false promise to bring order out of chaos. Science, he contends, is really a travesty of order.

Thurber does not deal with pure science, but is instead interested in the effects of clinical or applied science, including technology, on society. The anatomist of confusion demands to know what psychology, sociology, medicine, and the myriad mechanical devices cluttering our world actually do for (and to) the human beings trapped in the confusion. He answers this question in a complex statement that can be summarized in terms of two implicit conclusions of his work: Thurber essentially denies the possibility of ordering or explaining experience, and he even assigns a great measure of the blame for our perplexity to science and technology. In short, unlike Gatsby, the titular hero of one of his favorite novels, Thurber emphatically refuses to believe in the green light of progress, just as he fails to trust in Franklinian enterprise and invention.

Thurber's refutation of science is based in his essential doubts about our ability to deduce facts from constantly revolving experience. Science seeks not only to organize experience, but also to generalize, from observable data, about phenomena. In Thurber's world, however, generalizations are overturned constantly, as reality undergoes endless permutations; every experience is therefore different and distinct, as it is transformed by the limited, egocentric mind perceiving it.[33] Thurber's questioning of the powers of science is thus based in his conception of universal confusion: in science, he sees a particularly potent and pervasive false assumption about the ability of the human mind to understand, explain, and order experience.

Thurber was not, therefore, simply attacking the obvious inanities of scientism, which seeks scientific or factual answers to metaphysical questions, but was astonishingly refuting the most basic assumptions of scientific theory: the ability to generalize, assign causes, and arrive at conclusions. It is expectable for a humorist to ridicule the fertile territory of scientific smugness and jargon. Even more importantly, however, Thurber sees life as an inexplicable mystery, a monumentally involved and ambiguous predicament. According to the master anatomist of confusion, any attempt to explain life neatly or to order it simply crumbles in the face of experience. And technology, the stepchild of applied science that promised to simplify work, dispatch activity, and free humanity from the bondage of time, has ironically only further extended confusion, Thurber finds. The machine, a system created ostensibly to aid us, is rather a prime exemplar of our inner confusion and an irritating addition to the universal bedlam. Indeed, for Thurber science and technology are signal examples of the basic confusion in which the *corpus mundi* revolves.

To demonstrate the place of science in the anatomy of confusion, we will consider in chronological order Thurber's most important works that deal, first, with a criticism of science, and second, with the rejection of technology as a cure for humanity's chaotic predicament. Both of the early collections, *Is Sex Necessary?* (1929) and *Let Your Mind Alone!* (1937), ridicule the scientist. I wish to look closely at *Let Your Mind Alone!,* since it represents Thurber's most complete attack on the world of modern science.

The "scientist" that Thurber attacks in *Let Your Mind Alone!* is the social scientist, the "area" specialist, the popularizer (and banalizer) of everything from psychological analysis to learning techniques. These specialists are people who, with scant sense, no regard for human limitations, and even precious little understanding of science, attempt to transform human experience into a series of clever tricks. Their sententious tomes suggest to the unwary reader that if only one can decipher the "game" of life and arrive at the "correct" formula for playing it, all will be happiness, success, and fulfillment. Never one to let such comfortable assumptions alone, the humorist-anatomist intrudes upon this placid scene. His ensuing dissection of this part of the *corpus mundi* is unsettling, insightful, and hilarious. As its title suggests, *Let Your Mind Alone!* is a declaration of war against those modern psychologists and sociologists who pretend to explain the human condition with formulae, or to "treat" it with simplistic schemes. The particular impetus for these attacks was

Thurber's reading some of the "success manuals" written by a legion of pop psychologists during the twenties and thirties.[34] Since most American bookstores of the 1980s are filled with texts on how to cure everything from pickles to cancer, *Let Your Mind Alone!* could not be more relevant even today, a half-century after Thurber decried this trend in American culture. The anatomist does not have to strain to debunk such masterpieces of confusion; all he has to do is quote them.

Always enraged by the how-to-make-your-life-perfect-in-five-easy-steps approach of many modern specialists, *Let Your Mind Alone!* is Thurber's greatest single effort to deflate these false promises. Although they employ parodic passages, the essays in this collection are not, strictly speaking, parodies, as *Is Sex Necessary?* had been. Rather, they are exquisitely logical, outrageously funny assaults on the "success experts" who attempt to organize life, explain experience, and give direction to human activity. *Let Your Mind Alone!* could be described as "James Thurber Against the Dale Carnegie Syndrome." Another way of putting this, of course, is that the book is just one more example of an American writer seriously questioning his culture's pervasive promise of progress.

Even the collection's first essay, "Pythagoras and the Ladder," demonstrates Thurber's sharp sense of the damage done by the proponents of easy answers and "successful living." He notes, in a sardonic aside, the profound irony that "it was in none other than the black, memorable year of 1929 that the indefatigable Professor Walter B. Pitkin rose up with the announcement that 'for the first time in the career of mankind happiness is coming within the reach of millions of people.'"[35] It was particularly brutal of Pitkin to offer this banal vision of the good life just around the corner to a world sinking into the Great Depression, but this melancholy realization is only intensified by our knowledge that general affluence does not produce general happiness. It is doubtful, however, that such realizations would be possible for the specialist who could glibly characterize human history as "the career of mankind." Pitkin spoke psychobabble, long before there was a name for it.

Another piece in the collection, "Destructive Forces in Life," attacks the promise of "Masterful Adjustment" that many of the psychologists offered. The anatomist says that he selected his subject for this essay entirely at random, mocking the exactitude claimed by scientists. The essay then denies the possibility of either a masterful adjustment to life or of a perfectly disciplined mind, because of the chaotic nature of this world: "The undisciplined mind runs far short of having its purposes thwarted, its plans distorted, its whole scheme and system wrenched out of line. The undisciplined mind, in short, is far better adapted to the confused world in which we live today than the streamlined mind."[36] This essay is perhaps the crucial statement of Thurber's antiscientism, asserting as it does the fundamental impossibility of adjusting to life or organizing experience. In a different context, Otto Friedrich observed that "Thurber's view of life in the age of terror and confusion is based on the premises of *The Last Flower:* there can be no real adjustment to life on the edge of a cliff."[37] Since Thurber's men and women seem always to be acting out the last stages of civilization on the edge of that cliff, any adjustment to, or final explanation of, such a precarious existence is indeed impossible.

The facile promises of self-discipline and social organization crumble in the face of universal confusion, as "Anodynes for Anxieties" demonstrates. Thurber here easily reduces David Seabury's "How to Worry Successfully" to the full, uproarious level of its absurdity. It seems that Dr. Seabury had suggested, as a cure for worry, that people randomly associate "any possible idea" with the source of their worry. This, he maintained, would lead to a solution of their "problem." (These specialists always speak of "problems," because they wish to imply that the conditions under consideration are somehow solvable.) Thurber concludes commonsensically that not only is Seabury's method ineffective as a cure for worry, but that it is ironically the cause of much confusion. As he dissects Seabury's faulty method, the anatomist discovers delightfully that it is "Marxian," which is to say, in Thurber's punning lexicon, that it is the method used by the Marx brothers in constructing dialogue. To prove his point he cites the famous scene in which Groucho says to Chico that the missing picture is in the house next door and Chico replies that there is no house next door. Groucho, true to Seabury's irrational logic, concludes, "Then we'll build one," in an absurd attempt to justify his initial, nonsensical statement.[38] The point is that Groucho's proposal is as logical as solving problems through random association.

In the same essay, Thurber has the wit to destroy Dorothea Brande's advice that a person who forgets things should write innumberable reminders. (She does not address herself to the other, more serious problem of how such a person would remember to write these reminders.) Her solution reminds Thurber of "one of those elaborate Rube Goldberg contraptions, taking up a whole room and involving bicycles, shotguns, parrots, and little colored boys, all set up for the purpose of eliminating the bother of, let us say, setting an alarm clock."[39] As our attempts to simplify and order life become more elaborate, our confusion only intensifies and multiplies.

Let Your Mind Alone! resoundingly rejects the ever more complicated, extravagant, and unsuccessful attempts to order life and to "solve" the human enigma. In "The Sample Intelligence Test," Thurber distills the quintessence of confusion. Here he is especially indignant about the publication of a dollar edition of Dr. Sally Shellow's book, for, he says, this inexpensive edition of "How to Develop Your Personality" sadly "puts the confusion. . . [which was formerly only in Dr. Shellow's mind] within the reach of everyone." The anatomist then proceeds mercilessly to take apart Shellow's shallow "system" for personality development, which he describes in a typically ambiguous phrase as "so mixed up that it becomes magnificent." Magnificent is hardly the word that one expects at the end of this sentence, but Thurber was always simultaneously attracted to and repelled by confusion. In his methodical and delightful taking apart of Shellow's "paradise of errors" (to quote another ironic phrase), Thurber underscores the fundamental inability of the "wonderland of psychology" to make life more sensible or less difficult. Dr. Shellow, unfortunately for her but marvelously for Thurber's readers, had published a primitive intelligence test, replete with grammatical and logical errors, which Thurber masterfully dissects to its rickety skeleton. His own essay, which anatomizes the confusion, is the creation of reason and logic. Shellow's work is indeed a paradise for the anatomist of confusion, and this essay reveals Thurber at his funniest as well as his most serious. Notice, for example, his humorous attack on two serious mistakes made by Dr. Shellow: her grammatical absurdity and, even worse, her consummate trust that she has made herself perfectly clear:

> In Chapter I, first paragraph, Dr. Shellow gives the dictionary definition of "personality" as follows: "The sum traits necessary to describe what is to be a person." Unless

I have gone crazy reading all these books, and I think I have, that sentence defines personality as the sum total of traits necessary to describe an unborn child. If Dr. Shellow's error here is typographical, it looms especially large in a book containing a chapter that tells how to acquire reading skill and gives tests for efficiency in reading.[40]

Wordsmiths are so picky.

In "An Outline of Scientists," Thurber finally voices the theme of the entire book as "Thurber's Law": "Scientists don't really know anything about anything." He derived this flagrant generalization, we are told, from reading an offensive article about bloodhounds (first cousins of the noble Thurber dog). To his horror, the scientific article had concluded that bloodhounds repel people because they are "terrible to look at and terrible to encounter." Thurber needs very little encouragement to deny scientific theories, anyway, and this callous and nonsensical remark leads him to see that "*all* scientists are the same man. Could it be possible that I had isolated here, as under a microscope, the true nature of the scientist? . . . I have never liked or trusted scientists very much, and I think now that I know why: they are afraid of bloodhounds. . . . This must be the reason that most of them withdraw from the world and devote themselves to the study of the inanimate and the impalpable."[41] In this particularly revealing moment of introspection, the anatomist realizes that he has identified a telling image of the *corpus mundi;* he has delineated a crucial part of his anatomy of confusion. While criticizing and rejecting the scientist's position, Thurber uses a scientific metaphor for the artist's role, ironically suggesting a basic similarity between science and art. Yet, unlike the scientist, Thurber studies the pulsating, ambiguous human scene. Therefore, although he is an anatomist, scrutinizing the chaotic *corpus mundi* under the glass of humor, he retains a sense of humanity that the scientist seems to lack. While assembling his anatomy, he seriously and insistently questions the power of human reason, but he does not revel in insanity or in the rejection of common sense, as Walter Blair has charged.[42] Rather, he asserts the supremacy of individual experience and observation, which is the bias of art generally, but he does so with an equally strong caveat about the inherent limitations of such observations. Distilling all of these conflicting propositions into a rigorous, disciplined prose that is the product of both reason and imagination, the paradoxical nature of life itself generates Thurber's most careful analysis of disorder, his great anatomy of confusion.

Throughout the anatomy, Thurber argues that science offers inadequate solutions for both the great problems of the world and the trivial difficulties of everyday life. In "Women Go on Forever," he laments that the scientists have not discovered the "fact" of female dominance, because, "with their eyes on the average, they fail to discern the significant." Conversely, art reveals the significant: the grimly funny essay, "After the Steppe Cat, What?," predicts that it will be a poet, not a scientist, who will be able to "detect. . . [the] minute portents of the approaching end" of human life on earth.[43] Adumbrating the indictment of specialists in *The White Deer*, Thurber here argues that only the poet can perceive truth or make sense of nonsensical experience. Science is especially open to attack from the anatomist of confusion because it pretends to such clarification while only adding to the confusion. Implicitly, Thurber's work demonstrates that the only real anodyne for our anxieties is the keen sensibility and incisive wit manifested by his narrators and poet-heroes.

Science, in its peculiarly narrow vision, bases facile answers and naive optimism on little real knowledge of human nature. To correct this, a few years after *Let Your Mind Alone!*, Thurber wrote his own "Footnote on the Future," which criticizes the easy optimism of the "scientists, who look beyond the little menaces of the mundane moment, [and who] are, quite naturally, cheerful." As an artist, Thurber knew well that human history is a complex chain of many mundane moments, and he believed that art had to deal with the cumulative burden of daily life. Looking carefully at this evidence, he rejects the happy conclusion of some scientists, who think that if people learn to use all of their brain cells, this will necessarily create a happier, more virtuous life:

> In the history of mankind the increase of no kind of power has, so far as I can find out, ever moved naturally and inevitably in the direction of the benign. It has, as a matter of fact, almost always tended in the direction of the malignant; don't ask me why, it just has. This tendency, it seems to me, would be especially true of the power of the mind,

since it is that very power which is behind all the deviltry
Man is now up to and always has been up to.[44]

This argument isolates the crucial difference between Thurber and
the scientist: Thurber questions the usually unquestioned powers of
reason and concludes that human reason has, in fact, led man into
some of his most destructive acts. In *Let Your Mind Alone!* he perhaps exaggerates this idea in the statement that "sixty minutes of
thinking of any kind is bound to lead to confusion and unhappiness,"[45] but his systematic debunking of apparently reasonable
human behavior is quite convincing. Thurber's questioning of the
powers of human reason is offensive, if at all, only until we study
his definitive anatomy of man, the irrational animal.

Ironically, for all his rejection of science, Thurber displays some
of the best traits of the scientific, as well as the educated, mind. He
is an expert researcher, capable of extremely close observation of
phenomena and of equally astute conclusions from his observations.
He is unusually interested in different explanations of human history,
and the anatomy of confusion is filled with references to theories
from anthropology and the natural sciences. Insatiably curious, he
observes with a keen eye for detail, as "A Gallery of Real Creatures"
shows.[46] His lifelong interest in the natural world and in human
nature connects him with the highest goals of science, which are to
explain man and the universe. Thurber's probing of the nature of
reality is remarkably as close to Einsteinian physics and Jamesian
psychology as to the work of his fellow generators of *belles lettres*.
And brilliantly comical though his dissections of modern science are,
Thurber grew uncomfortable with his position, perhaps because
some critics noted that his attacks on science sounded like "Mark
Twain talking from the grave."[47] This specter probably forced
Thurber to rethink his antiscientism and helped cause his move away
from scientific parody after *Let Your Mind Alone!*

The important thing is that Thurber realizes the inadequacy of
science to answer the fundamental questions of human existence.
And, unlike most modern people, he argues that it is the function
of the artist, not the scientist, to interpret human life. With the
Romantic poets, Thurber believes that only the poet or artist has
the organizing vision, the synthesizing understanding, that can make

sense of a chaotic experience.

As Thurber became less preoccupied with science per se, he broadened his satire into an attack on what could be called the "systemless systems" of modern life. His criticism of these systems is directly related to his debunking of scientific thinking, however, because underlying his objections to both is the strong sense that life, as infinite mystery and eternal enigma, is always prey to complexity, complication, and confusion. Like science, these other systemless systems just add to the universal confusion which they unsuccessfully seek to mitigate.

The White Deer (1945) is the representative piece dramatizing Thurber's conception of systemless systems. Although the tale's King Clode begs constantly for help from his advisors (who are, in the accepted fashion of modern societies, specialists and scientists), neither he nor they can make sense out of the "false flux of fact and form" in which their world languishes. Clode is, in fact, the prototypical modern man, painfully aware that reality is constantly changing and eluding him, but unable to do anything about his chaotic predicament.[48]

If the scientist and the specialist are unable to end this confusion, Thurber does not place any more hope in the metaphysician's power. A rejection of philosophy, as one of the systemless systems that confuse the *corpus mundi,* is a consistent, if minor, theme in Thurber's work. As early as 1939, he decried the ineffectual and "curious indulgences," including religion and philosophy, which people contrive to understand themselves.[49] Thurber sees all of these efforts as failures, and in his last collection of fables (1956), he sardonically defines a philosopher as "one who seeks a magnificent explanation for his insignificance."[50] Thurber regards all human systems—whether scientific, religious, philosophic, social, cultural, or political—as elaborate mix-ups, akin to the contraptions of Rube Goldberg in both their complexity and their uselessness. Thus, each failed system has a place in the anatomy of confusion.

A powerful fable called "The Last Clock," published in Thurber's last completed collection (*Lanterns,* 1960), reveals the anatomist's fear of specialization and his disdain for intellectual arrogance at their most devastating levels. In this fable, mankind is abandoned in the bleak world of *The White Deer,* but here is without a poet, in fact, without language at all. Therefore, there is no chance for salvation of any kind. Time runs out because an ogre has eaten all the clocks. No one, none of the hundreds of self-satisfied bureaucrats or specialists, can save this ailing civilization. Their inability to articulate the nature of their predicament exemplifies the disease from which they all suffer:

> Three weeks to the day after the ogre had eaten the last clock, he fell ill and took to his bed, and the ogress sent for the chief diagnostician of the Medical Academy, a diagnostician familiar with so many areas that totality had become to him only a part of wholeness. "The trouble is," said the chief diagnostician, "we don't know what the trouble is. Nobody has ever eaten all the clocks before, so it is impossible to tell whether the patient has clockitis, clockosis, clockoma, or clockthermia. We are also faced with the possibility that there may be no such diseases. The patient may have one of the minor ailments, if there are any, such as clockets, clockles, clocking cough, ticking pox, or clumps. We shall have to develop area men who will find out about such areas, if such areas exist, which, until we find out that they do, we must assume do not."[51]

Although grim, this description of decadent modern society is also funny, because the imbecilic double-talk is but a slight exaggeration of the language we hear everyday. Especially when read aloud, the mock-medical language in this passage is both superbly funny and frightening, because it parodies so well the tangle of suffixes in which medical jargon wrestles for meaning. The parody becomes even funnier and yet more real because some of the coinages are puns on well-known disease names. Thurber thus reveals the complex connection between the decadence of a culture and its clouding of thought and mangling of language. A complete and breathtaking glimpse of "the Awful," the fable ends with the death of human civilization—the final failure of specialism and science to cure the ever-growing confusion in the *corpus mundi*.

"The Last Clock" provides a grim view of the fate of an over-specialized, insular society, but a work from the same period, *The Years with Ross* (1959), maintains an amused, detached perception of human confusion and our befuddled attempts to transcend it. In this book, Thurber remembers Harold Ross and his ineffectual attempts at order: "From the beginning Ross cherished his dream of a Central Desk at which an infallible omniscience would sit, a dedicated genius, out of Technology by Mysticism, effortlessly controlling and coordinating editorial personnel, contributors, office boys, cranks, and other visitors. . . . This dehumanized figure, disguised as a man, was a goal only in the sense that the mechanical rabbit of a whippet track is a quarry."[52] Perhaps Thurber's own bitter experience of trying to fulfill Ross's dehumanized fantasy as an editor during the early days of *The New Yorker* helped to solidify his conception of perplexed and perplexing human experience. At any rate, the figure of Ross, both real and mythic, continued to dominate Thurber's imagination long after he ended his formal association with *The New Yorker*. Thurber's Ross, a representative modern man, innocently yet vainly dreamed of the miracle system that was to come "out of Technology of Mysticism," a phrase describing a central American myth as only Thurber could. Like the vain hope that science would provide the answer to the human riddle, Americans have trusted that technology would organize and simplify human existence. The vagueness of this phrase and its unconscious coupling of the material and the spiritual only underscore the impossibility of the dream itself.

The mechanical and the scientific are connected in Thurber's anatomy, not only because technology is an outgrowth of scientific investigation, but also because, like science, technology appears to make order possible. After all, the social historians tell us that the technological revolution freed human beings from trivial work, allowed them time for pleasure and leisure, and aided them in the involved business of living. Not so, says Thurber, a remarkable conclusion that he demonstrates throughout his anatomy.

Thurber's chaotic world is cluttered with grisly gadgets and macabre machines. His characters are people who "have never taken a successful shower," and those who cannot operate an automobile without courting disaster.[53] They suffer lifelong memories of terrifying encounters with cream separators, and come from families uniformly scarred by experiences with the mechanical marvels of the modern age: "My mother, for instance, thought — or, rather, knew — that it was dangerous to drive an automobile without gasoline: it fried the valves, or something. 'Now don't you dare drive all over town without gasoline!' she would say to us when we started off.

Gasoline, oil, and water were much the same to her, a fact that made her life both confusing and perilous."[54] A classic example of Thurber's understatement, this passage also isolates with great precision a basic confusion in the *corpus mundi*.

Living ever on the brink of ignition or explosion, these jittery creatures fly from disaster to disaster as easily as cranking a car's engine or turning on an electric light. In the brave new world of twentieth-century America, the old experience of natural torment and perplexity is unmitigated; rather, it is made worse by multitudinous experiences and contraptions that are, sometimes quite literally, shocking. In this technological age, human beings are not only at the mercy of unkind fate and time's caprice, but are also the helpless "victims and martyrs of the wild-eyed Edison's experiments."[55] Like Harold Ross, who imagined a "mystical technology," these benighted people assign godlike significance to the perplexing technological kingdom in which they struggle to live. Always seemingly harassed by something beyond their ken, there is nothing more incomprehensible or foreboding to Thurber people than the machine.

The comedy of the machine is, of course, a conventional device. Not only does Bergson base his theory of laughter upon our perception of the mechanical in human activity, but much American literature takes an antimachine and generally antiprogress position. From Irving, Hawthorne, and Melville to Benchley, White, and Thurber, American writers expose the menace of the machine and deride the newfangled. Thurber could, in fact, have written Katherine Walker's 1864 essay, "The Total Depravity of Inanimate Things,"[56] which links, in its remarkable title, the Puritan definition of man with the heap of rubbish that surrounds him. A peculiarly American juxtaposition, perhaps it reveals what a "fallen world" is. Morsberger has noted that Thurber is similar to Benchley in that "both authors are victimized by inanimate things,"[57] but beyond Benchley's certain influence there are other likely sources and analogues for Thurber's portrayal of menacing machines: in Thoreau's rejection of the railroad of progress, in Rube Goldberg's cartoons, and in Charlie Chaplin's gloomy vision of *Modern Times*. American art is as likely to debunk progress and technology as American society is to foster belief in them.

Thurber's dramatization of our fear of the mechanical is not only a literary or conventional device, however. Mrs. Thurber has said that this is one aspect of his work that is grounded firmly in autobiographical fact, since Thurber himself was truly intimidated by the mechanical, and his letters bear poignant testimony to his feeble attempts at driving as blindness approached.[58] Yet, as a humorist, Thurber was able to convert his personal fear into a universal artistic situation, thus delineating the common dread in representative images. Indeed, his humor allows us both the delight and the insight of the comic distance, from which we may study our fears and frustrations displaced in others.

Even in an age of general terror and anxiety, the automobile engenders a special fear, probably because of its relative size, sophistication, and power, and also because of its crucial role in modern life. A car is the basis of one of the central memories dramatized in *My Life and Hard Times,* a book that depicts the early days of this century when the automobile was revolutionizing the way Americans live. The narrator of "The Car We Had to Push" recalls with great relish the time the Thurber boys duped their father into believing that the family car was falling apart. Actually, the boys had attached a package of kitchen utensils underneath the car, to be dropped at a particularly serene moment:

> This was a little scheme of Roy's to frighten father, who always expected the car might explode. It worked perfectly. That was twenty-five years ago, but it is one of the few things in my life I would like to live over again, if I could. . . . Roy twitched the string in the middle of a lovely afternoon on Bryden Road near Eighteenth Street. Father had closed his eyes and, with his hat off, was enjoying a cool breeze. The clatter on the asphalt was tremendously effective: knives, forks, can-openers, pie pans, pot lids. . . fell, beautifully together, in a lingering, clamant crash. "Stop the car!" shouted father. "I can't," Roy said. "The engine fell out." "God Almighty" said father, who knew what *that* meant, or knew what it sounded as if it might mean.[59]

The car is a mystical, frightening experience to father, for he is unable to understand or control it. A human creation, it has become a dangerous and almost diabolical force in the world.

The little Thurber man of the thirties is thus besieged by the mechanical: the middle-aged man on the flying trapeze drives a car

American Male Tied up in Typewriter Ribbon

only under duress, and then only to the distress of those around him.[60] Nothing better probes the meaning of his distressing predicament than the masterful essay, "Sex ex Machina," in *Let Your Mind Alone!* Combining Thurber's rejection of science with his hatred for the machine, this essay distills his thoroughgoing criticism of the crazy systems of the modern world.

"Sex ex Machina" mimics both the social historian and the clinical psychologist. Using the mature, world-weary, and detached voice so familiar to the reader of Thurber's essays, the work explores our fear of the mechanical. Its latinate title and case history form suggest a scientific approach to what Thurber defines as "the problem": "a world made up of gadgets that whir and whine and whiz and shriek and sometimes explode." Trying to establish the etiology of the general human disease, or the source of our ever-worsening confusion, the pathologist concludes: "No man . . . who has wrestled with a self-adjusting card table can ever be quite the man he once was. If he . . . hesitates, wavers, and jumps at every mechanical device he encounters, it is . . . only because he recognizes the menace of the machine as such."[61]

Confused *Homo sapiens* is not helped by the technological advances he has made, but is only further perplexed by them. His world is complicated infinitely by the confusing gadgets and systems he has introduced to it. And no one is free from the universal modern curse:

> Everybody, from the day of the jumping card table to the day of the screaming klaxon, has had similar shocks. You can see the result [of such contrivances] . . . in the strained faces and muttering lips of people who pass you on the streets of great, highly mechanized cities. There goes a man who picked up one of those trick matchboxes that whir in your hands; there goes a woman who tried to change a fuse without turning off the current; and yonder toddles an ancient who cranked an old Reo with the spark advanced. Every person carries in his consciousness the old scar, or the fresh wound, of some harrowing misadventure with a contraption of some sort.

These are the wounds that curious, bumbling, and mixed-up human beings inflict upon themselves while searching for organization,

serenity, and ease. As sufferers of the general human disease of
confusion, they only exacerbate their chaotic condition by trying to
explain or dispatch it. Once Thurber defines the difficulty, that "so-
called civilized man finds himself today surrounded by the myriad
mechanical devices of a technological world," he is doubly enraged
by the Freudians, who try to extricate man from this predicament
through "scientific" analysis. To Thurber's horror and dismay, these
specialists have only confounded the issue by confusing, for example,
automobiles with sex.[62] The only one who really learns from all the
mayhem wrought by such crazy creatures is the anatomist-*cum*-
pathologist, who dissects the decadent organism of modern life in
order to understand and describe it. After such analysis, of course,
he is able to synthesize his data and produce the work of art.

As late as 1956, in a fable called "The Grizzly and the Gadgets,"
Thurber indicted the mechanization of our age for strengthening the
rule of disorder. This satiric fable tells the story of a bear, once
victimized by the gadgets of a middle-class American home, who
finally rebels and destroys the pile of junk in which he is imprisoned:
"Enraged, infuriated, beside himself, seeing red and thinking black,
the grizzly bear began taking the living room apart," until he crushed
all of the gimmicks and gadgetry of a typical twentieth-century
American household. The fabulist then appropriately chooses to
rephrase that great hater of technology, Thoreau, in his summation:
"Nowadays most men lead lives of noisy desperation."[63] With what
trash and noise do we confound our little lives, attempting to hide,
even from ourselves, the nature of our predicament. And with what
fury do we thus speed up the chaotic revolutions of the *corpus mundi*.

Thus, from the ridiculing of psychology in *Let Your Mind
Alone!* to the attack on mechanization in "The Grizzly and the
Gadgets," Thurber's work consistently and roundly denies the
efficacy of science and technology in dealing with human life. This
is why his stories are filled with characters who cringe at the sight
of an automobile, and why his essays so often dismantle the illogical
systems of the scientific community. All of these attacks are but pieces
of Thurber's larger work, the anatomy of confusion, in which he
analyzes the types and causes of human confusion. Science is both
a principal example and a prime instigator of that confusion.

This investigation into the role of science and technology in
Thurber's anatomy will end with a look at perhaps his best story,

and certainly his most famous, "The Secret Life of Walter Mitty," for Mitty's confusion is emblematic of people's difficulty with modern life. Mitty retreats into his secret life, at least partially, so that he may be safe from the irritating and frightening contraptions of the modern world. Dwelling largely in "the intimate airways of his mind," he is not forced to back the car up correctly or remove tire chains with grace. Instead, he has the luxury of easily flying a vaguely-constructed airplane or of matter-of-factly performing a delicate but undefined operation while his dream patient snores off on an ambiguous "anesthetizing machine." The fine irony is that Mitty flees from a dreadful, machine-ridden world into a fantasy filled with machines that are even larger and more confusing. Suggestive of his radical confusion, all the gadgets in his dreams make the same "ta-pocketa" sound as they variously hum away or fly apart.[64] Mitty is, of course, the confused stepson of the father in *My Life and Hard Times,* who also just knew how it sounded when a car fell apart. Like the world of Thurber's reminiscences, Mitty's predicament is not simply personal or trivial, however. While he is bombarded with the minute and the mundane, the personal and the petty, Mitty is also perplexed by news photographs showing the wartime destruction of cities in Europe. Placed subtly in his social context, Walter Mitty suffers from the malaise that informs the entire *corpus mundi,* whether it takes the form of perplexing automobiles and chaotic personal relationships or predatory militarism.

He also suffers as the weaker participant in the universal battle of the sexes. If the machine does not get him, the Thurber woman will. This brings us to the final type of confusion studied in Thurber's anatomy of the *corpus mundi,* the place where human confusion is at once more apparent and more awful. It represents the very essence of confusion, or, as Amy Lighter says to Charles Grantham in "The Beast in the Dingle," it is actually "the predicament within the predicament—the predicament of you and me." From the social manifestations of human confusion, let us descend into the domestic war zone and examine at closer range the confusion between men and women. Our consideration of this species of confusion will begin by investigating how it functions in the quintessential Thurber story, "The Secret Life of Walter Mitty."

The War between Men and Women

In many ways, "The Secret Life of Walter Mitty" typifies Thurber's fiction of the thirties and early forties. In its brief pages, the anatomist examines the inarticulate, suffering, impotent world of modern urban America—and identifies the very distillate of that chaotic state, the impossible marriage of untrue minds. All of the elements of the Thurber world are here: the chaotic personal relationships and the muddled understanding of them; the menacing machines; the perplexing specialists; the failed myths of a decadent culture; and the abiding apprehension of a "twitchiness at once cosmic and mundane." More than anything, "Walter Mitty" exemplifies Thurber's fictional rendering of one particular species of confusion: the war between men and women. In this great story, he pictures the Thurber man and the Thurber woman of the early period.

Walter Mitty is inept, inactive, impotent, and unknowing. He is at the mercy of everything in his environment, including and perhaps especially his wife. She seems to hover over him, even as he dreams of flying successfully through the worst storm in naval history. A prototypical modern man, Mitty is the victim of banality and boredom: he succumbs to his "fate" during his wife's weekly trip to the hairdresser, and the only bloodshed suggested is in his fantasy of his own death, which he sees in clichéd images from grade-B Hollywood films. At the same time, Mrs. Mitty mothers Walter, reminding him to wear overshoes and threatening to take his temperature when they get home. Hollywood's version of this story did not, therefore, invent the "motherly" dimension of her character, but did pervert the entire story and the meaning of a Thurber wife by making Mrs. Mitty into Walter's literal mother and by giving Mitty a sweet, young mate. The Thurber wife of this period is not sweet, nor is she really a mate and peer, but rather an omnipotent, threatening power.[65] She is the predatory female, spawned—like the perplexing machines around her—by an industrialized and advanced culture, a culture so advanced that its people are left with nothing to do but create objects for their neurotic energy. Mitty is the sedentary and bewildered remnant of American manhood; his wife, the pioneer woman gone haywire in the absence of tangible frontiers to conquer. The Mittys are, therefore, representatives of an important class generated by American progress during the last century:

the middle-class, middle-brow inhabitants of cities who had acquired, for the first time in history, enough leisure to discover different ways of destroying themselves. Although some people have had such luxury in the past, only modern America has put it within the reach of many.

Mrs. Mitty is, therefore, a perfect historical piece: the bourgeois woman caught between real responsibility and real freedom. As both exile from and prisoner of the system, she is relegated to chipping away at the social and domestic edifice that entraps her. In fact, both of the Mittys are victims of their culture's worn-out definitions of sexual roles, with Walter attempting to play the tired role of "the imperturbable" Western male, and his wife becoming a caricature of a woman and a human being. Like robots, they mouth empty words and make empty gestures, as in the following scene, which is emblematic not only of the wide gulf separating men and women, but also of the terror lurking beneath the surface of a world without genuine human activity:

> Something struck his shoulder. "I've been looking all over this hotel for you," said Mrs. Mitty. "Why do you have to hide in this old chair? How did you expect me to find you?" "Things close in," said Walter Mitty vaguely. "What?" Mrs. Mitty said. "Did you get the what's-its-name? The puppy biscuit? What's in that box?" "Overshoes," said Mitty. "Couldn't you have put them on in the store?" "I was thinking," said Walter Mitty. "Does it ever occur to you that I am sometimes thinking?" She looked at him. "I'm going to take your temperature when I get you home," she said.[66]

This is a classic report from the war zone. As it demonstrates, the sexual conflict is really a cold war, fought in confusion with innuendo and psychological torment. In this confused and confusing world, the only form of communication seems to be the non sequitur, and any attempt at social intercourse only serves to highlight the essential alienation of human beings. In "Walter Mitty," as in his studies of men and women generally, the anatomist discovers the core of confusion, the basic predicament within the general predicament in which the *corpus mundi* is caught. The war between men and women is, therefore, both the distillation of human confusion and its most apparent form.

Having said that Mrs. Mitty is the culmination of the Thurber woman of the early period, let us now try to discern how Thurber arrived at this character by examining the images of women in some of his important cartoons and early stories. Later, we shall also attempt to discover where Thurber went after creating Mrs. Mitty, and why.

Although anyone familiar with Thurber's drawings has probably developed some theory about his view of men and women, the significance of this relationship is the most misunderstood aspect of his art. The popular view, which is shared by some critics, is that Thurber, like Twain, was a misogynist in both letters and life.[67] As I am not interested in Thurber's life in this study, I will attempt to delineate only the view of woman presented in his art. Woman, is, in fact, a very important creature in the *corpus mundi*, and we must understand her if we are to understand Thurber's anatomy of confusion.

"The War between Men and Women" is, of course, Thurber's phrase, the title he gave not only to a series of classic drawings but to a whole cultural phenomenon. Until now, when I have spoken about "man" in Thurber's world, I have meant humanity or mankind, in keeping with the traditional biases of our language and Thurber's usage, and without reference to gender. Now, however, I will be speaking about men and women as distinct creatures in Thurber's imagination. Since Thurber is much more interested in women than in men, our discussion of the war between men and women will necessarily focus on the female side of the battlefield.

In his delicate dissection of the war between the sexes, Thurber discovers the very heart of human confusion, the predicament within the predicament, the region of the *corpus mundi* where human failures and limitations are magnified by the lens of proximity and familiarity. And, we shall also learn that, although Thurber is best known for depicting the daily skirmishes in this war, his view of the battle of the sexes does change. A final truce is never declared, but Thurber comes to see creative possibilities for the misspent energies of men and women. In his last decade, he even suggests that woman may be the solution for man's history of confusion, a vital force bringing life and order from cycles of death and destruction. But, since the most common view of the Thurber woman is based on his cartoons, let us begin our discussion of her there.

Thurber did most of his cartoons during the thirties and early forties, before blindness made drawing impossible. His drawings, instantly recognizable and consistently provocative, were nonetheless done in extreme haste. Helen Thurber susbstantiates Thurber's claims that he did not take drawing seriously and often used it as a source of entertainment. He could do numerous drawings in one evening, and more often than not, gave them away to friends.[68] Therefore, the complexity and subtlety of his prose studies of marriage are in marked contrast to the primitive, almost spontaneous portrayal of the same subject in his drawings. Even so, when studied as pieces of the anatomy of confusion, Thurber's drawings do present a revealing view of the crazy cosmos about which he wrote.

The women in Thurber's cartoons are, like Mrs. Mitty, distinguished by their determination, vitality, and strength, even more than by their dowdiness, homeliness, or size. Thurber often suggests their dominance and forcefulness by adorning them with wildly arched, determined brow lines and exaggerated snarls that overwhelm their faces and the scenes in which they act. Manifestly aggressive, his women sometimes wear hats that resemble weapons, as though they must always be ready for the next encounter with a Thurber man.[69] These women seem to be either in motion or idling, with their motors running, waiting to charge out again. They are in marked contrast to Thurber's men, who are bewildered, sedentary, and assaulted by the world. In fact, Thurber inverts the traditional view of men as doers, giving this active role to his women and causing laughter because of the surprising switch. Such a radical difference between men and women is also one of the reasons that they fight their perplexing war.

Even as a sexual creature, the Thurber woman is more active and alive than her mate. Although almost no Thurber man has a hair on his head, the Thurber woman's hair is perhaps her dominant feature. (One would hardly call it her crowning glory, however). It is as wild and restless as her actions. Indeed, if such a thing is possible, it resembles exposed and stimulated nerve endings as it radiates from her great head and charges the atmosphere around her. Often naked, or clothed in vaguely ancient garments that barely cover, these women display an undisguised, if unappealing, buxom sensuality.

"Have you seen my pistol, Honey-bun?"

They have come, it seems, directly from the caves of the collective unconscious.

By comparison, Thurber men are almost desexualized, although their gender remains distinct. In contrast to the nearly naked women, they usually have almost no skin exposed. Repressed and constricted, Thurber men wear the uniform of the middle-aged, middle-class, middle-brow at the middle of this century: the illfitting and nondescript suit, the bow tie, and often the pince-nez. Sometimes adorned with a civilized mustache, the typical Thurber man has no other hair on his body, a detail suggesting both his lack of sensuality and his difference from the Thurber woman. Indeed, it is probably confronting the wildly undisguised sexuality of the female that frightens the Thurber male into his armchair.

Thurber women are forceful, if banal; dynamic, if vulgar. Unlike the men with whom they spar endlessly in claustrophobic domiciles, these women seem able to meet a crazy world on their terms: they throw bowling balls; they hear real seals barking in bedrooms; they carry shotguns to bed, prepared for the certain insurrection; they overpower everything, including and especially the men, on the scene.[70] In this sense, they are true ancestors of Elaine Vital, the mythical future woman that Thurber was later to envision in an apt pun on Bergson's theory of the comic life force, or the *élan vital*.

Surprising as it may be, Elaine Vital is the direct descendant of a woman portrayed in the very early series of drawings entitled "The Race of Life," which was published in 1932 in *The Seal in the Bedroom*. In this whimsical version of Dante's *Commedia*, it is the woman who guides her unknowing and weaker partner through the perilous journey. Even though this is an early work, its male-female relationship lacks the feeling of hostility and estrangement that characterizes most of Thurber's earlier pieces. The woman begins the journey and gets progressively farther ahead of the man: she is, we learn, "The Pacemaker" in the race of life, as well as the leader in its "Spring Dance," a maytime fertility celebration that requests continuation of the species. She is the life force—willingly carrying the man when he is unable to continue alone, protecting him from "The Menace," and staying "On Guard" while her weaker and slower partner must sleep. At the end of their journey, she is still full of vitality, while her mate seems incapable of reaching "The Goal." We trust that this disarming, gibbous female will help him across, though, especially as we see them strike an unusual Thurber pose: in a drawing called "Sunset," they sit arm in arm—placid, trusting lovers on the primeval beach of life.[71] Thurber's respect for woman's strength, resiliency, and courage is thus revealed even in this early series. Although this respect does not become a dominant theme until much later in his career, "The Race of Life" shows that Thurber's attitude toward the female of the species was always complex. It also demonstrates Thurber's wistful longing for another time and another place—a place where men and women would work together, not against each other, as they do in the modern world.

The more familiar profile of the Thurber woman is captured in a single untitled cartoon that has come to be known as "Home," a drawing in which a nightmare image incorporates a woman's body into the facade of an ordinary American home.[72] This woman, who represents Thurber's Everywoman of the early period, seems to grow out of the very structure of the house. She turns toward the shrivelled man, presumably her husband, with her great arms outstretched, not in a welcoming embrace, but in a menacing swathe that seems ready to swallow up the tiny male figure that is approaching timorously. There is no joy in her impending victory, however; she only seems grimly determined to get her man. In this single drawing, Thurber dramatizes not only the dominance of the American male by the female, but also the total identification of the modern bourgeois woman with her home. This woman, lying in wait for her easy prey, has no identity except that which we perceive: she is a house-woman, an identity that gives neither man nor woman any joy. If her husband seems the pathetic victim of her aggressive stare and smothering embrace, she is just as victimized by the house that imprisons her. She is, therefore, not only an archetypal image in Thurber's anatomy of confusion, but also in the history of American culture.

A series called "The War between Men and Women" presents a whole gallery of such images. Here, the anatomist portrays a class war between the sexes: this is not the one-to-one combat suggested in "Home," nor the insidious war of nerves fought by the individual couples in the short stories, but a picture of general bedlam. In "The War between Men and Women," Thurber gives a provocative name to, and creates a series of inimitable images for, an age-old conflict. The battle erupts at that most revealing and barbaric of modern

Untitled drawing of woman/house, called "Home."

rituals, the cocktail party, when a man throws a drink in a woman's face; it rages on through equally mundane settings from the modern world: the grocery, the "club," and finally, the well-kept suburban lawns where men and women fight out the final stages of domestic disaster. Society's basic unit, the family, has failed, its demise fittingly brought about within the context of our routines and our affluence. The series ends in a temporary "Surrender," where the women's general appears to surrender her club to the men. We must not understand this final drawing to mean an end to the sexual war, however, for there is a strong suggestion in the woman's defiantly arched eyebrow that she is about to club the unwitting fool on the head. (See *Men, Women, and Dogs,* p. 205.) There is certainly no reason to believe that these frames represent anything but prototypical segments in an ongoing war. In these drawings, Thurber discovers the simmering violence underlying the cold war that men and women fight everyday; the actual bedlam here is but the explosion of this usually unspoken aggression and misunderstanding through the brittle surface of modern life. Forty years after Thurber gave us a name for it, the war rages on, in ways that make his vision seem only too prophetic. Like his fables, Thurber's drawings depict the timeless and the typical in human experience.

Thurber captures moments of perfectly normal madness in his drawings of men and women, but in his short stories he plumbs sexual conflict in all its complexity. From the first well-drawn Thurber couple, Mr. and Mrs. Monroe of *The Owl in the Attic* (1931), to Mr. and Mrs. Mitty, the fiction of Thurber's early period is filled with couples at war. John Monroe's inane posturing adumbrates Mitty's fantasies, and the ironically named "Little Mrs. Monroe" is really a bombshell of the proportions of the housewoman in "Home." In fact, Monroe is so enervated by his little bombshell that he is unable to execute a planned indiscretion without her supervision.[73] This, clearly, is domination.

Throughout the Monroe stories, the reader senses that these people are funny and sad, not only because John must rely upon his stronger partner and his fantasies to get through life, but also because only the form of marriage remains in a tired atmosphere that is distinguished by a lack of desire and pleasure. Robert Morsberger appropriately compares John Monroe to other impotent males in modern American fiction, especially Jake Barnes in *The Sun Also*

Rises. Even more important, however, is how this situation becomes humorous in Thurber's stories. In his "Notes on the Comic," Auden remarks that although marriage is not a comic institution per se, it "becomes comic if social emotion is the only motive for a marriage, so that the essential motives for marriage, sexual intercourse, procreation, and personal affection, are lacking."[74] In the Monroe stories, the cartoons, and "The Secret Life of Walter Mitty," sex and personal affection are not only lacking but are hard to imagine. When children appear occasionally in the drawings (none of Thurber's fictional couples is "blessed with issue"), one wonders how they managed to get there. As we have seen, by the time of *The Last Flower,* Thurber begins stressing the importance of sexual motives and pleasure in human life, but earlier he is most interested in describing the situation of sterility and boredom in the modern world.

The influence of Henry James on Thurber's style is quite apparent in the earliest of his stories,[75] but it is also likely that his knowledge of James helped Thurber form his concept of the war betwen men and women. In both writers, this war is usually fought beneath the facade of polite manners, a battle of submerged nerves and quivering nuance. Indeed, what could better describe the typical Thurber couple than Isabel Archer's characterization of her own miserable life with Osmond: "They were strangely married, at all events, and it was a horrible life."[76] Furthermore, James's derisive pictures of looming and zooming American women are mirrored in the Thurber woman, who overshadows everything on the horizon. In a sense, it is Henry James who is the godfather of Mrs. Mitty, "little" Mrs. Monroe, and Ulgine Barrows (in "The Catbird Seat.").

As he matured, Thurber's attitude toward the war between men and women became more complicated and more subtle. Two exceptionally fine short stories, "The Breaking Up of the Winships" and "A Couple of Hamburgers," published in *Let Your Mind Alone!* (1937), dramatize the familiar battleground, but in these stories the anatomist moves further from caricature and closer to real life. The consequence of this shift is that the stories become at once more ambiguous and more disquieting. In "Winships," Thurber pictures for the first time a marriage of relatively attractive people who seem equally responsible for what happens to them. In a ridiculous but immediately recognizable argument over whether Donald Duck or Greta Garbo is the greatest genius of the modern age, these two ordinary, basically likable people destroy their life together. That all of this happens as easily as saying "quack, quack," only underscores the tenuous nature of the relationship between men and women and the fragile hold that anyone has on rationality. Thurber is always at his best when describing the extraordinary confusion resulting from ordinary situations, and this story is one of the finest examples of Thurberian confusion.

The initial argument between Gordon and Marcia Winship is humorous because it is trivial and we are able to witness it through the eyes of a detached Jamesian narrator. From this safe distance and with this fine sense of irony, we laugh at the nonsensical confusion before us. As the story quickly moves on, however, Thurber employs battle imagery ("She had recourse to her eyes as weapons") to enhance the feeling of aggression in the situation. When the Winships separate and leave the restaurant where their argument erupted, with "their resentment swelling, their sense of values blurring," the reader foresees their doom. At a party a few days later, Gordon meets Marcia's angry gaze with, we are told, the greatest of all resentments, "the resentment of the misunderstood husband." Marcia compounds the conflict when she senses that her position in the contest is "a part and parcel of her integrity as a woman." Thus, the Winships remain estranged and hostile because of their rigid definition of themselves as man and woman—definitions so far apart that an unbridgeable gap exists between them. As the story is presented, the breakup of the Winships is the inevitable resolution of a sequence of ordinary events from normal life.[77] The story's ultimately serious effect relies on our knowledge that all couples do argue, that people quickly become irrational when they argue, that drinking only adds to the irrationality, that people misconstrue situations based upon preconceived notions, and that the wounds of such bitterness and hostility often never heal. The most unsettling thing about "The Breaking Up of the Winships" is that two such people, in such ordinary circumstances, can watch their lives fall apart and, in the confusion between men and women, become overwhelmed and lost.

"A Couple of Hamburgers" portrays a much less attractive couple driving down the road of life, arguing and needling each other, as the narrator reminds the reader of the passage of time. Like most of Thurber's pictures of marriage, this story is a report from the war zone, not, as the Winships' story had been, a retelling of the final defeat of a relationship. The people in "Hamburgers" are caught somewhere between the beginning of a marriage, which seems a dim memory, and its seemingly inevitable failure. As we watch them fight the cold war of nervous attrition, Thurber's fine-tuned prose makes us feel the atmosphere of frustration and hostility in which they wrestle:

> He finished his hamburgers and his coffee slowly. It was terrible coffee. Then he went out to the car and got in and drove off, slowly humming "Who's Afraid of the Big Bad Wolf?" After a mile or so, "Well," he said, "what was the matter with the Elite Diner, milady?" "Didn't you see the cloth the man was wiping the counter with?" she demanded. "Ugh!" She shuddered. "I didn't happen to want to eat any of the counter," he said. He laughed at that comeback. "You didn't even notice it," she said. "You never notice anything. It was filthy." "I noticed they had some damn fine coffee in there," he said. "It was swell." He knew she loved good coffee. He began to hum his tune again; then he whistled it; but she knew that he knew that she was annoyed. "Will you be kind enough to tell me what time it is?" she asked. "Big *bad* wolf, big *bad* wolf — five minutes o' five — tum-dee-doo-dee-dum-m-m." She settled back in her seat and took a cigarette from her case and tapped it on the case. "I'll wait till we get home," she said. "If you'll be kind enough to speed up a little." He drove on at the same speed. After a time he gave up the "Big Bad Wolf" and there was a deep silence for two miles. Then suddenly he began to sing, very loudly, "H-A-double-R-I-G-A-N spells Harr-i-gan-." She gritted her teeth. She hated that worse than any of his songs except "Barney Google." He would go on to "Barney Google" pretty soon, she knew.[78]

The explosive tension that is barely under control here finally bursts through the surface in a story written for *The Thurber Carnival,* and I wish to end this discussion of Thurber's early portrayal of men and women by looking at "The Catbird Seat."

By the time Thurber put together this retrospective in 1945, his work was ranging out from stories and essays into fable, parable, and fairy tale. About this time, and associated with his experimentation in these new forms, he began concentrating less upon the horrors of marriage in the modern world and became more interested in the possibility of men and women living together peacefully in the distant worlds of fairyland and the far future. As he was turning to this vision of qualified happiness between men and women in the fairy tales, however, Thurber wrote "The Catbird Seat," a classic short story in which undisguised sexual hostility allows the destruction of the hideous female caricature that Thurber's early work had created.

In a story written a few years before "The Catbird Seat," Walter Mitty dreams of his own death as a way out of the battle of the sexes, but Erwin Martin has the temerity to act out his hostility toward Ulgine Barrows. Although Martin rationalizes that what he hates about Mrs. Barrows is her bringing confusion to the organization where they both work, we know better, for we are told that "the faults of the woman as a woman kept chattering on in his mind like an unruly witness." Barrows, like the female vulgarians ridiculed by James, has faults that are impossible to overlook; she is banal, loud, and crass, galloping around the office as "a circus horse," greeting the fastidious Martin with a "braying laugh. . .like the report of a shotgun." What is so marvelous about this story is that Martin eventually "kills" Barrows with cleverness; she is declared a lunatic because Martin convinces her that he is a heroin addict, an impossible "fact" that she promptly repeats to everyone at F & S. Martin, who drinks milk while plotting Barrows's "murder" and has never been seen smoking a cigarette, is the victor in this little sexual game and, like the meek husband in "The Unicorn in the Garden," has the rare last laugh for a Thurber male.[79] Since neither Martin nor Barrows is an attractive character, we are able to view dispassionately the effects of the cruel sexual joke they play. Indeed, any story that makes both characters attractive or sympathetic ("Winships") or both unattractive ("Catbird") will have this effect. With Ulgine Barrows mercifully squashed (we want her dead as much as Martin does), Thurber can move on to another kind of woman.

In his early cartoons and stories, then, Thurber is preoccupied with the unending confusion between men and women in the modern world, focusing upon marriages in decline. The anatomist dissects the *corpus mundi* to its very heart, revealing at last the predicament within the predicament — the war between men and women. In some of his early essays, including "Courtship Through the Ages" and his chapters in *Is Sex Necessary?*, the noted anthropologist, Dr. James Thurber, studies the history of sexual behavior and concludes that it was the making of sexuality into a mere game that ruined the human relationship between men and women. He even coins a term, "Pedestalism," for a basic cultural phenomenon in the western world: the unnatural, enslaving reverence for women.[80] This is an appropriate choice of words, for objects on pedestals are easily broken and invite potshots. This image also suggests the fragility and unreality of male-female relationships in the modern world, as is starkly portrayed in Thurber's cartoons of men and women. Typical of his delicate balancing of pathos and humor, Thurber calls the long history of misunderstanding and game-playing between the sexes "a bright and melancholy story." In Thurber's deft hands, the anatomy of such a debacle is both bright and melancholy, enlightening and saddening, amusing and frightening. In this characteristically enigmatic phrase, the anatomist suggests why he is so driven to analyze the terrible confusion between men and women.

The emphasis is upon the brighter side of the male-female relationship in Thurber's only completed play, *The Male Animal* (1939), which he wrote with Elliott Nugent, a friend from student days at Ohio State. Perhaps because of the conventions of theatrical comedy in this country, *The Male Animal* deals rather lightly with some standard Thurber themes, themes that he probes with more subtlety and less expectable results in his fiction: the battle of the sexes, the impotence of modern man, the superiority of the "lower" animals, and the central role of free expression in human life. Professor Tommy Turner, the play's reluctant hero, learns in the space of a weekend that "he's a male animal," meaning that he, like the males in the wild animal kingdom, must defend his home or his kind when attacked; he must act, not simply talk. As we have seen, action is unusual for any Thurber man, and this play also has a rather unusual resolution for a Thurber plot: Turner saves his marriage by assuming dominance over his "little woman," a character who is closer to the stock American wife of Broadway and Hollywood than to Thurber's fictional women. It is likely that Thurber was influenced not only by his collaborator, who had extensive experience in American theater, but also by the assumed expectations of mainstream theater-goers. The most characteristic Thurber touches in this play are the depiction of Turner before his change into a "male animal," when he reminds one of Mitty and Monroe in his inability to find matchboxes or keep up with football players, and later, as a newly-emerged "animal," when he talks about the kinship between man and other beasts.[81] Outside of these elements, the play is not typical either of Thurber's tone or his portrayal of men and women.

At the end of the thirties, Thurber began experimenting not only in a variety of new forms, but also with many old ideas. It is difficult to say which of many factors most influenced this change, but it is likely that each of the following had an effect: the developing economic and political crisis that was to culminate in the Second World War; Thurber's own aging, which was exacerbated by a number of physical problems, especially his blindness; his personal success, and tentative adjustment to it; and, perhaps in ways too subtle to calculate, his successful second marriage.[82] Beyond these, as an artist Thurber must have been motivated to explore new forms and to devise new ways of addressing perennial subjects. After all, in "The Secret Life of Walter Mitty" he had written the definitive "Thurber story." Rather than continuing to rewrite the same story, as lesser artists would do, it appears that Thurber instinctively chose to develop and change. At any rate, with *The Last Flower* and the fairy tales we see Thurber beginning to focus on the glimmer of brightness in the melancholy scene. It seems no longer enough for him to paint—with fine irony and great insight—the actual hell of the modern world. Now he seems driven to ask more difficult questions in his art: "If human life *was* ever thus, what now? Is it possible to rejuvenate this dead world, to change it? Most particularly, can men and women *ever* learn to live together?" If the answer to this last question should be "yes," then it would be possible to strike confusion at its core and perhaps to cure the *corpus mundi* of its ancient disease. Thus, the anatomist of confusion must investigate the possibility.

As we have seen, Thurber always perceived woman as strong, vital, and determined. Indeed, she is the *first* sex in Thurber's anatomy. This recognition of her strength and vitality is often attended in the early work by a sense of fear and horror. In *The Last Flower,* however, the Thurber woman moves beyond aggressive domination of the male. She begins doing the work of mother earth, functioning as the *élan vital* and, with her mate, creating the world as she goes along. At this time, therefore, Thurber begins to perceive woman's strength as a positive force—the last hope for the rejuvenation and continuation of a decadent world. At last, the Thurber woman discovers an object great enough for her strong will and boundless energy: the entire world. Since she remains, above all else, strong and alive, hers is a consistent character that changes, develops, and mellows—not a series of radically different or conflicting images. As early as "The Race of Life," Thurber had celebrated woman's strength, resiliency, and vitality; over the years, he became increasingly inclined to regard her strength as a cause for hope, not fear, and as a generator of joy, not sadness. Walter Mitty was brutalized by Mrs. Mitty's misdirected energy, but the heroes of Thurber's fairy tales are complemented by their strong female partners. This integration effects at least a momentary end to the confusion in which each tale begins. Ultimately, Thurber suggests that the female life force that he personifies as "Elaine Vital" may be able to create such an order in the future world. At least, his parables and tales argue, she will continually recreate the world after man's destruction of it. We can regard *The Last Flower* as a kind of transitional work, one that connects Thurber's pictures of marital tension and horror from the thirties with the images of qualified happiness presented in his fairy tales of the forties and fifties.

As noted in our discussion of Thurber's social criticism, *The Last Flower* begins after World War XII has destroyed the world, in the familiar Thurber landscape of dissolution. This "Parable in Pictures," is, therefore, the graphic representation of the abyss toward which the early works had always been edging. Significantly, it is the picture of a world in which "boys and girls grew up to stare at each other blankly, for love had passed from the earth." It is, in fact, the living hell that was adumbrated in the impotence and emptiness of the Monroes and the Mittys.

The Last Flower is really the story of that indefatigable, creative woman described earlier in "The Race of Life" and "Women Go On Forever." When the young girl reestablishes a fertile landscape, both pleasure and procreation come back into the world with the rebirth of human sexuality. It is apparent in this book's frank acceptance of sensuality that Thurber did not despise either women or sex. Indeed, woman is the source of life, joy, and pleasure in *The Last Flower*. It is men who become soldiers and fake "liberators" and destroy the fragile world she has nurtured against all odds. In the end, all that is left of humanity is the lonely trio of one man, one woman, and one flower, suggesting an eternity of cyclic death and rebirth. Without woman, the parable foresses no end to death and destruction: in her absence, we may assume, there would not even be the cycle of life, death, and rejuvenation, but only a grim regressive spiral. In this sense the girl in *The Last Flower,* like the "mature" Thurber woman generally, is a comic hero.[83] This is to say, she makes order possible and brings the world to life.

These mature females—mature because they are products of Thurber's deeper understanding of the sexes—appear only in his parables and fairy tales. When Thurber writes about the real world of twentieth-century America, he deals only with the hell of the early stories: sterile, suffering, and inarticulate. After 1939, however, Thurber's work takes place increasingly in the distant worlds of fable and fairy tale. In these tales, the men (at least the heroes) are brighter, less bumbling, and generally more attractive than their counterparts in the short stories; the women are remarkably bright, loving, and appealing. And here, for the first time in Thurber's world, men and women do live and work together peacefully, using their energy to make new worlds instead of destroying existing ones. It is chiefly because of this remarkable change in the relationship between men and women that these stories are so different from Thurber's early fiction and drawings. Even in his later work, Thurber perceives the *corpus mundi* as a state of chaos, but woman is no longer cast as the instigator of confusion or as the enemy of man. Instead, she functions as the maker of peace, understanding, and order. No longer "the enemy," she is friend, partner, teacher, and mate. She is life itself. A brief review of the women in Thurber's fairy tales should demonstrate this.

Although women are not especially important in either *Many Moons* (1943) or *The Great Quillow* (1944), in *The White Deer* (1945) Thurber presents his first completely attractive fictional woman, the Princess Rosanore. Her mate is Prince Jorn, the poet who "sang that love, not might, would untie the magic knot," thus foretelling that it would not be a simple victory of muscle that would end the confusion in his world. Only Jorn is able to accept the Princess as she really is, only Jorn loves her in spite of the fact that she was once a deer. When he tells Rosanore this, Jorn voices the eternal, enigmatic hope of marriage: "What you have been, you are not, and what you are, you will forever be." This ideal, but not idealized, woman is Jorn's true mate because she matches his great endurance, valor, and honesty. Rosanore is "as wise as she is lovely," and the book stresses her intelligence and honesty even more than her beauty, thus adding special seriousness to a superficially traditional fairy tale character. As Jorn and Rosanore dance their wedding dance together, the blind clockmaker Tocko recites an incantation suggesting that this marriage of true minds signifies triumph over the confusion and mutability of the world: "As slow as time, as long as love: the rose, the fountain, and the dove."[84] This scene is a long way from "The War between Men and Women" in the chaotic modern world. Only in his last three fairy tales does Thurber use the traditional comic ending of a marriage feast to represent the institution of life and order in an unruly world.

Five years after *The White Deer*, in *The 13 Clocks,* Thurber writes once again about the marriage of a poet and a wise and lovely lady. In this apparently conventional plot, a damsel in distress must be rescued by an attractive young prince. According to a witch's spell, the Princess Saralinda is imprisoned by the evil Duke of Coffin Castle, who may hold her until her twenty-first birthday, at which time he may enslave her in a different way by forcing her to marry him. As a part of the spell, however, the Duke must also allow other suitors to compete for Saralinda's hand by performing terrible tasks. No one, until Prince Zorn, is successful. Zorn succeeds with help from both his friend, the Golux (or light), and Saralinda herself (or love); he therefore achieves his goal by using both his head and his heart, and by working with, not against, a woman. Like Rosanore, Saralinda is described in terms of life and vitality, in juxtaposition with the cold duke, for "she was warm in every wind and weather," and resembled the rose. Perhaps no other woman in Thurber's work less matches the popular conception of "the Thurber woman" than Saralinda: "The Princess Saralinda was tall, with freesias in her dark hair, and she wore serenity brightly like the rainbow. It was not easy to tell her mouth from the rose, or her brow from the white lilac. Her voice was faraway music, and her eyes were candles burning on a tranquil night. . . . The Duke. . . held up the palms of his gloves, as if she were a fire at which to warm his hands."[85] To remind the reader how remarkable this passage is, Saralinda was created just five years after Thurber's scathing portrait of the braying and stomping Ulgine Barrows in "The Catbird Seat."

Yet, even in this most romantic of all Thurber's fairy tales, with its emphasis on the powers of love and its conventional description of a beautiful woman, the Golux (the teacher) advises Zorn and Saralinda to "keep warm, ride close together. Remember laughter. You'll need it even in the blessed isles of Ever After." Since Thurber believed that laughter derived from our painful knowledge of the chaotic and finite nature of life, this advice qualifies the vision of happiness and order represented in the marriage of Zorn and Saralinda. In his description of their ride out to Yarrow to begin their new life, the narrator hesitates to affirm without reservation the power of human love, while still voicing his wistful hope that it is possible: "A fair wind stood for Yarrow and, looking far to the sea, the Princess Saralinda thought she saw, as people often think they see, on clear and windless days, the distant shining shores of Ever After. Your guess is quite as good as mine (there are a lot of things that shine) but I have always thought she did, and I will always think so."[86] Like the fragile hope for life that ends *The Last Flower*, Thurber here suggests that, in the absence of absolute love and complete happiness, we must still bravely attempt to love and to push on toward the shores of happiness that are ever just beyond the horizon. By coupling the ideal and the starkly real, the fantastic and the mundane, Thurber continually causes the reader to connect fairy land with the imperfect modern world and, thus, to comprehend the remarkable reality of human existence. It is a bright and melancholy spectacle indeed — its brightness glimmering even more significantly against its deeply melancholy background.

Thurber's last fairy tale, *The Wonderful O* (1957), uses neither a conventional fairy tale plot nor a conventional maiden as heroine. Rather, in the last period of his life when he was stating in essays that women must take over for the human race to survive, Thurber tells the story of a man and a woman who are equals. Their names, Andreus and Andrea, indicate that though their genders remain distinct, they are peers. Their shared role in resolving their predicament also implies that both the male and female sides of the human personality are necessary for a coherent existence. *The Wonderful O* is not really a love story, but an argument for human freedom and true communication. Not a woman, but a whole society is imprisoned in this tale, and it takes a man and woman working together, not merely a charming young prince, to free this society from bondage. In view of Thurber's early depictions of marriage, what is most important about *The Wonderful O* is that there is no sense of competition or hostility between the sexes here: Andrea and Andreus cooperate to overthrow the tyrants who have enslaved their world by banning the letter "O." Even though they marry, the notable image at the book's end is not the ringing of wedding bells, as in *The White Deer,* but the resounding bell of freedom. Like her distant sisters in "The Race of Life" and *The Last Flower,* it is Andrea who finds the book of magic that tells her people how to break the curse over them, and it is she who bravely teaches them to speak clearly and humanly once again: "'Be not afraid to speak with O's,' said Andrea at last. 'We cannot live or speak without hope, and hope without its O is nothing, and even nothing is less than nothing when it is nthing.'"[87] As his anatomy of the *corpus mundi* dramatizes, Thurber envisioned a deeply flawed, tragic world—a world perhaps as bleak as Lear's, where it is not only abundantly clear that "nothing will come from nothing," but more remarkably, that less than nothing is possible. The essential bleakness of Thurber's vision only makes his tentative suggestions for peace, order, and love more poignant and more noble. If he dared to face the awful emptiness of human existence, he also had the courage to see more than nothing. Finally, he dared to see beyond a vast world revolving in perpetual chaos, and to devise something upon which to celebrate life's meager feast.[88] He even dared at last to see an end to the war between men and women—if for just a moment.

Thurber's parables and tales continually connect women with hope, love, freedom, and life. In *The Last Flower,* a young girl doggedly protects the future of human existence; in *The White Deer,* Princess Rosanore's honesty and courage enable her mate to end the confusion in their world; in *The 13 Clocks,* Saralinda's rose, a symbol of eternal love, helps Zorn through the forbidding forest of life, and Saralinda herself starts the frozen thirteen clocks, thereby bringing life into Coffin Castle. Finally, in *The Wonderful O,* a woman is directly responsible for establishing human values and bringing order out of chaos. Since Thurber pictures such women and such marriages only in his fairy tales, it could be argued that he thought them impossible among real human beings. Yet, the fact that he even postulated an end to the battle of the sexes is evidence of his hope that it could happen. At least for the moment of artistic creation, in the final image of each of his fairy tales, peace between men and women is a reality. And when they are at peace, the whole world turns peacefully quiet. Thurber reserved this possibility for the far future and for fairy land. The more familiar Thurber woman lives in the actual modern world, which is a living hell.

Almost as if his experimentation with the idea in fairy tales permitted him the freedom, Thurber's last essays state directly his theory of the strong and creative woman as a positive force. He could still embellish an old Thurber scene by satirizing the considerable irritations of a young Mrs. Malaprops,[89] but the emphasis at the end of Thurber's life is emphatically on the beneficent characteristics of women. Two of the most successful pieces in the autobiographical *Thurber Album* (1952) are portraits of the strong-willed, vibrant women who shaped Thurber's early life, his mother and Aunt Margery Albright. "Lavender with a Difference" describes his mother as the dominant character in the explosive Thurber household, a prototype for the mother in *My Life and Hard Times*. Her personality was so strong, in fact, that she dominated any group, and an aging Thurber openly relishes her independence and power. He also recalls with delight that she had the "gift of confusion," an essential trait for any inhabitant of the Thurber carnival who wishes to survive. "Daguerreotype of a Lady" captures a sharp image of Margery Albright: "An active woman who got things done" in a "time of stouthearted and self-reliant women." Ironically, Thurber's nostalgic pieces seem to hum, "Give me some women who are stouthearted women." Margery Albright is associated closely with her garden in Thurber's memory, a fact that suggests her alliance with both beauty and fertility.[90] It is probable that Thurber's memories of such strong women helped form his basic impressions of feminine strength, which inform even his early works, and that, as he aged, he needed to explore the meaning of these memories.

In many of his final statements, Thurber expresses directly his trust in woman's strength. His second retrospective collection, *Alarms and Diversions* (1957), begins with an essay about the strength and superiority of women. In keeping with the fashion of the 1950s, the piece is called "The Ladies of Orlon." The anatomist concludes that woman, made of tougher fiber than man, "is now definitely here to stay, whereas the decline of the male, even the actual decadence of the insecure sex, has been observed." This image of the future recalls Thurber's early prediction in "Women Go On Forever":

> Socially, economically, physically, and intellectually, Man is slowly going, I am reliably told, to hell. His world is blowing over; his day is done. . . .
> Each expert, in his fashion, has analyzed the decline of mankind and most have prescribed remedies for the patient. But none of them, I believe, has detected the fact that although Man, as he is now travelling, is headed for extinction, Woman is not going with him. It is, I think, high time to abandon the loose generic term, "Man," for it is no loner logically inclusive or scientifically exact. There is Man and there is Woman, and Woman is going her own way.[91]

This is a theme that Thurber was to repeat again and again during the last years of his life. In studying the unending chaos on earth, Thurber tried continually to find a way out of the confusion, an end to disorder, and in woman he saw one possibility. Appropriately, his last collection of fables dramatizes the gap between men and women as well as the creative possibilities of the "secure sex." The opening fable, "The Sea and the Shore," recounts the genesis of life according to Thurber. In his history of the human race, it is the female who first climbs out of the sea and onto land—in fact, she is roughly "a couple of eons" ahead of the male. The moral is clear and reflects a truth about all Thurber couples, happy or sad: "Let us ponder this basic fact about the human: Ahead of every man, not behind him, is a woman."[92] The last fable in the collection, "The Shore and the Sea," pictures the end of the society started by that far-seeing female. The collapse of civilization is instigated by a male lemming who irrationally urges his kinsmen to rush back into the sea and drown. The drama reenacted in these two fables is, of course, another version of the plot of *The Last Flower*: cycles of creation and destruction, of life and death, with woman acting for life in each story.

Although a sensitive reading of Thurber's work reveals the crucial place of woman in his anatomy of confusion, he finally explains her relationship to his "comic theory" in *Lanterns & Lances*

(1961): "I am more interested in Thurber's theory of Elaine Vital, the female life force, than in Bergson's theory of Élan Vital, the masculine life force. . . . Elaine Vital, if properly directed—that is, let alone—may become the hope of the future."[93] An end to chaos and destruction is always only a possibility for Thurber, but especially at the end of his life, he urgently explores the creative powers of the female as one possibility for ensuring the survival of the race.

It is a long, hard way from Little Mrs. Monroe to Elaine Vital, or even to the princesses in the fairy tales. Both Elaine Vital and Princess Rosanore remain mythical women, images from the faraway worlds of fairy land and the distant future where Thurber dares to glimpse an end to the war between men and women. Yet, there are some consistent qualities in the Thurber woman, from beginning to end, and they are strength, power, and vitality. Most of his women are also allied wth natural or sensual things. In any Thurber cartoon or short story, therefore, you may see the distant ancestor— unrefined, misdirected, sometimes barely recognizable—of Elaine Vital, of the young savior of the race in *The Last Flower,* and of the equally strong, wise, and lovely women in the fairy tales. In much of his work, Thurber emphasizes the imperfect marriage and the hostility between men and women because, within the context of present confusion, they are reality. When he looked into the future, however, Thurber saw the great energy and vitality of the female eventually bringing life and order to a chaotic, destructive universe. If one needs to label it, this is perhaps a sexist view of men and women, but it is one that is at least as close to contemporary feminisim as to traditional misogyny.

Thurber best summarized his complex conception of women in a rare public speech:

> Somebody has said that Woman's place is in the wrong.
> That's fine. What the wrong needs is a woman's presence
> and a woman's touch. She is far better equipped than men
> to set it right. The condescending male, in his pride of
> strength, likes to think of the female as being "soft, soft
> as snow," but just wait till he gets hit by the snowball.
> Almost any century now Woman may lose her patience
> with black politics and red war and let fly. I wish I could
> be on earth then to witness the saving of our self-destructive

species by its greatest creative force. If I have sometimes seemed to make fun of Woman, I assure you it has only been for the purpose of egging her on.[94]

The really horrible Thurber women — Ulgine Barrows, Mrs. Mitty — are horrible because, in an inversion of sexual roles, they assume the most deplorable traits of conventional men: they are hostile, aggressive, full of hatred. They are destroyers in humanity's long history of destruction. Thurber never really relents in his vision of unending chaos, but, in his desire to find a way out of the human predicament, he suggests that woman's immense power can at least keep the cycle of life going, inevitably rebuilding after the equally inevitable destruction.

Besides all of these endlessly perplexed and perplexing human beings, there are a few less alarming creatures in the Thurber carnival. We shall complete our tour of the *corpus mundi* with a note on them.

Sane Canines, or Sound Creatures in a Crazy World

As we have seen, Thurber's world is a macrocosm of bedlam filled with disintegrating societies, disordered households, mad specialists, perplexing machines, confusing theories, and warring couples. Standing just outside the chaos, the anatomist can see and focus for others the rampant confusion in the *corpus mundi*. In Thurber's depictions of this world, we see all human systems, institutions, and relationships crumble, while man himself glides, as an erratic star, through the universal chaos. From his vantage point as detached observer of life's bedlam, Thurber is able to perceive the irrational human animal at the very center of the world's confusion. Therefore, when he compares *Homo sapiens* to other beasts on planet earth, the comparison only underscores humanity's essential craziness and imperfection. Often, Thurber's dogs seem able to perceive the cloudy chaos surrounding them; they, too, are anatomists of confusion, humorous spectators in a dismal human world. Thus, the Thurber menagerie is included in his anatomy of confusion not simply as an afterthought, an embellishment, or a bit of whimsy, but as an essential means to clarify and intensify our profound sense

Untitled drawing of man, woman, and dog.

of human confusion. It unforgettably presents Thurber's images of the few sound creatures in this crazy world.

Despite the justifiable popularity of the Thurber dog, the plethora of animals in his work has probably been the main cause of Thurber's being wrongly and widely considered "elfin," "zany," or "whimsical," to use a few of his own least favorite words from reviews.[95] Such a misunderstanding is especially unfortunate, for Thurber uses animals to focus a serious, often grim world view. Thurber's greatest indictment of the corruption and confusion inherent in human nature is implied in his protrayal of the more noble and reasonable "lower" animals. Since the dog is the best known and the most important member of the Thurber menagerie, we will begin this inquriy into the importance of animals in Thurber's world by discussing representative pieces from *Thurber's Dogs* (1955), the collection that includes most of his stories and essays about the species.

In his introduction to this collection, Thurber bemoans the woes that have befallen the noble dog, those painful effects of the arrogant attempts of people to make the dog over into their image. To Thurber's dismay, the dog has been leashed, clipped, bred, shown, and fed in a manner suited to human beings not dogs. Mercifully, for both of them, the dog has simply been amused by the silly ministrations of his inane "master": "The list of his woes could be continued indefinitely. But he has also had his fun, for he has been privileged to live with and study at close range the only creature with reason, the most unreasonable of creatures."[96] All of Thurber's beasts—the dogs in his cartoons, the imaginary animals in "the New Natural History," the lone wood duck over the busy highway, the dolphins in the essays—are included in his anatomy to emphasize the unreasonableness of the "the rational animal" and to highlight the nature of his predicament.

The presence of these noble beasts in a chaotic world makes our knowledge of human nature both more awful and more acceptable. It seems more awful because humans, in their rampant imperfection, are discovered beneath the "lower" animals. Yet, it is easier to accept this dismal vision because it is relieved by the presence of animals less complicated and more appealing than *Homo sapiens*. Indeed, a trip through the Thurber carnival is not depressing, even though it is disquieting, because we may catch glimpses of his remarkable bestiary along the way. Somehow, Thurber people are easier to face with these less alarming creatures nearby.

As the existence of a full volume on them testifies, references to dogs fill Thurber's stories and essays, and they are ubiquitous in his drawings. There is the story of "The Dog That Bit People" and memories of "Canines in the Cellar" (in *My Life and Hard Times*). Even the wretched Mittys have a dog (it eats, we presume, puppy biscuits), as do the Monroes and poor Emma Inch. Thurber's first story was about a dog, and later in his life he researched the species, reporting his findings in essays such as "Lo, the Gentle Bloodhound." There are also moving obituaries for a number of Thurber's real dogs, which is no wonder; he admitted to having owned and loved over fifty-five dogs in his lifetime. With the notable exception of Muggs, the dog that bit people, they seem to have been an attractive crowd.[97]

Thurber remarks in an essay called "Christabel" that the poodle is "the most charming of species, including the human . . . [because] they happily lack Man's aggression, irritability, quick temper, and wild aim." Incapable of war and destruction, the poodle is outside human confusion. Equally important, she escapes confusion because she is a "humorist," as her sensible behavior at a dog show demonstrated: after being fixed up in a foolish manner, "The poodle instantly began to howl . . . to express disapproval of the judge, the bedlam, and the whole distressing spectacle." Like the anatomist, the poodle sees the insanity of the human spectacle and is, therefore, a "humorist" according to Thurber's definition. Detached from human society, she consequently can really see it, and thus howls in disapproval at its mad rituals. The poodle is so separated from the bedlam, in fact, that she remains untouched by the foolish addiction to gadgets and gimmickry that plagues human beings: she "doesn't like unnecessary sounds; she likes quiet and tranquility." In another essay on dogs, Thurber asserts that anyone who will admit the truth knows that "Man is troubled by what might be called the Dog Wish, a strange and involved compulsion to be as happy and carefree as a dog."[98] Certainly many dog owners may be heard voicing just this wish.

Because Thurber acknowledges the innate limitations of human beings, he is not suggesting, in his paeans to dogs, that we would be better if we could return to the innocence of nature. A poem written during Thurber's adolescence to mourn the deaths of two of his dogs says that the dogs are in "some canine paradise," because they were "innocent of human crime and sin." Indeed, it is because dogs are radically different from human beings that Thurber loves and respects them. Charles Holmes is correct when he says that "Thurber's dogs are his contact with peace and innocence,"[99] but Thurber was not suggesting that people could become more like dogs and thereby end the confusion and corruption in the *corpus mundi*.

Thurber's most comprehensive statement on the dog is his moving "Memorial," a eulogy to his first poodle. In this short, compressed, and poignant essay, he states his essential conviction that dogs are saner than people: "She tried patiently at all times to understand Man's way of life: the rolling of his wheels; the raising of his voice; the ringing of his bells; his way of searching out with lights the dark protecting corners of the night; his habit of building his beds inside walls, high above the nurturing earth."[100] This passage connects Thurber's distrust of human nature and of what we commonly call "progress" with his admiration and affection for the dog. This connection must be kept in mind if we are to understand the significance of these sound creatures in a crazy world. Indeed, Thurber's dogs are always implicitly compared to their environment, which is suffused with the madness and degradation of human beings.

Though he does not believe that people can become more dog-like, Thurber postulates half-seriously that perhaps one day the poodles will take over the world:

> The poodle I knew seemed sometimes about to bridge mysterious and conceivably narrow gap that separates instinct from reason.... There were times when she seemed to come close to a pitying comprehension of the whole troubled scene and what lies behind it. If poodles, who walk so easily upon their hind legs, ever do learn the little tricks of speech and reason, I should not be surprised if they made a better job of it than Man, who would seem to be surely but not slowly slipping back to all fours.[101]

This description of Thurber's poodle as coming close to "a pitying comprehension of the whole troubled scene" explains the function of the Thurber dog, that genuine humorist, in the drawings and stories generally. The anatomist, of course, is ever interested in comprehending the troubled scene and in understanding what lies behind the chaos.

The well-known Thurber dog is not a poodle, however, nor an accurate representative of any particular breed. Rather, he is a sort of generalized hound dog, combining the stubby legs and massive body of the basset hound with the ponderous head of a bloodhound. Thurber said that his dog's legs were so short because, in the doodling that led to the dog's creation, he ran out of space on note pads. The Thurber dog may have started as an idle doodle during *New Yorker* editorial meetings, but as things seem to happen for genuine artists, it eventually assumed its rightful place in the body of Thurber's work. Thurber himself realized the dog's full significance years after his first sketches of it, as he told an interviewer: "I've always loved that dog. . . . Although at first he was a device, I gradually worked him in as a sound creature in a crazy world. . . . If I have [by comparison] run down the human species, it was not altogether unintentional."[102]

To understand what Thurber means by calling his dog "a sound creature in a crazy world," all one need do is study the cartoons in which both dogs and people appear. One drawing that exemplifies the dog's role in Thurber's anatomy of confusion is entitled "Cocktail Party—1937." Here the dog sleeps peacefully in the foreground of a wildly animated room full of people who are in various stages of inebriation[103] The dog seems to be a tranquil, inviolate island separated from the frenetic crowd by his self-possession and sanity. Of course, he also looks better than any human being in the scene. The trouble with these people is not that they are "acting like dogs," but that they are not.

The Thurber dog often appears perplexed, shocked, or disgusted by human behavior. In the drawing of a woman saying ridiculously into the telephone, "Well, if I called the wrong number, why did you answer the phone?," the woman's husband and dog react with similar dismay at her faulty logic. In another drawing, another witless woman asks, "Who is this Hitler and what does he want?," as her dog registers appropriate disgust at her ignorance. In a caricature of Thurber himself, working frantically with discarded note cards, his dog seems amused by the vanity of human wishes and the insanity of human routines.[104] Indeed, the dogs in each of these frames have all the sense, sanity, and calmness that Thurber people so completely lack. Thurber's depiction of human beings and animals is humorous because he inverts our comfortable assumptions that our world is ordered, sane, and purposeful, and then gives the so-called "brutes" the admirable qualities of sensibility and nobility. Yet, as his essays

Cocktail Party, 1937

show, this comic inversion dramatizes a serious belief.

Many of Thurber's drawings have only dogs in them, and these are particularly appealing because they make no overt comparison between the noble dog and brutish man. In both "The Hound and the Bug" and "The Hound and the Hare," the dog appears center stage in a little drama that reveals its practicality and lack of aggression. In each series, the hound pursues a bug or a rabbit until it is clear that he will not capture it, when he calmly gives up and goes to sleep. As students of Thurber's anatomy, we know that a person would continue in this futile battle until someone was destroyed.[105] Thurber's dog is, in fact, the only character in his drawings who acts with Huck Finn common sense, which emphasizes Thurber's essential distrust of human nature.

Perhaps the best Thurber dogs are those who simply curl up at the foot of a page or end of a story. Very often, they are the only bright spots in a dim anthology of human behavior. In their innocence and disregard for the wild human spectacle, they serve as an effective counterbalance to the confusion and sadness in the pages surrounding them. The most memorable of these drawings shows a dog opening the front door to see if it is snowing; it is. With the bewildered and disappointed look of an innocent in a savage world, he stares up into the stormy heavens and seems to wonder, "Why?"[106]

As a humorist, Thurber constantly deflates human pride and destroys human smugness, and all of his comparisons of people and animals happily achieve these ends:

> They say that man is born to the belief that he is superior to the lower animals, and that critical intelligence comes when he realizes that he is more similar than dissimilar. Extending this theory, it has occurred to me that Man's arrogance arises from a false feeling of transcendency and that he will not get anywhere until he realizes, in all humility, that he is just another of God's creatures, less kindly than the dog, possessed of less dignity than the swan, and incapable of becoming as magnificent an angel as the black panther.[107]

There is great opportunity for laughter in such a view, since an unflattering comparison of people and other animals denies the reader's expectations. The Thurber dog is surprising because we do not expect great wisdom, calm, insight, and nobility even in a dearly loved and commonly accepted domestic animal. Yet, Thurber does not sentimentalize his animals, as Disney does, or make them into people, as many children's stories do. Thurber's animals retain their specialness and distinction by his constantly preferring them to the erratic human race.

The notable exception to this usually clear distinction between human beings and animals is Thurber's only play, his collaborative effort with Elliott Nugent, *The Male Animal*. As mentioned before, this play is rather uncharacteristic of Thurber, perhaps expectedly because it was a joint venture in a form that Thurber had not attempted since undergraduate days. Indeed, the play's main statement — that human males should act as all other male animals do — would seem to result more from the writers' need to bring the comedy to a satisfactory conclusion than from Thurber's sense of the distance between human unreason and the reasonableness of the "lower" animals. What is consistent, of course, is the parallel insistence upon the relative sanity and attractiveness of the natural order.

Comparing man and other beasts leads Thurber to some of the most perceptive and delightful essays in *Lanterns & Lances,* where he demonstrates for the last time just how serious and funny this subject is. In "The Trouble with Man is Man," the humorist notes disdainfully that "Man has come to blame his faults and flaws on the other creatures in this least possible of all worlds," but he argues that man is, as usual, mixed-up about his situation:

> The human being says that the beast in him has been aroused, when what he actually means is that the human being in him has been aroused. A person is not pigeon-toed, either, but person-toed, and what the lady has are not crow's-feet but woman's wrinkles. It is our species, and not any other, that goes out on wild-cat strikes, plays the badger game, weeps crocodile tears, and sets up kangaroo courts.

In control of both his subject and his form, Thurber moves masterfully in this passage from an amusing, but inconsequential, remark about a cliché to an increasingly awful revelation: we can easily dismiss the "slander" of pigeons by person-toed people, but kangaroo courts are another matter. Thurber is here using the old comic device of literally interpreting metaphors, but he manages to make even a playful investigation of language carry a serious theme: "The English and American vocabularies have been vastly enlarged and, I suppose, enriched by the multitudinous figures of speech that slander and libel the lower animals, but the result has been the further inflation of the already inflated human ego by easy denigration of the other species."[108] All of Thurber's work is a systematic assault on that inflated ego. He accomplishes this by demonstrating the essential flaws in man's greatest sources of pride, his reason and his ability to organize experience, and by consistently comparing him unfavorably with his fellow creatures on planet earth.

Animals play a crucial role in the execution of an important Thurber theme, the collapse of civilization. Indeed, when Thurber pictures our decadent world, which is ever on the brink of extinction, he often dramatizes the predicament by noting the rupture between man and other beasts. In the wasted landscape of *The Last Flower, The White Deer,* and "After the Steppe Cat, What?" all life on earth seems doomed to annihilation. *The Last Flower* tells the story not only of the destruction of human civilization, but also of nature. Emblematic of man's degradation when war came into the world, *The Last Flower* recalls, "the dogs deserted their fallen masters" in disillusionment and disgust.[109] Hostility toward the natural order is also characteristic of the villains in the fairy tales; the world of *The White Deer* reels in bleak confusion because the King's sons have "depleted their kingdom of wildlife," and we are told that the evil Duke in *The 13 Clocks,* who has destroyed humanity in Coffin Castle, also likes "to tear the wings from nightingales."[110] The real world of twentieth-century urban America seems just as hostile to the natural order, as even "The Wood Duck" cannot survive the destruction of his habitat by mechanized human society.[111] By implication, if there is no room for the other beasts on earth, this is no world for frail human beings, either.

The demise of humankind and the collapse of civilization are always just around the corner in Thurber's imagination, and sometimes he regards the prospect with sardonic delight. "Here Come the Dolphins" is a late essay that expands on Thurber's hypothesis that perhaps poodles should take over the earth. Upon further investigation, it seems that dolphins are a more likely choice:

> It neither alarms nor surprises me that Nature, whose patience with our self-destructive species is given out, may

have decided to make us, if not extinct, at least a secondary
power among the mammals of this improbable plant. . . . I
mourn the swift mortality of Man that will prevent him
from reading *The Decline and Fall of Man* by B. N.
Dolphin. What I am saying, of course, will be called satire
or nonsense. Professor Dolphin can deal with that when
the time comes.

With perfect comic timing, the essay makes a familiar Thurber point:
throughout the *corpus mundi* something is terribly awry, and something other than man will have to right it.

Thurber is indeed edging into satire in this essay, as he attacks
the savagery of supposedly refined human rituals and habits: "Man,
being Man, doesn't care much for submissive victuals, but loves to
beat the hell out of some of his main dishes, and has devised a dozen
weapons with which to kill them. . . . The penguin and the dolphin,
beholding the dismaying spectacle of human beings at table, will
surely exclaim, when they learn English, 'What foods these mortals
eat!'"[112] With this particularly apt pun, Thurber reveals what fools
these mortals be.

In his fables, Thurber uses animals conventionally, that is, to
represent human beings, with two notable exceptions. The first of
these, in the early collection of fables, is called "The Tiger Who
Understood People," and this corrupting knowledge is his doom.
Thurber's fable reveals not the familiar bromide that the "civilized"
world is "a jungle," but an even more dismaying truth: that animals
in a real jungle should be warned; "It's human society out there—be
careful!" When the poor tiger tries to apply human standards to the
relatively quiet jungle, he is literally eaten alive. The grimly funny
moral of the tale admonishes, "If you live as humans do, it will be
the end of you."[113] It is, after all, dangerous enough for a human
being to be human. A fable in Thurber's second collection compares
human beings to dinosaurs in a setting "ages ago in a wasteland of
time and a wilderness of space." Even faced with his inevitable
extinction, the dinosaur accepts his fate and foretells humanity's
shameful future in one grim statement: "there are worse things than
being extinct. . . and one of them is being you." With heavy dramatic
irony, Thurber has the human being smugly enumerate the reasons
that the dinosaur is inferior:

"You cannot even commit murder," he said, "for murder requires a mind. . . . You and your ilk are incapable of devising increasingly effective methods of destroying your own species and, at the same time, increasingly miraculous methods of keeping it extant. . . . In your highest state of evolution you could not develop the brain cells to prove innocent men guilty, even after their acquittal."

As bitter as Swift's indictment of human nature in his "Journey to the Country of the Houyhnhnms," Thurber's essay ends with the ironic moral: "The noblest study of mankind is Man, says Man."[114] We may call this satire, but that is not to say that its author does not mean what he says, only that he means it in a more complicated and indirect way.

When Thurber organized the 1948 collection that he titled fittingly *The Beast in Me and Other Animals,* he really described the terrain of the entire Thurber carnival: the first section of the book, "Mainly Men and Women," consists of stories about the confusion in human society; the second section, "Less Alarming Creatures," is a gallery of the saner, more attractive beasts on planet earth. Whether they appear in "The Gallery of Real Creatures" or in Thurber's imaginary bestiary, the "New Natural History," the very existence of these animals in the midst of this collection puts the predicaments of Charles Grantham and Amy Lighter, of Americans suffocating in a "Dewey Dewey Fog" or suffering under the delusions of "Soapland," into perspective. The sanity, tranquility, and undiluted pleasure of the animal world offsets and relieves the madness in the human spectacle. Thurber knows this, of course, as he reveals ironically in the self-deprecatory introduction to the book:

Take the imaginary animals in this book, for example. No labor of ingenuity could fit them into a continuable pattern. They emerged from the shameless breeding ground of the idle mind and they are obviously not going anywhere in particular. Faced with this fact, the author tries the desperate expedient of pulling the bestiary out of his pages only to discover to his dismay that it serves as the legendary thread that stubbornly unravels the whole.[115]

We can now see that Thurber's legendary beasts are woven inextricably into the pattern of his art, effecting a unity not only within this collection but also within the Thurber vision of chaos.

In his thirty year career of anatomizing the confusion of the world, Thurber chose to clarify his vision with the dog, "a sound creature in a crazy world," whose very presence adds a necessary perspective from which to view the bedlam and carnival of human life. In order to dramatize the chaotic nature and rampant imperfection of human beings, Thurber continually compares people with "lesser," even nonexistent, animals: the dinosaur, the poodle, the dolphin, the wild animals of the jungle and the receding American frontier. In his inimitable galleries of real and unreal animals, Thurber implicitly contrasts the joy and beauty of these animals to the dismaying human scene. The frequent appearance of such animals in the Thurber carnival serves to intensify and yet relieve, to focus and yet distance, the reader's knowledge of the perpetual confusion among human beings. It is clear, then, that Thurber's use of animals cannot be dismissed as nonsensical fun or "elfin" charm; it is a serious, consistent, and integral device in his anatomy, the means by which he puts the world's confusion into perspective and evokes the wise laughter of recognition and acceptance.

At the end of this tour of the Thurber carnival, it seems likely that his animals may adjust their own fur coats and march off quietly in dismay and amusement at the sorry spectacle. But they will always return—to comfort human beings in their terrible loneliness and watch them perform their crazy activities. Unscarred by human reason, they are ever separate from the cycles of human chaos and destruction.

This brings us to a consideration of Thurber's investigation into the causes of human confusion: his anatomy of the *corpus mentis,* or his analysis of the imperfect human mind that informs the chaotic *corpus mundi* and generates endless confusion. In order to understand fully the nature of human confusion, we must turn from the external manifestations of this confusion to the internal source of human perplexity, the *corpus mentis.* In the next chapter, we shall follow the anatomist's delicate dissection of this fragile organism.

3 *Corpus Mentis*
Psyche under the Knife

Human dignity, the humorist believes, is not only silly but a little sad. So are dreams and conventions and illusions. The fine brave fragile stuff that men live by. They look so swell, and go to pieces so easily.
— *Enjoyment of Laughter*

These things happen in a world of endless permutations.
— *Let Your Mind Alone!*

The world of Thurber's creation is distinguished by dense and striking images of chaos, and the preceding discussion concentrated on the external manifestations of that chaos: social disorder, mass hysteria, marital tension, and the organized disorder of modern science and technology. We turn now to a consideration of the origin of confusion, to the psychological and intellectual sources of confusion: the essential chaos studied by the anatomist in the "moonlit marges of the mind."

If the carnival of human life, the *corpus mundi*, is the material existence dissected by the humorist-anatomist, then the human mind, or the *corpus mentis,* is what infuses that body with life. It is the very spirit and essence of confusion. In seeking the defining image for his anatomy, the anatomist is driven inward, toward the seat of knowledge and the cause of our chaotic state: the imperfect human mind. Thurber described this movement inward in the seriously comical epigraph to his 1948 collection, *The Beast in Me and Other Animals:*

There is the tiger that lurks in motor cars, crouches in sealed envelopes and prowls between the doorbell and the phone, ready to pounce upon the dreamer by day, the reveler by night, or any man at any hour; but *I am concerned with the beast inside, the beast that haunts the moonlit marges*

of the mind, never clearly seen, never wholly lost to view,
never leaving, in its wanderings, pawprints sharp enough
to follow. (italics mine)

The ironic fact is that Thurber must look for just these tricky "paw-prints" as he works on the *corpus mentis.* Societies and institutions in disorder are but symptoms of the human disease; in order to investigate the etiology of human chaos, Thurber must finally ply the steel of his art through the obscure tissue of thought known as the mind. The anatomist thus places even the psyche under his knife, and it is a delicate surgery. The resulting anatomy is, necessarily, a more subtle and ambiguous art than the dissection of the *corpus mundi,* for the anatomy of the *corpus mentis* reveals the ultimate and inclusive confusion in Thurber's great anatomy of confusion: the confusion in the individual's perception of the world, the ambiguous clash of illusion and reality.

The terms illusion and reality are perhaps nebulous, but for my purposes here, I will consider reality to be whatever exists outside the mind, the material or actual world. Illusion is that which exists within the mind; ideas, dreams, conceptions, and judgments. Clearly, then, these are neutral terms as I use them. Within my definitions, illusion will include the perception of reality or all that is known of reality by a human intelligence in any given instance. Thurber's anatomy of the *corpus mentis* shows that reality, or what we know of it, is transformed and, in a sense, created by each eye perceiving it.

In a 1937 letter to E. B. White, Thurber described his realization of the subtle relationship between consciousness and reality: "It came to me today . . . that *the world exists only in my consciousness* (whether as a reality or as an illusion the evening papers do not say, but my guess is reality). The only possible way the world could be destroyed, it came to me, was through the destruction of my consciousness."[1]

Kenneth MacLean has noted that Thurber's work is generated by "the revolving imagination that is constantly changing life, building it up anew. It is the seat of irony, where something is always turning into something else, death into life, the impossible into the suddenly possible." When Peter De Vries established Thurber criticism in his essay, "James Thurber: The Comic Prufrock," he similarly observed that "reality in Thurber undergoes filtering and transmutations as curious and abrupt [as in Eliot's poetry]." De Vries perceived

Thurber's intentions and subjects as supremely serious, while admiring his comicality; or, as he more felicitously phrased it, he saw Thurber as our "jester in Axel's Castle."[2] The careful student of Thurber is indeed more apt to compare him to Eliot—or to Joyce and James—than to superficial comics of any period. Thurber's attention to metaphysical questions, including the meaning of reality, is one of the things that distinguishes his work from that of many humorists and from formula fiction writers.

The preponderance of dreams and fantasies in Thurber's world has led some of his readers to identify his work with the Romantic conception of the imagination. Morsberger and Tobias, for example, regard his rejection of scientism as the outgrowth of a preference for imaginative intelligence over a prosaic, narrowly factual reading of experience.[3] This is appropriate, not only because of Thurber's early works, which stress the superiority of daydreaming, reverie, and fantasy over a literal and mundane understanding of experience, but also in view of his consciously Wordsworthian definition of humor as emotional chaos recollected in tranquility. Holmes argues that the distinguishing mark of Thurber's mind is "the tension between a strong sense of fact and a strong bias toward fantasy."[4] These comments are helpful, but Thurber's concern with illusion and reality goes beyond his emphasis on "fantasy" or his belief in the powers of the imagination, and the significance of illusion and reality in his work extends far beyond the fairy tales and the stories with dream sequences.

Although Thurber had a Romantic strain, which occasionally surfaces in the early work and in the fairy tales, a more important and persistent literary influence was Henry James.[5] All twentieth-century writers of fiction in English are indebted to James, of course, but I wish to make a case for Thurber's special indebtedness to him. This debt is rooted in Thurber's lifelong preoccupation with James, and is represented in his numerous Jamesian parodies, imitations, and allusions. Thurber's link to James was conscious, direct, and wide-ranging: the claustrophobic domestic scenes, the endless wars of nerves and egos, the delicate probing of the modern temperament, the overriding sense of predicament and perplexity, the self-conscious characters, the clash of men and women—all the essential Thurber images and preoccupations are but one step removed, through humor, from the work of his master, Henry James. In fact, Thurber's ultimate goal, which is to cultivate perception and raise awareness of reality, is linked inextricably to his knowledge of James. And the consistent dramatization of the clash between illusion and reality in his work probably owes more to the Jamesian concept of consciousness than to any other source, as it demonstrates effectively James's thesis that "humanity is immense, and reality has a myriad of forms."[6]

The anatomy of confusion reveals that all individual perceptions of reality are, in a sense, distortions. They are distorted because they are selective, limited, and individual, as James suggests with this potent metaphor in the preface to *The Portrait of a Lady:*

> The house of fiction has in short not one window, but a million—a number of possible windows not to be reckoned, rather; every one of which has been pierced, or is still piercable, in its vast front, by the need of the individual vision and by the pressure of the individual will. These apertures, of dissimilar shape and size, hang so, all together, over the human scene that we might have expected of them a greater sameness of report than we find. They are but windows at the best, mere holes in a dead wall, disconnected, perched aloft; they are not hinged doors opening straight on life. But they have this mark of their own that at each of them stands a figure with a pair of eyes, or at least with a field glass, which forms, again and again, for observation, a unique instrument, insuring to the person making use of it an impression distinct from every other.

The consciousness of the artist, then, perceives the immense, moving field of reality as through a field glass, an image which describes not only the Jamesian artistic consciousness but the aesthetic distance from which Thurber, the humorist-anatomist, views the world. James was interested in scrutinizing the development of such consciousness in those characters capable of approaching, though perhaps never reaching, "an immense sensibility"[7] with which to read experience. As the house of fiction metaphor makes clear, the Jamesian aesthetic sensibility is finally superimposed above his fictional "centers of consciousness," those characters capable of developing awareness, like Archer and Strether.[8] In Thurber's world, such a consciousness resides in the artist himself, often in the guise of narrator. Rarely is such sensibility represented in the action of a Thurber story; in fact, the poet-heroes in the fairy tales are

Thurber's only characters with refined sensibilities.

Thurber's implicit goal is to develop a wider awareness, a finer perception in his reader. For as the eye transforms experience, experience transforms the eye. Like all art, Thurber's world becomes a part of our experience and thus changes our eyes. For Thurber, the essence of humor is that hysterical laugh evoked by facing "the Awful," and his art often causes such recognition and laughter, signs of a developing awareness. Paradoxically, this wider awareness only intensifies our perception of the ambiguous nature of reality, of the limitations of knowing.

Thurber's view of the human comedy is filtered, like James's, as through a field glass, from a distance, necessarily selective and removed. The frame of the lens is the order imposed upon the chaotic field under study. The vision in the frame receives the special Thurber touch in that, here, reality is transformed by what could be called the kaleidoscopic action of his humor. In the Thurber kaleidoscope, images of reality are ever shifting at the slightest provocation. These endless permutations of reality are humorous because the sudden shifts in vision result in conventional comic effects: incongruity, doubleness, surprise, even fear. As human experience is seen in the Thurber kaleidoscope, nothing is quite what it appears to be, all is ambiguity, flux, and confusion. Here is the record, most often written in everyday, understated language, of human illusions, dreams, and expectations—suddenly and irrevocably going to pieces before our eyes. Thus transformed, experience inside the Thurber carnival is paradoxically frightening and exhilarating, funny and sad, clear and muddled. It is a particularly modern, ironic, and tragicomic vision. Since tragicomedy is essentially a "bi-focal vision of experience,"[9] it is the most appropriate form for a writer who considers reality to be an ever-shifting, elusive entity. Thurber's pictures of life, like the images in a kaleidoscope, show reality constantly shifting and changing before our eyes, the ultimate expression of confusion. These myriad permutations of reality—or more properly, the infinite number of perceptions of reality—are the very essence of Thurberian confusion, since the diverse forms taken by reality not only cause confusion, but are its essential expression. In order to discover the place of the *corpus mentis* in Thurber's anatomy, we must look at representative works in which the clash of illusion and reality, of expectation and experience, is most important.

Three major aspects of Thurber's use of illusion and reality will be discussed. First, Thurber characters who are either ignorant of themselves, those who are "fundamentally absentminded" in Bergsonian terms, or who have purposefully deluded themselves about reality, will be discussed as comically unconscious people. Their separation from reality is especially important as a key to understanding the bedlam in *My Life and Hard Times* and the chaos in the two collections of fables. The first section of this chapter will deal, therefore, with the absentminded and the deluded. Second, Thurber's wider concept of the ambiguous nature of reality will be discussed as a means of understanding his world view. In the humorist's own terms, this second section will deal with the distinction between the factual and the possible in human experience. Finally, the chapter will relate Thurber's intense and overriding interest in language to his conception of an ever-revolving, changing reality.

The absentminded and the deluded fill Thurber's pages, as they do many writers of comedy and humor. In *Laughter,* Henri Bergson concludes that "a comic character is generally comic in proportion to his ignorance of himself. The comic person is unconscious." This type of character, radically separated from even a muddled perception of reality, possesses what Bergson terms a "fundamental absentmindedness" which enables him to ignore both himself and the world about him, thus inelastically and unprofitably moving through his experience.[10] Often Thurber's characters seem to have an elaborate system by which they encourage and intensify their absentmindedness, so that they become not only ignorant or unconscious, but actually deluded about themselves and their world. These characters are especially prominent in *My Life and Hard Times* and the *Fables*.

My Life and Hard Times is based on Thurber's memories of a youth filled with mistaken impressions, delusions, false expectations, and misnomers. This pseudoautobiography, itself a sham, includes stories about "The Night the Bed Fell," in which a bed does not fall, "The Day the Dam Broke," in which there is no dam, and "The Night the Ghost Got In," in which, presumably, there is no ghost. All the characters in this book, in fact, seem confused about what is going on around them. In "A Note at the End," the narrator "Thurber" explains that "until a man can quit talking loudly to himself in order to shout down the memories of blunderings and gropings, he is in no shape for the painstaking examination of distress and the careful ordering of events so necessary to a calm and balanced exposition of what, exactly, was the matter."[11] In order to understand exactly what is the matter in *My Life,* we will examine in some detail the first story in the collection, "The Night the Bed Fell," as a prime example of Thurberian confusion resulting from the mixed-up minds of its participants.

"The Night the Bed Fell" is the story of, not the night the bed fell on Thurber's father, but the night that everyone thought the bed had fallen. His father liked to sleep in the attic, it seems, "to be away where he could think," which does not surprise the reader of these riotous stories. On the night in question, Father had gone upstairs, disregarding the objections of Thurber's mother, who "opposed the notion strongly because, she said, the old wooden bed up there was unsafe: it was wobbly and the heavy headboard would crash down on father's head in case the bed fell, and kill him." Thus, from his mother's initial, mistaken expectation—that his father would be killed in bed—flows an ever-widening, incomprehensible rush of confusion. What actually happened, the narrator coolly assures us twenty years later, was that little Thurber's own cot collapsed, causing him to roll under it. His mother, however, "came to the immediate conclusion that her worst dread was realized: the big wooden bed upstairs had fallen on father." She awakened everyone in the house with her screams of "Let's go to your poor father," and they rushed to the attic in a wild flood of "banging and confusion" only to find father sleeping soundly.[12]

The narrator begins this story with the slight apology that it "is admittedly a somewhat incredible tale," but follows with the justification that "still, it did take place." The persona in these early tales, who is a fictionalized Thurber, often seems to be telling a twentieth-century version of the tall-tale, but the difference is in the quiet understatement, the droll wit, the measured urbanity and maturity of his voice. The story of "The Night the Bed Fell" is somewhat incredible, but the tale as Thurber presents it is exceptionally believable because of his pointed references to levels of consciousness, false expectations, and misconceptions in the minds of the characters. Even the reader has a false expectation, since the title of the story promises a lively but straightforward tale; from it, one would expect a story, however, humorous, about the bed's falling one night during Thurber's boyhood. The story's multilevel irony is rooted, therefore, in the reader's false expectation. Following this red herring, Thurber places a remarkable, seemingly extraneous gallery of family portraits, which establishes the fundamental eccentricity and absentmindedness of the entire Thurber clan. Notice the insistent references (italicized) to the congenital misapprehension from which they all suffer: "We had visiting us at this time a nervous first cousin of mine named Briggs Beall, who *believed* that he was likely to cease breathing when he was asleep. It was his *feeling* that if he were not awakened every hour during the night, he might die of suffocation." Not present in the household on the evening in question, but described here in order to prepare the reader for the bedlam to follow, are the likes of Aunt Melissa Beall, who "suffered under the *premonition* that she was destined to die on South High Street," and Sarah Shoaf, "who never went to bed at night without the *fear* that a burglar was going to get in and blow chloroform under her door through a tube." We are told that Aunt Gracie Shoaf "also had a burglar *phobia. . . .* she was *confident* that burglars had been getting into her house every night for forty years."[13] This is not a family to be confused by the facts of their existence.

These endearing family vignettes are related before the actual narrative begins, and the narrator, mimicking a voice telling a tale, soon chides himself for "straying from the remarkable incidents that took place the night the bed fell on father." Such devices make Thurber's fiction seem effortless, casual, even impromptu, but what discipline lurks beneath this facility. By repeating the phrase "the night the bed fell," the narrator reinforces the reader's misunderstanding and intensifies the false impression that these caricatures of Thurber's relatives are entertaining but off the point. After the story begins, however, the narrator admits that "it was my mother who, in recalling the scene later, first referred to it as 'the night the bed fell.'"[14] At this point, the reader begins to sense the essential confusion in the Thurber household, and, by extension, in the Thurber world. The narrative that ensues is simply an orchestration of the confusion which results from misconceptions and false expectations like the "crochets" of Thurber's aunts.

The understated narrator says drolly that his cot was of the type that could collapse at any time; "that is, in fact, precisely what happened, about two o'clock in the morning" of the "night the bed fell on your father."[15] Since only the narrator and the reader are aware of what is going on, we are able to stand back with the humorist and enjoy the pandemonium resulting from the ordinary occurrence of an army cot collapsing on a little boy. It is important to note that, throughout the story, everyone has a mistaken idea of what is going on. Thurber reminds us continually of the personal idiosyncrasies which prevent any character in the action from seeing what is actually happening.

The story is told by a narrator who was present the night the bed fell (by the person who was under the cot, in fact). Therefore, his memory of the events is in itself a filter and a distortion of reality. His point of view is the closest thing to an understanding of "reality," however, even though he admits that he was literally unconscious at the beginning of all the activity. When the clamor began, he says, "I did not wake up, only reached the edge of consciousness and went back," thereby admitting severe limitations on his view of the events. As members of the household are awakened, the narrator stresses the misconceptions of each; I again italicize key words that relate to individual perceptions of the events. Notice the knife of Thurber's humor as it cuts through the mass of confusion in order to reveal its elements. His mother "came to the immediate *conclusion* that her worst dread was *realized:* the big wooden bed upstairs had fallen on father." Her shouting immediately made brother Herman *think* she was "for no *apparent* reason, hysterical," and cousin Briggs, who had been afraid that he would die in his sleep, "came to the quick *conclusion* that he was suffocating and that we were all trying to 'bring him out.'" The narrator admits that he was "*conscious* of what was going on, *in a vague way,* but did not yet *realize* that I was under my bed instead of on it. . . . *Foggy with sleep,* I now *suspected,* in my turn, that the whole uproar was being made in a frantic endeavor to extricate me from what must be an unheard-of and perilous situation. . . . I *think* I had the *nightmarish belief* that I was entombed in a mine."[16]

The confusion of this night is possible, therefore, only because of the confusion inherent in people's minds. Specifically, the external confusion is the result or material demonstration of the disparity between their mistaken expectations and the actuality of their lives. The banging, shouting, and running (all irrational) are only manifestations of inner confusion. What Thurber has portrayed so well here is the basic tendency of human beings to relate all external experience to their individual, eccentric, and flawed "understanding." Thus, since Mother had *thought* and in a sense *willed* the bed to fall on father, any sound became to her the sound of the bed falling on father; in the commotion, the other members of the household similarly assumed that their own special fears or suspicions had been realized.

Father was as confused as the rest, for when he heard their battering on his attic door, he promptly "decided that the house was on fire. 'I'm coming, I'm coming!' he wailed in a slow, sleepy voice—it took him many minutes to regain *consciousness.*" Mother, trapped in her idiosyncrasy and "still *believing* he was caught under the bed, *detected* in his 'I'm coming' the mournful, resigned note of one who is preparing to meet his maker." It was not until all of these confused and misguided people converged on the attic and found father perfectly all right that the confusion was momentarily squelched. When father opened the door to see his family standing before him in wild and unfounded anticipation of his death, he posed the central question of the story: "What in the name of God is going on here?"[17]

Who could have told him? The fact that the incident was always referred to as "the night the bed fell" shows how stubborn and inelastic people's misconceptions and perceptions can be. Thurber's mother is still completely unaware of reality at the end of the story. As the ultimate irony, the narrator repeats without embellishment his mother's final irrational statement about the incident: "'I'm glad,' said mother, who always looked on the bright side of things, 'that your grandfather wasn't here.'"[18] As soon as the reader recalls that not only had nothing happened, but that it was, in fact, only grandfather's absence from his attic room that made the bedlam possible (since only when grandfather was away could father sleep there), the story ends, as it began, in an impression of profound mental confusion.

The narrator "Thurber" grew up, however, and became a mature artistic consciousness, so that "the situation was finally put together like a gigantic jigsaw puzzle."[19] Only the artist is thus able to make sense out of nonsensical human experience. The resulting gestalt is the story as we have it—the synthesis of discordant and conflicting points of view, distilled into one telling image of the human psyche by the superior sensibility of the artist. In his quiet recollection of chaos, the anatomist is able to approximate saying

"You said a moment ago that everybody you look at seems to be a rabbit. Now just what do you mean by that, Mrs. Sprague?"

what, exactly, was the matter.

This fine perception of chaos informs the whole of *My Life*. All of the other stories in the collection describe the confusion resulting from false expectations, mistaken impressions, and mental perplexity. In "The Car We Had to Push" Thurber's mild-mannered father, who does not really understand cars at all, is "convinced" that the engine fell out of the car. It does seem strange that the car is operable without its engine, but father refuses to get bogged down in such details. Similarly, Thurber's mother "knew" that it was dangerous to drive a car without gasoline (to say the least) and "had an idea" that the Victrola would blow up — all because machines were mysteries to her. When the old family car finally does fall apart, we are told that grandfather "*gathered,* from all the talk and excitement and weeping, that somebody had died. Nor did he let go of this *delusion.*" The magnificent tradition of confusion will be carried on, for the Thurber boys just "knew" that there was a ghost in their house. Herman had "always *half-suspected* that something would 'get him' in the night," and on the basis of this expectation, he "raised such a hullabaloo of *misunderstanding*" that the event was always referred to as "The Night the Ghost Got In."[20]

Such misunderstanding follows Thurber into adulthood. In "University Days," remembering that he could never see anything under the microscope in botany lab, he isolates the total idiosyncrasy of perception. His professor concluded that Thurber's difficulty in seeing "was the result of not adjusting the microscope properly, so he would readjust it for me, or rather, for himself. And I would look again and see milk." Each eye is unique and eccentric and, therefore, flawed. Young Thurber's inability, as an individual consciousness, to see any material reality under the scrutiny of the lens is symbolized in his own "adjustment" of the microscope. When he finally focuses the lens on something he can see, the professor realizes to his dismay that "you've fixed the lens so that it reflects your eye!"[21] To mother, the noise of a cot collapsing easily becomes the calamity she has expected; to father, the sound of kitchen utensils falling on pavement immediately becomes the sound of a car's engine falling out; to the student, the slide of a plant cross-section remarkably becomes an image of his own cloudy perception. It is only the vision of the humorist-anatomist, superimposed above all these deluded specimens, that can properly focus the lens: an older, mature Thurber, looking back on this nonsense, is able to make it coherent. In order for life to be transformed into art, experience must be thus recollected in tranquility, distanced from its own peculiar time and place and made universal and articulate.[22]

Thurber's characters, willing participants in bedlam and confusion, are not only unconscious of themselves, but are also deluded about the world around them. Their expectations and conceptions are so misdirected and inelastic that they seem, in Thurber's inimitable phrase, victims of some "trivial mental tic"[23] that leads to an overpowering, universal confusion at the slightest provocation. The seeds of confusion are carried, it seems, in our personalities, minds, and humanity. The timeless humor of *My Life and Hard Times* resides in Thurber's kaleidoscopic vision of reality which perceives confused individuals as perpetually surprised and surprising, with reality constantly turning into something else in the endless revolutions of chaos. That these permutations of reality happen so easily, so quickly, so unexpectedly, and yet so mundanely is peculiarly Thurberian—and all demonstrate how close laughter and fear, sense and nonsense, and triumph and defeat are in Thurber's world. As "The Catbird Seat" dramatizes, the most bizarre possibility is what is believable in this crazy world, while simple truth often seems the strangest fabrication.

Thurber continued to delineate the web of illusion and reality in his *Fables for Our Time,* but the subjects and tone of these parables make them richer and more devastating than much of his earlier work. The *Fables* operate by establishing series of expectations, expectations that are then denied or radically transformed, so that the face of reality shifts before the reader's eyes. This constantly changing face of reality creates the great irony and ambiguity of Thurber's fables. Even in their morals, the fables surprise us, because the reader expects some well-worn or trite bit of philosophy at the conclusion of a fable. Instead, in their humorously reworded morals, Thurber's fables completely overthrow conventional thinking. Adding yet another ambiguous stroke to the generally divided canvas of the fables, their morals are made strangely familiar by a deliberate garbling or punning on famous phrases, axioms, or proverbs. To demonstrate how the fables economically dramatize Thurber's kaleidoscopic view of reality, I will discuss two of the finest fables in the first collection in some detail, and then note some similarities between the early and late fables.

"The Green Isle in the Sea" is the story of an old man who goes to his favorite place, a city park near his home, after being robbed and mauled several times. The park, the reader realizes, is a kind of last resort for the kindly old gentleman. In the park, however, the old man becomes an easy target for a sky full of ominous bombers.[24] The narrative progresses much more complexly than this outline suggests, and I want to show how the fable's great artistic tension and power result from Thurber's slowly revealing to the reader the endless permutations of reality. By the end of this ironic and shocking tale, neither the old gentleman nor the reader sees anything as he had seen it before.

First, the reader is impressed by its exotically peaceful title, "The Green Isle in the Sea." As in "The Night the Bed Fell," the reader's high expectations are soon dispelled, yet the ironic first sentence of the fable only intensifies the original impression: "One sweet morning in the Year of Our Lord, Nineteen hundred and thirty-nine, a little old gentleman got up and threw wide the windows of his bedroom, letting in the living sun." This is the beginning of a fairy tale, an incantation of the golden age. The careful Thurber vocabulary, which can always evoke many sensations with a few well-chosen words, deliberately includes "sweet," "Lord," "gentleman," and especially "living" to promise so much that is about to be denied systematically by the fable. First, the mood is broken when a black widow spider "slashed at him." This is a foreboding image, but is quickly dismissed since the spider missed. The little old man then goes down to "a splendid breakfast." Just as the word "splendid" again encourages hope in the reader, the man's grandson pulls his chair out from under him. This cruel and non-sensical act is requalified, as the earlier episode with the spider had been, because "the old man's hip was strained but it was fortunately not broken."[25] The word "fortunately" is especially ironic because had the old man broken his hip earlier in the day, he would not have been "fortunate" enough to be killed later. This reminds the reader of mother's ridiculous comment about grandfather's absence on "The Night the Bed Fell," but here the irony is more bitter. In the world of the fables, people (or animals representing people) suffer the consequences of their mis-apprehension and confusion. In this sense, "The Green Isle in the Sea" is, curiously, closer to real life than is *My Life and Hard Times,* and is at least as close to tragedy as to comedy.

As the morning progresses, we find that not only are our expectations overturned, but the old man's illusions are crumbling before his eyes as well. When he leaves the breakfast table, he goes "toward a little park with many trees, which was to him a green isle in the sea." The juxtaposition of what the park has been to him, that is, what he has perceived it to be, and what it is now transformed into, what it really is, constitutes the major irony of the fable. As the old man approaches his "green isle in the sea," we again expect that some respite from the world's harassment will be found there. Near the park, however, he is tripped by a "gaily-colored hoop sent rolling at him. . . by a grim little girl" and later he is robbed of all his valuables, including "a gold ring his mother had given him when he was a boy."[26] The terrible irony of human experience is underscored by the fact that it is a "gaily-colored" hoop that nearly kills him and that it is thrown by a "grim" little girl. These are two adjectives one would not expect, the first shocking because it couples a pleasant, vital image with an instrument of assault, and the second at least incongruous because it unconventionally describes the little girl as "grim." When the gold ring is finally wrenched from the old man, the clash between the reader's expectations and the brutal reality of the man's experience becomes so great that a feeling of hideous defeat and outrage is experienced. These things happen, Thurber warns, on a "sweet" morning, in "the Year of Our Lord," under a "living sun," and to a nice old gentleman. If there were one thing about the old man or his surroundings that could explain or justify his experience, the intense energy of this fable would be diminished severely. So, too, would its richly ambiguous truth be trivialized and corrupted. But Thurber does not allow such diminution.

The reader, teased along by the narrator, by his own desire for justice, and by his experience with fables and with the literature of the happy ending, continues hoping for refuge or even retaliation. But the fable's final vision is unrelieved in its savage denial of all illusions:

> When at last the old gentleman staggered into the little park, which had been to him a fountain and a shrine, he saw that half the trees had been killed by a blight, and the other half by a bug. Their leaves were gone and they no longer afforded

any protection from the skies, so that the hundred planes which appeared suddenly overhead had an excellent view of the little old gentleman through their bombing sites.[27]

No matter what has happened before, the reader is not prepared for this last glimpse of "the Awful"; there is something so irrational, so horrible about the now cosmic harassment of this innocent old man that one's breath is taken away.

Until the first sentence of the paragraph quoted above, the reader still has some hope that all will be righted for this bewildered but appealing old man. The words "at last" suggest another refuge to the reader, as do the words "fountain" and "shrine." Finally, however, the little old man sees, when the reader sees, what the artistic sensibility sees and seeks to recreate: the apocalyptic vision of a wasteland in which even a kind old gentleman cannot survive. In Joycean terms, the reader and the old man simultaneously experience an epiphany at the conclusion of this fable. The gentleman's illusions about himself and his existence, symbolized in his pathetic misconception of the arid, brutal park as a "fountain and a shrine," are devastated just as the reader's hopes for him and the unwitting humanity he represents are devastated.

Nothing is what it appeared to be, as the moral of the fable demonstrates: "The world is so full of a number of things, I am sure that we should all be happy as kings," it innocently promises, only to follow with this qualification, "and you know how happy kings are."[28] (The reader must remember that this fable was written at the end of the 1930s, when being a king certainly did not guarantee happiness.) Reality, presented in a series of contradictory revelations, has shifted before our eyes so many times that, by the end of the fable, the "living" sun has become the glaring light in which the old man is seen from the bombers overhead. This fable is so successful because, just as the reader's illusions or expectations are overturned, the gentleman's illusions about his park, "the green isle in the sea," are savagely unmasked. His park is not a fountain and a shrine — not a source of and tribute to life — but a wasteland. His bright, fragile dreams of peace and sustenance are replaced by material bombers, leafless trees, and death. The clash of illusion, or the mind's version of experience, and reality, or the material world, could not be greater. And, as Thurber said of Conrad's Lord Jim, "There is no running away"[29] from this awful revelation: the fable mercilessly presses our noses against a window on the world's starkest terrain, offering only scanty, nervous laughter as relief.

Thurber's most famous fable, "The Unicorn in the Garden," also operates through a profound clash of illusion and reality. Like "The Green Isle in the Sea," this fable begins in a halcyon setting, also described in an exotically beautiful opening line: "Once upon a sunny morning a man who sat in a breakfast nook looked up to see a white unicorn with a golden horn quietly cropping roses in the garden." Both the language and the picture are remarkable. When the husband tells his wife about seeing the unicorn, she replies with the factually true statement that "The unicorn is a mythical beast." But the fable does not justify her "realism." Even though she calls the police to carry away her "crazy" husband, it is she who ends up being carried away to the booby-hatch.[30] The imagination wins out, in a complete rejection of common sense and ordinary expectation.

Thurber manages to create a high amount of tension in this fable by making the reader identify immediately with the quiet husband's reverence for beauty, reverie, and myth, while at the same time encouraging the reader to expect the wife and common sense to triumph. When the husband first tells his wife about the unicorn, her response is jarring to the reader only because of its harsh tone, especially as it is compared to the husband's quiet civility: "She opened one unfriendly eye and looked at him. 'The unicorn is a mythical beast,' she said." The reader is still seeing double, sympathizing with the husband while having to admit the truth of the wife's statement, until the husband repeats the story of the unicorn to his wife. This time, without justification, she threatens him: "'You are a booby,' she said, 'and I am going to have you put in the booby-hatch.'"[31] The reader's feeling of suspense is then focused on whether or not this nice but perhaps eccentric man will be put in a booby-hatch just for seeing a beautiful unicorn. (What has gone on before this morning to bring the couple to such a place is left to the reader's speculation.)

All our expectations are then reversed in the tense description of the wife's conversation with the police, which ends with the police carrying off the lucid, factual woman to the booby-hatch. When the police ask the husband if he had, in fact, told his wife that he had seen a unicorn in the garden, he replies with her cold realism: "the unicorn is a mythical beast." In the space of this short fable, roles and attitudes have been reversed, the impossible has happened, the mythical has been seen and has just as mysteriously disappeared, and all expectations and truisms have been flatly denied by experience. Even the moral's meaning shifts before our eyes, because it is a pun: "Don't count your boobies until they are hatched."[32] The reader of Thurber's fables laughs, if at all, in response to the wordplay in the morals and the incongruity created by the seemingly endless series of unexpected events and revelations. Reality, or what we see and know of it, constantly revolves and redefines itself. The only resolution of all this flux and contradiction is, paradoxically, a consistent sense of the ambiguity and confusion inherent in human experience. We probably sympathize with the husband in "The Unicorn" because, along with Thurber, he acknowledges the illusory and mythical aspects of life.

Most of the other fables in this collection also depend on overturning the reader's expectations—especially expectations that result from a knowledge of truisms, earlier fables and tales, and ordinary experience. In "The Little Girl and the Wolf," it is the wolf, not the little girl, who gets killed; in "The Moth and the Star," it is the "irresponsible dreamer" who lives a long and satisfying life; and in "The Patient Bloodhound," the bloodhound's patience is his shortcoming, not his salvation.[33] As a humorist, Thurber always enjoyed denying smug assumptions and twisting clichés and axioms, and this humorous debunking is part of his fables' goal. More is involved in the basic world view expressed in the fables, however. In the fables, Thurber is essentially denying the validity or possibility of human knowledge; in these disillusioning fables, no previous fact or directive can prepare one for life in a world of endless permutations, for no constant is capable of being isolated.

This point is made in a brief but devastating fable, "The Fairly Intelligent Fly." The verbal irony is particularly pointed, of course, because the fabulist uses the adjective "fairly" to describe a fly who is not intelligent at all. The implicit comment seems to be that this fly is as intelligent as anyone else. Priding himself on his wariness, the fly refuses to enter a spiderweb in which many flies have been trapped and died. Once again, we would expect the story to have a happy ending, especially when the fly says cautiously to the spider, "I never light where I don't see other flies and I don't see any other flies in your house." This is a reasonable, even clever conclusion, but when the fly sees a large number of flies in another location, he kills himself with his cleverness. A bee warns him that the swarm of flies is actually stuck on a piece of flypaper, but the deluded fly says "Don't be silly...they're dancing." The profound limitations of perception and reason are stressed in the fable itself, while the moral overturns yet another comforting axiom: "*There is no safety in numbers, or in anything else.*"[34] There is also no decision, no conclusion, no expectation that can be justified by experience. Most important, reason and judgment cannot be trusted to tell people much about their experience.

Thurber continued this manipulation of point of view to dramatize the failure of expectations in his second collection of fables. One of his finest late fables, "The Rose and the Weed," matches the intense energy of the best of the earlier fables, and demonstrates the immense artistic control that Thurber still had over his subject matter and the persistence of his preoccupation with the clash of illusion and reality. The narrative concerns an encounter between a rose and a weed in which each plant disparages the other's characteristics in a verbal war of personalities and "social" class. The rose, of course, presents the conventional view that the weed is inferior to a beautiful, cultivated flower: "You are an unwelcome guest, and unsightly of appearance. The Devil must love weeds, he made so many of them," she says. This seems true enough until the weed suggests that flowers smell worse than weeds when they fester. The haughty rose replies that weeds have ugly names, whereas she is named "Dorothy Perkins." The reader's bifocal vision continues as the weed asserts that some weeds have even prettier names, like jewelweed and candyweed, so, who can say what is beautiful? In a denigrating pun, we are told that "the weed smiled a weedy smile. 'At least,' he said, 'I do not come from a family of climbers.'"[35] As these quotations show, the argument of this fable is effective because it is based in antithetical views of reality which, when taken in isolation, appear true. The artistic sense of reality is superimposed above the two, however, and in a sense derives from their juxtaposition. Thus, the essential comment of the fable seems to be that all perception is limited and everything is ambiguous. This is also a major implication of *The Ambassadors*, of course, but Thurber's fable must make the point in a few hundred words.[36]

All authority is brought into question by Thurber's fables. When the rose begins citing Shakespeare's lines about roses, a wind comes up and "Dorothy Perkins' beautiful disdain suddenly became a scattering of petals, economically useless, and of appearance not especially sightly." The fable is not so simple as only to overturn our programmed response in the weed-versus-rose controversy, however. In the last sentence, all is suddenly and profoundly altered when a gardener snaps the weed "out of the ground by the roots, before you could say Dorothy Perkins, or for that matter, jewelweed." The timing in this sentence is masterful, especially the inclusion of the phrase, "for that matter," because even within the sentence itself, our expectations are abruptly denied. Like the first collection of fables, this fable's moral presents the ultimate ambiguity and changefulness of experience: "*Tout,* as the French say, in a philosophy older than ours and an idiom often more succinct, *passé.*"[37] In the world of Thurber's fables, not only does our perception shift constantly as expectations are denied and axioms are disproven, but reality itself seems to be ever-revolving, revealing itself forever in surprising and different permutations. The only constant here is change; the only order, chaos.

The perpetual transformation of reality is also the subject of "The Rose, the Fountain, and the Dove," a fable in which a dove is goaded by malcontents into leaving his serene valley. The rose and the fountain, it seems, are frustrated by not being able to leave the valley. "'It is always the same wherever one is,'" complains the rose. The wise dove, who could fly anywhere but chooses to remain in the peaceful skies over the quiet valley, replies, "'To my eye, it is always changing.'" The eye thus transforms the action; the individual perception creates the reality. When the dove makes the mistake of flying away from the valley, he is killed.[38] He has mistakenly sought out diversity when all life is diversity itself.

The complex fable "The Truth about Toads" attacks not only human vanity but the greatest source of human pride, the mind. This is the story of an evening at the Fauna Club, where all the animals are congregated, each brashly touting his own mistaken importance: the rooster brags that he causes the sun to come up, the stork that he is responsible for everyone's being born, and the ground hog that he ends winter. There is a strong rejection of both individual vanity and cultural folkways and myth in this fable. When a raven prophetically hangs a sign above the bar which reads "Open most hearts and you will find graven upon them Vanity," none of the insular and deluded animals thinks that the saying applies to him. An arrogant toad joins the crowd and swears that he will not get drunk drinking "fireflies" because, he says, "nothing can make me lightheaded. I have a precious jewel in my head." He assumes that, as a "rational animal," he is not prey to the weakness of all flesh. He later passes out, however; when a woodpecker opens his head in order to see the magnificent jewel of which he was so proud, he finds nothing: "open most heads. . . [and] you will find nothing shining, not even a mind."[39] All pretensions, illusions, and expectations crumble under the scrutiny of the anatomist's eye. In fact, the instrument of knowledge and the chief source of human pride, the mind, is itself limited, flawed, diminished.

Much of Thurber's work deals with the great disparity between what the imperfect, egocentric mind perceives and what is in fact reality. Thurber retains a high level of complexity, ambiguity, and humanity because he does not suggest a new formula or myth to replace an old, disproven one. Rather, he is most interested in raising awareness, so that the reader at least learns how little is actually known. The truth that Thurber's anatomy presents, the pattern it imposes on the chaos, is that reality changes constantly and takes myriad forms. Paradoxically, then, his only clear statement is that everything changes, is constantly qualified and restated, and is, finally, ambiguous.

The Thurber characters who seem particularly unattractive, evil, or corrupt are those who mistakenly think, in deliberate and elaborate self-delusion, that they have the answer, the interpretation, the real control over experience. These include the pseudoscientists, the tyrants, the dully prosaic wives. Others, like the eccentrics in *My Life and Hard Times* and the poor old gentleman in "The Green Isle in the Sea," are really unconscious of both themselves and their situation. No corrective is applied for them, because they are simply acting out the human comedy in all its inherent confusion and disillusionment. The humorist, wistfully yet sympathetically, watches them from the comic distance, seeming to sigh quietly to himself, "Lord, what fools these mortals be!" Thurber sometimes edges into satire, however, and thereby strongly indicts the purposefully deluded characters. This is sometimes the case in the fables, but it is nowhere more evident than in the fairy tales. *The White Deer,* which is a tale that dramatizes the impossibility of knowing and the constantly changing face of reality, also has a few characters who deliberately pervert whatever reality they could possibly discover. This is true of the Royal Astronomer, Paz, who invents a rose-colored lens for his telescope, and of the Royal Recorder, who is mesmerized by his own legalistic gobbledygook. Perhaps the most deluded character in this tale of delusion and trickery is the Royal Physician, who thinks, in a radical confusion of identity, that he is both physician and patient.[40] This confusion renders him neither physician nor person, and delights by approximating so closely many real practitioners.

Invoking the ghost of Alice in Wonderland, the Black Knight asks rhetorically of Prince Jorn, "When all is dark within the house, who knows the monster from the mouse?"[41] This provocative question not only implies the general lack of awareness in the deluded and unconscious people of this tale, but also expresses the severe and inevitable limitations of human perception. The human eye must attempt seeing in a dark world which is lighted only by ever-diminishing stars and reflections in trick mirrors. The world of *The White Deer* is the chaotic world of the specialist, the technician, the bureaucrat, the despot—a world not improved by any of these social functionaries, but increasingly debased by them. It is a world in which human beings see, at best, as through a glass darkly, a glass progressively obscured by the phantasms of incompetent saviors promising The Answer.

This enchanted forest and this fantastic court—through the time-honored devices of satire, parody, and parable—are immediately recognizable as the modern world. This close identification makes the story of *The White Deer* both funny and frightening, pitiful and frustrating. The response to this book is, in fact, something like the reader's feeling when Gulliver at last looks in the mirror and says of himself, "Yahoo!"—the self-recognition is so strong and disquieting. Yet Thurber's tale manages to effect more of an acceptance of human experience than Swift's great satire does.

Like *The White Deer,* many of Thurber's works stress, in addition to the limitations of individual perception, the larger idea of the essentially elusive nature of reality. The two are related, of course, but they have a hierarchical relationship. Thurber's unconscious or deluded characters are part of his evidence for the general law that reality takes myriad forms. I wish to explore this idea of the infinite mutability of reality, surveying primarily some of Thurber's works that deal explicitly with dreams or the imagination. In Thurber's own terms, the distinction I will be making is between the factual (or material reality) and the possible (or what the mind does with reality; that is, the illusions and dreams it creates).[42] Although factual reality, which exists outside the mind, may be immense and extremely diverse, it is finite. The mind, as orderer of reality, can recreate experience infinitely as it forces new interpretations and combinations on the stuff of reality. Any given eye, or individual perception, sees reality in a different way, thus augmenting reality by its seeing.

In one sense, as we noted in Chapter 2, Thurber suggests that the powers of the imagination are superior to the prosaic, factual knowledge claimed by scientists and others who smugly assume that they understand reality. The humorist resembles the Romantic poets in this preference for creative, synthetic intelligence over analytical reason.[43] He makes this point very well in several essays about the imagination in *Let Your Mind Alone!*. In "The Case for the Daydreamer," for example, Thurber suggests that daydreaming is a necessary part of life, even when the dream cannot become reality. Since all that is known of reality is in the mind, anyway, the daydream itself is a kind of reality: "The thing to do is to visualize. . . the dream so vividly and insistently that it becomes, in effect, an actuality." He concludes that "realists are always getting into trouble," and in view of the curiously distorted "realists" in *Let Your Mind Alone!*, this is a justifiable conclusion: these realists—the mixed-up scientists, psychologists, and sociologists—are people who, though smug about their "systematic" approach to experience, only think they understand reality. The daydreamer, who admits that reality is too much for him or that it is essentially incomprehensible, is at least attuned to the true vagaries of human life.[44] Like the prosaic wife in "The Unicorn in the Garden," the scientist's grasp of reality and his control over the situation crumble when he is confronted with the power of the imagination and the confusion of the world. Although the unicorn is a mythical beast, who can say, in this world of endless permutations, that myth, which is based in some part of reality, is not an adequate vision of the world or reading of experience?

Also asserting the primacy of the imagination, "The Admiral on the Wheel" relates Thurber's remarkable adventures one day when his glasses were broken. This "handicap," which blurred his perception of factual or material reality, intensified his mind's operations on what was seen: "The kingdom of the partly blind is a little like Oz, a little like Wonderland, a little like Poictesme. Anything you can think of, and a lot you never would think of, can happen there." In the world of Thurber's creation, which so consciously seeks to replicate the world of the mind's eye, these remarkable things are precisely what happen every day. He says that such things happen "there." Where is "there"? "There" exists nowhere but in the mind of the perceiver. What happens "there" is a matter of infinite possibilities, as the individual, eccentric eye looks through the kaleidoscope at the ever-shifting world: "I saw a Cuban flag flying over a national bank, I saw a gay old lady with a gray parasol walk right through the side of a truck, I saw a cat roll across a street in a small striped barrel, I saw bridges rise lazily into the air, like balloons."[45] Thurber's most humorous images are thus as close to surrealism as to Romanticism. By implication, if he had looked back at any of these images a second time, or if his eyesight had been slightly altered, the catalogue of visions would be different. Thus does consciousness create the world.

"The Secret Life of Walter Mitty" depends heavily upon dreams for its statement about the real world, but Mitty's greatest dream, revealed at the story's climax, is of his own death. In a mood of tedium, frustration, and ennui, the story follows Mitty through an ordinary day—a day, like Ivan Ilych's life, so simple and so ordinary that it is, finally, terrible.[46] Indeed, Mitty's existence is so brutal, so dead, so impotent, that he must retreat into his mind; his only life is there, in "the moonlit marges of his mind." Therefore, according to my definitions, he is living radically separated from reality and almost totally in illusion. More properly, he is living through his dreams so completely that they have, in an inversion of illusion and reality, become his actual existence. Ironically, the pictures of "the remote, intimate airways of his mind" in the dream sequences are far more vivid and detailed than any other aspect of his death-in-life existence. When his wife screeches at him to slow down, pulling him abruptly out of the heroic skies of Navy warfare, his reaction is that "she seemed grossly unfamiliar, like a strange woman who had yelled at him in a crowd."[47] Although his dreams are out of Hollywood epic and melodrama, they seem, even to the reader, better than life with Mrs. Mitty in this sterile landscape.

The student of Thurber must be careful not to confuse the fact of Thurber's dealing with the triviality of modern life with his being a trivial artist. "Walter Mitty" depicts the vacuous vista of the modern world, a world confronted daily by human beings incapable of understanding or mastering it. Like that quintessentially modern poem, "The Love Song of J. Alfred Prufrock," Thurber's work makes a profound comment on the banality of our times and a major point about triviality.

F. O. Matthiessen has said, in a review of writers who dealt with the subject of alienation after the Second World War, that escapism in modern literature flows from a "concern with escape, not from the real, but from the monstrously unreal."[48] I can think of no better description of the mundane and horrible reality of the typical Thurber scene than that it is "monstrously unreal."[49] The question at the end of "Walter Mitty" is whether Mrs. Mitty's fact or her husband's illusion is better. It is a question that goes unanswered, however, because neither choice is attractive or can be chosen freely. These characters seem trapped, as much by themselves as by their environment, and this great story, so close to real life, remains ambiguous. Much of its universal appeal must reside in this enigmatic quality.

Like Walter Mitty, Charlie Deshler moves to "A Curb in the Sky," retreating into the intimate airways of his mind in order to get away from the mundane brutality of his marriage. Because Deshler's wife corrects all of his statements, he starts talking only about his dreams, thinking that she cannot correct his fantasy. These dreams become, therefore, "the only life he had," and paradoxically, the retreat into his mind is the only action possible: "Any psychiatrist will tell you that at the end of the way Charlie was going lies madness. . . . You can't live in a fantastic dream world, night in and night out and day in and day out, and remain sane. The substance began to die slowly out of Charlie's life, and he began to live entirely in shadow."[50] Ultimately, the question must be, which is less unreal, the substance or the shadow? Like Mitty's "reality" or the blurred edges between illusion and reality that Matthiessen's comment suggests, the answer is ambiguous.

The question of what constitutes reality is, of course, one of the principal questions of modern art. Thurber's preoccupation with the question also places him firmly in the central tradition of American literature, which flows directly from the tales and romances of

"I wouldn't rent this room to everybody, Mr. Spencer. This is where my husband lost his mind."

Hawthorne, that prober of the psyche from whom James learned so much. Thurber often presents this serious, even profound, moral/aesthetic question in a comical tone, it is true, but the substance remains the same. And, I would suggest, at his best—in the fables, the fairy tales, and the classic short stories—Thurber dramatizes the dilemma with as much power and sophistication as these ostensibly serious artists.

In his essay on "Our New Sense of the Comic," Wylie Sypher discusses the relationship between this question of illusion versus reality and the comic tradition. He suggests that dreams and fantasy are an essential part of modern comedy because "the very incongruity of the dream world is comic." Incongruity is a stock comic device, but the incongruity between Mitty's dream-life and what we know of his actual existence—he lives not only in a world of brutal personal relationships but of bombed cities—is not simply comical. In fact, the incongruity of Walter Mitty's life is as pathetic as it is funny. Mitty's dreams are Thurber's means of revealing the awful face of reality itself; they accomplish this better than any literal transcription of Mitty's day could. As Sypher explains:

> Freud interprets the dream and the jest as a discharge of powerful psychic energies, a glimpse into the abyss of the self. We have learned to read our dreams to tell us what we really are, for we now find that the patterns of our conscious life have meanings that can be explained only by looking below them into the chaos of the unconscious life always there, old, irrational, and inarticulate except in the language of the sleeping self.[51]

Mitty, then, is neither the air pilot he imagines himself to be, nor the milquetoast that his wife perceives (since her perception is necessarily limited, also), but a person defined in the reader's mind by the incongruous juxtaposition of the two views. This juxtaposition is accomplished by a controlled artistic consciousness that perceives the myriad forms of reality but is able to grasp one image from the fluid chaos. The image that we have of Walter Mitty, who he is to us, is thus a composite sketch made by the humorist-anatomist, not only combining many individual "Mittys" into one "type," but also perceiving the ironic collision of several points of view on this "type." Thurber accomplishes this in a compact story told in "the language of the sleeping self," much as his bare bones drawings seem to be images from nightmares and daydreams. The images are immediately recognizable, however, because the people in them are the people we really are.

Not content to study the clash of illusion and reality in the "real" world of the short story, Thurber chose to plumb the subject in a form suited perfectly to his investigation: the fairy tale. His first tale, *Many Moons* (1943), is the simplest statement of his persistent theme that reality is an ever-shifting entity. This is the story of a little princess who wants the moon in order to get well. None of her father's royal advisors is capable of getting the moon for her until one day, the Court Jester—the wise fool—thinks to ask the princess herself what she thinks the moon is like:

> "How big do they say the moon is," asked the Court Jester, "and how far away?"
>
> "The Lord High Chamberlain says it is 35,000 miles away, and bigger than the Princess Lenore's room," said the King. "The Royal Wizard says it is 150,000 miles away, and twice as big as this palace. The Royal Mathematician says it is 300,000 miles away, and half the size of this kingdom."
>
> The Court jester strummed on his lute for a little while. "They are all wise men," he said, "and so they must be all right. If they are all right, then the moon must be just as large and as far away as each person thinks it is."

The little princess says that, to her, the moon is a golden disc the size of her thumb, because when she reaches her hand out toward it, her thumbnail just covers it. She is then given a small disc as the moon, and does not balk even when the actual moon rises in the sky. When the Jester asks her how the moon can be both in the sky and on a chain around her neck, she replies that, just as the cycles of nature constantly replenish and destroy the earth's flowers, so there must be many moons to rise in the sky. There are many dreams, many "realities." She has what she thinks is the moon, that is, her impression of reality, and the comment seems to be that there are as many "realities" as there are perceivers.[52] Thurber has by this time completely inverted the illusion/reality commonplace, thus demonstrating the ironic nature of both labels. Even in *Many Moons*, the simplest of all his fairy tales, it is obvious that Thurber was writing as much about adult experience as for children. Childhood is especially jarred by disillusionment, of course; a child often refuses to believe in anything after a myth or impression is shaken. A lie about Santa Claus, for example, becomes a traumatic experience that causes, in the naive new realism of the child, a rejection of all such myths or dreams. It is a mature, coherent personality that can accept the illusory nature of human life without either ranting about the unfairness of it all or demanding that a new "reality" take the place of the original delusion.

In *The 13 Clocks* the Golux, a magical man who is capable of dealing with a nonsensical world, plays with the theme of elusive reality: "'Half the places I have been to, never were. I make things up. Half the things I say are there cannot be found. When I was young I told a tale of buried gold, and men from leagues around dug in the woods. I dug myself.' 'But why?' 'I thought the tale of treasure might be true.'" This Golux, or light, that helps the story's hero, Zorn, on his journey for Saralinda's love, is Thurber himself, enunciating the essentially illusory and enigmatic nature of life. His tale, which is true even though he made it up, is art, a type of reality superior to life's mundane "realism." By implication we could say that Thurber worked at creating his own world—a world of frank illusion often more real and more truthful than the actual world—because he, too, thought his "tale of treasure might be true." This is a richly suggestive phrase about the creative impulse.

The action of *The 13 Clocks* proves the substance of illusion. Zorn pays for Saralinda's hand in Hagga's jewels, jewels that will turn back into tears in a fortnight. These illusory jewels trick the Duke, the consummate deluded character in Thurber, who ironically clutches the gems as though they were everything: "'Begone!'" the cold Duke screamed . . . and bathed his hands in rubies. 'My jewels,' he croaked, 'will last forever.'" In the epilogue, the Duke is startled when the gems melt before his eyes and he, too, must finally realize how quickly the facade of reality changes. "What slish is *this?*" he exclaims in horror and disgust. When he is totally disillusioned by the fact of his "precious gems turned to thlup" (which, of course, is what they have always been), he gives himself over to the Todal, the mysterious monster in the tale, and to death.[53] He who thought he knew so much, who had falsely felt in control of everyone and everything in Coffin Castle, is unable to accept the elementary truth the Golux teaches: that the only certainty is that life is illusory and changeful. Factually, a tale that was made up is not true, but in Thurber's world of endless permutations, the impossible constantly becomes the possible. The tale told by a magical man or by a creative intelligence may be more real than the monstrously unreal material world that denies its validity. Although ambiguous, this distinction in Thurber's view of reality was also drawn effectively by James in "The Art of Fiction":

> It goes without saying that you will not write a good novel unless you possess the sense of reality; but it will be difficult to give you a recipe for calling that sense into being. . . . Experience is never limited and it is never complete; it is an immense sensibility, a kind of huge spider-web of the finest silken threads suspended in the chamber of consciousness, catching every air-borne particle in its tissue. It is the very atmosphere of the mind; and when the mind is imaginative — much more when it happens to be that of a man of genius — it takes to itself the faintest hints of life, it converts the very pulses of the air into revelation.[54]

The intangible, incongruous, and indefinable thus become part of reality, constituting a superior reality of their own.

The face of reality can change when eye glasses are broken, or when Mrs. Mitty brutally forces Walter Mitty back into the corners of his mind, or when a long-held expectation or illusion is disproven by experience. Reality, or more properly, the individual's perception of it, is also peculiarly affected by language, the arbitrary and distinctively human system that is sometimes falsely assumed to be only rational and descriptive. For Thurber, language is the gateway to a whole new reality, a whole new level of awareness. Often, words — which were devised to describe certain things or concepts — assume lives of their own, as they are separated from the reality they normally denote. Thus, garblings of phrases become, in the mind's eye, images never seen before. They create a whole new order of reality.

The complicated relationship between language and life can be highly comical, as in the literal interpretation of common metaphors in "The Secret Life of James Thurber." Morsberger takes Thurber's point in this essay to be a demonstration of the Bergsonian doctrine that a figure of speech becomes comic when one pretends to take it literally.[55] When Thurber recalls that the "secret world of idiom" was his youthful refuge from mundane Columbus, Ohio, his literal images of a man "tied up" at the office or of a girl who was "all ears" are funny. They are macabre as well, but the story elicits more open laughter than does much of Thurber's fiction. There is more involved in this essay than comic literalism, however. Thurber purposefully chose "The Secret Life of Salvador Dali," the autobiography of the surrealist painter, to contrast with his own childhood memories. Dali, who is perhaps best known for his literal depiction of dreams, is a perfect choice for Thurber's travesty. One could say that both Thurber and Dali see the dream in the reality and vice versa: their work portrays the constant interchange of the real and unreal, the movement between the dream world and the actual world. Although Thurber protests too much that Dali has had a more lively and exotic life than he ("Let me be the first to admit that the naked truth about me is to the naked truth about Salvador Dali as an old ukelele in the attic is to a piano in a tree, and I mean a piano with breasts"), he gradually admits to a kind of kinship with the antic surrealist. As surrealism stresses the nonrational and subconscious significance of imagery and especially exploits unexpected juxtapositions, Dali and Thurber share a similar artistic vision of the ever-changing face of reality:

> It never occurred to me to bite a bat in my aunt's presence or to throw stones at them. There was one escape, though: my secret world of idiom.
>
> Two years ago my wife and I, looking for a house to buy, called on a firm of real estate agents in New Milford. One of the members of the firm, scrabbling through a metal box containing many keys, looked up to say, "The key to the Roxbury house isn't here." His partner replied, "It's a common lock. A skeleton will let you in." I was suddenly once again five years old, with wide eyes and open mouth. I pictured the Roxbury house as I would have pictured it as a small boy, a house of such dark and nameless horrors as never crossed the mind of our little bat-biter.

The "fantastic cosmos"[56] that Thurber inhabits as a result of the ability of language to transmogrify experience is haunted by an infinite number of such images and visions, visions that are often only slightly reminiscent of the literal or factual reality to which the words relate. A skeleton key, in no way a horror in the actual world, becomes an image of indescribable horrors.

Taking metaphors literally, as well as seeing actual experience as metaphor, is at least as important in the writing of poetry as it is in comedy. In fact, Thurber had a poet's understanding of the suggestive and connotative powers of language. In his consciousness, words, which are usually regarded as representations of ideas or things, themselves become a new order of reality. "The Black Magic of Barney Haller" is the masterful story of an eerie hired man working at Thurber's country house who, through weird garblings of ordinary language, transforms summer afternoons into wild thunderstorms and himself into a Teutonic savage:

> "Dis morning bime by," said Barney, "I go hunt grotches in de voods."
>
> "That's fine," I said, and turned a page and pretended to be engrossed in what I was reading. Barney walked on; he had wanted to talk some more, but he walked on. After a paragraph or two, his words began to come between me and the words in the book. "Bime by I go hunt grotches in de voods." If you are susceptible to such things, it is not difficult to visualize grotches. They fluttered into my mind: ugly little creatures, about the size of whippoorwills, only covered with blood and honey and the scrapings of church bells. Grotches. . . Who and what, I wondered, really was this thing in the form of a hired man that kept anointing me ominously, in passing, with abracadabra?[57]

Barney's potent abracadabra also transmogrifies the simple image of the hired man himself—the material reality—into a strange and unexpected creature: "I had a prefiguring of Barney, at some proper spot deep in the woods, prancing around like a goat, casting off his false nature, shedding his hired man's garments, dropping his Teutonic accent, repeating diabolical phrases, conjuring up grotches." Thurber pointedly refers to Barney as "a traveller back from Oz" and finally resorts to nonsense language to scare Barney away:

> "Listen!" I barked, suddenly, "Did you know that even when it isn't brillig I can produce slithy toves? Did you

happen to know that the mome rath never lived that could outgrabe me? Yeah and furthermore I can become anything I want to; even if I were a warb, I wouldn't have to keep on being one if I didn't want to. I can become a playing card at will, too."[58]

And, indeed, in the Thurber carnival, he can. In this special world anything can suddenly become anything else, and language is the most frequent catalyst of quick transformation. In the next chapter we will explore more fully the implications of Thurber's use of the language of confusion; for our purposes here it is sufficient to note the role that language plays in transforming reality.

One sentence in "Barney Haller" describes best the endless permutations of reality. After Barney says, "Once I see dis boat come down de rock," to a "faintly creepy" Thurber, the writer interjects: "It is phenomena like that of which I stand in constant dread: boats coming down rocks, people being teleported, statues dripping blood, old regrets and dreams in the form of Luna moths fluttering against the windows at midnight."[59] Factually, of course, a moth is a moth and statues do not drip blood, but often impressions, circuitously related to external stimuli, are more revealing and more "real" than the elusive fact itself. Dreams and illusions are products of an ever-expanding chamber of consciousness, and they are also telling glimpses into the abyss of the self, as Shakespeare knew when he put the dream of statues dripping blood into his character's head the night before Julius Caesar dies.

What is real? Where does human experience happen? Because the mind is the seat of all knowledge, and because the mind itself provides at best only a limited perception of reality, the answer is ambiguous. Thurber's kaleidoscopic view of reality transformed by a slip of the tongue or a slight personality quirk or an unexpected turn of events, resembles the Jamesian sense of muddlement in its essential, paradoxical clarification of the ambiguities of experience and the myriad forms of reality. Usually Thurber's narrators are detached from the action and fully understand the confusion of his characters. Occasionally, however, as in "Doc Marlowe," "The Breaking Up of the Winships," and "A Call on Mrs. Forrester,"[60] he experiments effectively with point of view by allowing the story to follow the developing awareness of the narrator himself.

In "A Call on Mrs. Forrester," the comparison with James is

overt, and I wish to look closely at this story's development of consciousness to conclude our discussion of the influence of James on
Thurber's sense of reality. The epigraph to this story explains that
it was inspired by a "rereading, in my middle years" of *The Ambas-
sador,* and the story constantly refers to the narrator's level of consciousness. The narrator says that, on his return to Marian Forrester's
town, the place "seemed to me, vulgar and preoccupied," in contrast
to his earlier and more favorable illusions about the place and the
lady herself. Before, he had "persisted in seeing only the further
flowering of a unique and privileged spirit" in the character of Marian
Forrester, for he "had built the lady very high, as you see."[61] The
story takes place entirely inside the narrator's mind, as his impressions
of Mrs. Forrester and her surroundings shift before his eyes and the
reader's simultaneously. Adding yet another level of ambiguity to
the story, the reader "sees" Thurber's story and the fiction of Henry
James and Willa Cather's *A Lost Lady* simultaneously, for the story
unabashedly borrows words, phrases, sentence patterns, subjects,
and characters from both James and Cather. The reader of any effective parody is always thus "seeing double," or in this case, triple.

The tormented Prufrockian narrator never actually calls on Mrs.
Forrester, but only views her house and her "presence" from a distance,
trying self-consciously to get his point of view straight:

> As I crossed the bridge, with the Forrester home now in
> full view, I had, all of a sudden, a *disturbing* fancy. There
> flashed into my *consciousness* a vivid *vision* of the pretty
> lady, seated at her dressing table, practicing in secrecy her
> little arts, making her famous earrings gleam with small
> studied turnings of her head . . . and, unhappiest *picture* of
> all, rehearsing her wonderful laughter.

This glimpse of "the Awful," a faint glimmer of awareness in the narrator's mind revealing the true woman beneath "the raiment of a lady,"
is followed by a swift succession of "ungallant fancies" in which the
lady becomes incredibly banal and her once beautiful house is transformed into a vulgar closet of the nineteenth-century Middle West:

> There would be an old copy of Ainslee's on the floor some-
> where, a glitter of glass under a broken windowpane,
> springs leaking from a ruptured sofa, a cobweb in a chande-

lier, a dusty etching of Notre Dame unevenly hung on the wall, and a stopped clock on the marble mantle above a cold fireplace. I could see the brandy bottle, too, on a stained table, wearing its cork drunkenly.

Just to the left of the front door, the big hall closet would be filled with relics of the turn of the century, the canes and guns of Captain Forrester, a crokinole board, a diavolo, a frivolous parasol, a collection of McKinley campaign buttons, a broken stereopticon, a table tennis set, a toppled stack of blue poker chips and a scatter of playing cards, a woodburning set.

Never content with simply overturning one expectation or illusion, Thurber intensifies the confusion and muddlement of this story by portraying another complete upheaval in the narrator's mind. Suddenly, just as his new impression of Marian Forrester the vulgarian has confidently replaced his earlier illusions about her grace and charm, his sensibility is shaken and another impression takes its place:

"I beg you to remember it was once said of Madame de Vionnet that when she touched a thing the ugliness, God knows how, went out of it." "How sweet!" I could hear Mrs. Forrester go on. "And yet, according to you, she lost her lover, for all her charm, and to a snippet of an applecheek from New England. Did the ugliness go out of that? And if it did, what did the poor lady do with all the prettiness?"

As I stood there in the darkening afternoon, getting soaked, I realized sharply that in my fantasy I had actually been handing Marian Forrester stones to throw at the house in Paris, and the confusion in my viewpoint of the two ladies, if up to that moment I had had a viewpoint, overwhelmed me.[62]

Thurber is laughing at James here, of course, but it is affectionate laughter born of kinship and his perception of the incongruity of James's "high seriousness" in the modern world. The parodies are the only stories in which Thurber indulges in the tortured complexity of James's later syntax, but often his deceptively simple prose creates layers as richly ambiguous as the master's.

The story ends with its narrator never even approaching the house, in a confusion of viewpoint which implies the fundamental ambiguity of experience. He is able to choose clearly neither Madame de Vionnet, with a sensibility so refined that she could pretend not to see an omelet in a guest's lap, nor Mrs. Forrester, the vulgarian who would at least have enough humanity to appreciate the comedy of an omelet on a civilized man's lap. Thurber has thus captured in this short story not only James's idea of character and perception, but the essential ambiguity in James's comparison of Americans and Europeans, a comparison that is often regarded simplistically by readers who expect a definite statement from the master of nuance and muddlement. The question of whether Madame de Vionnet is better than Mrs. Forrester (or Christopher Newman or Isabel Archer) is finally unanswered, unless the answer is that neither is better. In a large sense, all experience is muddled and all reality ambiguous.

Thurber's view of reality as an ever-shifting, ambiguous entity is not only evidence of his Jamesian influence, however. Sypher suggests that modern comedy is built upon a split vision of the world, depending as it does "upon double occasions, double premises, double values." Since we live in a world of irreconcilables, he asserts, modern comedy is the form that, even more than tragedy, best reveals truths to us: "After all, comedy, not tragedy, admits the disorderly into the realm of art. . . . and ours is a century of disorder and irrationalism."[63] The resultant art, attempting to effect order within disorder, is as ambiguous as life itself. Thurber's compendium of such split images, or his anatomy of the *corpus mentis,* is not the handiwork of a camera out of focus, but a series of carefully executed double, triple, even quadruple exposures showing the conflicting elements of life juxtaposed with one another — all in perfect focus, with the sharpness and clarity that only dreams or primal terrors have. Neither tragic nor comic, these images are the most essential expression of Thurber's fundamentally tragicomic vision.

Thurber admitted that he lived in a constant state of flux about reality and life:

> Intelligent persons are expected to formulate 'an integrated
> and consistent attitude toward life or reality;' this is known
> as a 'philosophy' (definition 2c in Webster's New Inter-

national Dictionary). Unfortunately, I have never been able to maintain a consistent attitude toward life or reality, or toward anything else. This may be entirely due to nervousness. At any rate, my attitudes change with the years, sometimes with the hours.[64]

This ambivalence leads Thurber constantly to qualify and requalify his position in his prose; it is also at least a partial basis for his depiction of many characters' elusive hold on any attitude, illusion, or perception. The inability to make a consistent or final statement about life is the ultimate result of Thurber's one consistent vision, that of the unending chaos and disorder of human life. It is also, perhaps, the necessary result of man's depending upon his faulty nervous system to process the information derived from his chaotic experience, as it is decoded with uneven success by the imperfect organ in his head. Like Prufrock, Thurber's characters live with endless visions and revisions which a minute can reverse. This is the burden of consciousness.

Paradoxical as it is, Thurber states clearly the fundamental ambiguities of human experience and substitutes a fine-spun superrealism for a factual, limited understanding of life. His wicked or truly unattractive characters are those who are deluded into taking illusion as reality. Thurber does not make the mistake of offering another inadequate formula to replace the old illusion, but is instead interested in elucidating the infinitely complex and even contradictory nature of life. The one fundamental illusion to be destroyed, then, is the belief that reality is ever self-evident. Peering into the abyss of the human mind, Thurber's anatomy of the *corpus mentis* attempts to discern, through a delicate dissection of thought and memory, the fragile and inadequate structures of meaning that hold our chaotic experience together. The Thurber carnival, an incongruous blend of the funny and the sad, the triumphant and the defeated, the real and the fantastic, is as rich and enigmatic as life itself.

As an epilogue to this discussion of illusion and reality, we may recall Prospero's haunting comments on the illusive human comedy:

> Our revels now are ended. These our actors,
> As I foretold you, were all spirits and
> Are melted into air, into thin air;

And, like the baseless fabric of this vision,
The cloud-capped tow'rs, the gorgeous palaces,
The solemn temples, the great globe itself,
Yea, all which it inherit, shall dissolve,
And, like this insubstantial pageant faded,
Leave not a rack behind. We are such stuff
As dreams are made on, and our little life
Is rounded with a sleep.[65]

And, with no further ado, let us move on to a consideration of the elusive medium which describes and defines our little, insubstantial lives: the language of confusion.

4 The Language of Confusion
Thurber's Anatomy of *Homo Loquens*

Ours is a precarious language, as every writer knows, in which the merest shadow line often separates affirmation from negation, sense from nonsense, and one sex from the other.
— *Lanterns & Lances*

As our exploration of Thurber's anatomy of the *corpus mentis* has revealed, the world perceived through the anatomist's lens is a precariously balanced world indeed. This world is so tentatively balanced because the human mind, which seeks to understand experience, is essentially flawed, limited, and changeful. Here, only "the merest shadow line" temporarily separates fear from laughter, life from death, or sense from nonsense, thus ordaining irony-within-irony and creating endless visions and revisions of experience.

Most specifically, the Thurber carnival is a world of confused and confusing language. Since the frail human mind is the seat of all knowledge, the basic material of thought—language—is the most common catalyst of confusion. When human beings think, that is, when they imagine, name, recall, foresee, analyze, comprehend, explain, or characterize their experience, they do so in words. Because the use of language is central to human experience and is, in fact, what distinguishes humans from other beasts, Thurber's anatomy of confused human existence concentrates on this activity above all others. Throughout his career, the master anatomist particularly studies the species *Homo loquens*,[1] behaving in his habitat, doing his distinctively human thing, in order to arrive at the most revealing image of humankind for the anatomy. Thus, if we want to enter the world of Thurber's creation, language must be the key. Having acquainted ourselves with the social and mental confusion in which humanity languishes, let us now consider Thurber's language as the best way of gaining full access to that special world charted in his anatomy of confusion.

In our investigation, we shall discover that, even though he is from the beginning careful and gifted as a stylist, Thurber becomes increasingly inventive during the three decades of his writing career. Always fascinated with delineating the characteristics of *Homo loquens,* Thurber comes to see human life as synonymous with language, which in turn, affects his style and form. Finally, he explores and exploits language to the point that it becomes, not only his glorious medium and insistent subject, but also a character in the human comedy. In *The Wonderful O,* which is, in a sense, the culmination of all his exploration, language is personified, with essential moral and cultural roles to play. Like Orwell's *1984,* Thurber's mature work shows that the state of a language is equivalent to the general health of its culture. This is to say that Thurber discovers that language is experience, is life.

Although it has become almost axiomatic to say that Thurber wrote a "lucid, correct, and expensively simple English,"[2] admirers of his style often fail to realize that simplicity only partially describes Thurber's language. Even more often they fail to see the intimate, intrinsic relationship between his use of language and both his subject matter and his artistic credo. The more extreme consequences of his linguistic obsession have been regarded generally as a minor fault or a major idiosyncrasy, at times obscuring meaning rather than aiding it. Critics with this view usually notice the growing concern with words and sound after the advent of Thurber's blindness in the early 1940s, and the increasing role of word games in the later books. Some critics find the language pieces offensive from the beginning of Thurber's career, but the more common judgment seems to be that only the later pieces are overwhelmed by punning, esoteric jokes, and other kinds of wordplay.[3]

Yet Thurber's interest in language, in its power and its limits, is consistent throughout his career (although much intensified in his last two decades, as he became more of what he called an "ear writer"[4] and worked in new forms). I propose that this predilection, far from being a mere quirk or tangential indulgence, is related fundamentally to his other subjects, his view of human life, and his perception of the artist's role. Interest in language is continuous and integral in Thurber's art. Indeed, his greatest contribution to life and letters is his passionate devotion to discovering sense in a world of nonsense, and his creation of a distinct, authentic voice in which to speak of it. He liked to refer to himself as a "word man,"[5] and from the beginning he viewed language as both a possibility for achieving the most precise balance in a chaotic world and as a probability for triggering bedlam. And we shall find that, as Thurber grew and developed as a writer, his perception of this essential paradox deepened, and his understanding of how best to render it changed.

Despite random praise from other writers and most of his reviewers, Thurber's language has been seriously neglected.[6] The following discussion will explore the basic relationship of Thurber's linguistic obsession and fine prose style to his themes and subject matter, an exploration that will require another look at some works cited previously, with the emphasis now on a scrutiny of language. Although Thurber understood the world to be in perpetual confusion, he regarded language as both a prime instigator of that confusion, and paradoxically, as our only means to surmount it. Through language, Thurber suggests, we can attempt to say what, exactly, is the matter; we can attempt to close the gaps which necessarily exist between muddled, perplexed, and hostile people; we can recapture the past, in memory, and make it new again, in art; we can at least register our recognition (and, often, our disapproval) of the awful reality of our world. This conception of language, which emerges from studying the body of Thurber's work, is but a corollary of his concept of the artist as one who brings grace and measure to chaotic experience. In his own calm, precise, and amazingly creative language, Thurber recollects and recreates the bedlam and carnival of human life.

Note, for example, the tonal and temporal distance between the narrator's voice, droll, controlled, and analytical, and the events that he is describing in this characteristic passage from *My Life and Hard Times*: "I suppose that the high-water mark of my youth in Columbus, Ohio, was the night the bed fell on my father . . . [it is] a somewhat incredible tale. Still, it did take place. . . . It happened, then, that my father had decided to sleep in the attic one night, to be away where he could think." The language here is distinctly conversational, yet cultivated, measured, and radically understated. Compare the tone and detachment of this passage, written at a distance of thirty years from the "events," with the cacophony in the Thurber household on that infamous evening: "My mother, still shouting, pursued by Herman, still shouting, was trying to open the door to the attic. . . . Roy and the dog were now up, the one shouting questions, the other barking".[7] In Babel, the multiplicity of voices only increases the confusion, and even the dogs bark without comprehension. It is left for the artist alone to decipher the meaning of human activity.

Thurber knew that detachment or distance is necessary to establish a comic voice in fiction: the lens of time and space makes possible our perception of the comicality of events. Therefore, what I am suggesting about Thurber's prose style is intrinsic to his humor, and the connection of the two helps to explain the peculiar sound and structure of a Thurber sentence or anecdote. In fact, the feeling of fragility that one often gets in reading a Thurber line results, in part, from his tenuous hold on experience during the delicate dissection of events that makes possible his story.

Regarding language, Thurber really provides two anatomies: one, the body of his work, or the anatomy of confusion, is the result of his method, which records and analyzes the human spectacle in a calm, detached, exacting, and inventive way; the other, the anatomy of *Homo loquens,* or Thurber's analysis of man the talker, is the result of his choice of subject—that is, of his most important subject, language. These two anatomies are linked inextricably, of course, since the anatomy of *Homo loquens* is but a part, albeit the most important part, of Thurber's anatomy of human life.

As *My Life and Hard Times* shows, Thurber's early stories reveal the world of linguistic confusion. But late in his life, in a casual essay called "The Case Book of James Thurber," he reflects on his method, explaining directly and succinctly the ideas about language that he has been developing over the years. Here, "Dr." Thurber cites several typical cases from his long study of chaos. Reporting in clear, investigative prose, he follows climactic order in arranging these cases, introducing the last with this remarkable passage: "The Anatomy of Confusion is a large subject, and I have no intention of writing the standard treatise on it, but I offer to whoever does, the most singular of all my cases." Thurber is hedging ironically here, of course, because the body of his work, although unannounced as such, does present the perceptive reader with this "Anatomy of Confusion." What is most significant is that, as Thurber offers a phrase that perfectly describes the entire body of his work, he cites examples of verbal confusion. For Thurber, language was the secret source

*A Garble with an
Utter in its claws.*

of human chaos, as well as the buried treasure of human joy. As the "Case Book" reveals, his is a world of slurred pronunciation, garbled names, and wildly flexible words—a world where the Gloucester telephone supervisor becomes, breathily, "the Gloucester Sympathizer," and a cocker spaniel turns, quite innocently, into a "cockeyed Spaniard."[8] It is a world at once frightening and exhilarating, perplexing and funny. And language is its key.

Surveying human chaos, the anatomist uses and analyzes language itself. Language is the only chance to end or forestall confusion, but it, like all human endeavors, often fails. In fact, since we can know our experience—including language—only through inadequate words themselves, failure is much more likely than success. This chapter is concerned especially with the unique Thurber rendering of these failures, or with "The Language of Confusion": humanity's mistaken, garbled, inaccurate, and insufficient attempts at communication. However, we shall also see that, as Thurber anatomizes the disorder of language and life, he constructs an order of his own, thus revealing an essential paradox at the base of human experience: that language is both the *cause* and the *cure* of the "human disease." His implied statement seems to be that only the poet or artist can make sense from the language of confusion, create with it, or use it as a weapon in the unending war against chaos. A roughly chronological account of Thurber's language and style should help to clarify these points.[9]

From *Is Sex Necessary? or Why You Feel the Way You Do* (1929) to the posthumous collection, *Credos and Curios* (1962), the history of Thurber's art is the story of his developing linguistic obsession. When Thurber collaborated with E. B. White on his first published book, *Is Sex Necessary?*, he established firmly the use and abuse of language as one of his basic subjects. Like much of Thurber's writing, *Is Sex Necessary?* is heavily parodic, and the book also employs such future style markers as frequent neologisms, especially mock jargon coinages, and groups of words or phrases that are not normally used together.[10] The language of confusion resonates throughout its pages.

Is Sex Necessary? is an extended parody, and it is the particular kind of parody that Thurber was to favor—next to the literary parody—over all others: parody of the scientific (or pseudoscientific) treatise.[11] In Thurber's use of parody in this book and the later "scientific" parodies of *Let Your Mind Alone!*, he differs from the parodic tradition which assumes that the imitator admires his model, at least partially.[12] Although Thurber later uses parody in this richer, quasi-complimentary sense when he imitates Henry James, the earlier parodies of scientific and political language are attacks denigrating what Thurber understood to be the inadequate conclusions of these areas of human activity.

Since Thurber saw language as a way of comprehending the essence of a person, the parody was a natural form for him. The person that he wants to discover in the early parodies is the specialist, that most common of modern men. Like *Let Your Mind Alone!*, *Is Sex Necessary?* is a spoof of self-help manuals written by specialists for the masses: the "sex books" or popularized psychology of the 1920s. Thurber, who was attracted to scientific methodology as a way to construct a literary text, uses mock case histories as his form. Note the carefully parodic record of "patient" George Smith:

> Aged 32, real estate operator. Unmarried, lived with mother. No precocious mother fixation. Had freed his libido without difficulty....formed an attachment in 1899, at the age of 29, with a young virgin. Her protective reactions....lasted over a period of three years, during which he never held her hand. Defense Devices: usually euchre (four handed)....Definite and frequent fudge-making subterfuge.[13]

This passage is humorous because it provides the reader with a comical "double-vision" of experience:[14] the language seems both correct (or nearly so) and hideously incorrect, enough to cause a laugh or a wince in the reader. As we have noted, Thurber's humor causes most often only a wince or a sigh, not the guffaw incited by low comedy. The nearly correct language ("Defense Devices") leaves the small jolt, or the "laugh," until the end, where the seemingly technical description ends with a reference to fudge-making. Of course, Thurber is not just satirizing modern science (or, more properly, its manifestations in applied science and scientism). He is also attacking particularly its involved yet empty language, language which reveals an essential confusion and inability to deal with human problems. This is to say nothing of his implicit attack on the readers of such tomes, many of whom, I suspect, have bought *Is Sex Necessary?* under the erroneous impression that the book would provide an answer to its titular question.

In the preface to *Is Sex Necessary?*, a mock anthropological voice, buried in confusing verbosity, intones: "Almost immediately the two halves of the original cell began experiencing a desire to unite again — usually with half of some other cell."[15] The shift down in tone in the last phrase of this sentence is a hallmark of Thurber's comic prose style, and here it confuses the sentence enough to cause the reader to question all scientific reporting. Thus, the confusion one senses in reading this line is not the result of mere gimmickry, but of an attempt to show, through language, the state of a mind and, in a way, the state of the world.

Even the neologistic games that Thurber plays with the reader of *Is Sex Necessary?* continue the subtle deflation of specialists and their language. We are delighted to learn that, in Thurber's lexicon, "Schmalhausen Trouble" describes the problems of "close families," but such verbal tricks have a serious side, too. They expand our thinking about technical language by subjecting it to analysis and ridicule. So, too, do Thurber's "new" definitions of standard terms: we learn that "narcissism" is the "attempt to be self-sufficient, with overtones." The anatomist of language is taking apart sentences, phrases, and words, attempting to see what lies beneath their surface. All of this is wildly humorous, probably because Thurber is using the established comic technique of setting up expectations which he then does not fulfill.[16]

In the midst of puncturing jargon, therefore, Thurber has called attention to several important aspects of our way of life: science, scientism, learning, and language. He even deals with the significant subject of the inability of the sexes to communicate. His "treatise" on "The Lilies-and-Bluebird Delusion" is an early, humorous rendition of the communication gap that prefigures the near-horror of such confusion in later stories like "A Couple of Hamburgers," "The Breaking Up of the Winships," and most prominently, "The Secret Life of Walter Mitty." "The Lilies-and-Bluebird Delusion" recounts the "case" of a young couple who cannot communicate because of adherence to stock phrases, old wives' tales, and superstition. Due to inadequate sex education, a young wife believes that procreation is effected by flowers being brought into her bedroom (this is what her mother had told her, after all). Her husband attempts to explain, first in English, then in French, but finally admits, "I just don't know enough words."[17] Language, the only hope for ending human confusion, is itself painfully flawed and limited. By the end of the piece, the home of such mute partners is as foreboding as it is funny; in this arid landscape, unknowing and inarticulate couples are able only to clump together, waiting for death. It is a pervasive and dominant scene in Thurber's fiction, planted at the beginning of his career. Thus, in his first book, Thurber has already begun to plumb language's creative possibilities, while also revealing that he is acutely aware of its limits. In a sense, *Is Sex Necessary?* is a study of the creaking mechanism of language itself.

Following *Is Sex Necessary?* in 1931 was Thurber's first collection of short stories, *The Owl in the Attic and Other Perplexities.* Here, the first of the well-drawn Thurber couples, Mr. and Mrs. Monroe, suffer from the language of confusion. Also parodic (in this case, their imagery invokes Henry James), the Monroe stories continue Thurber's portrayal of inarticulate couples, but this time their inability to communicate is the focus of the story.

Mr. and Mrs. Monroe play involved games with one another instead of really living. John Monroe is daydreaming his way through life (he thus introduces a "type" in Thurber's fiction), reflecting his inordinate interest in popularized philosophy and its jargon. His attraction to such language leads Monroe into exquisitely involved confusions. "Mr. Monroe began to feel pretty much the master of his fate. Non-fiction, of a philosophical nature, always affected him that way, regardless of its content." Thus persuaded, John Monroe lives the dangerous life of the language victim. In "The Imperturbable Spirit," for example, he turns the adjective over and over in his head, until everything appears imperturbable. The incantatory properties of language trick John Monroe into thinking that he is imperturbable. His life is as meaningless as the slogans he believes, but as a specimen of confused *Homo loquens,* he sees neither the irony nor the emptiness of his situation. Only the anatomist studying him is really able to see him, to recognize that he has turned both life and language into a mere game, thus making all of his attempts at communication only brittle, vacuous noise. In his native habitat, the language of confusion rules.[18]

Since language is the distinctively human activity, other animals usually experience neither its successes nor failures. Therefore, "The Pet Department" includes only one question about language. In answer to why a police dog would act strangely after being asked continually the inane question, "if you're a police dog, where's your badge?" Thurber (in the persona of a newspaper columnist) answers: "the constant re-iteration of any piece of badinage sometimes has the same effect on present day neurotic dogs that it has on people."[19] Like poor John Monroe, even the dog, through his domestication, has been forced into perplexity by language.

"The Ladies' and Gentlemen's Guide to Modern English" connects language directly with human experience. The "Guide," Thurber tells us, was inspired by Fowler's dictionary of *Modern English Usage,* that bible of New Yorker editors and other modern stylists. Thurber's "Guide," as a parody/commentary on Fowler, is an excursion into the labyrinth of language, and, more than ever, it is clear that his delving into language is an inquiry into the nature of meaning. In the "Guide," Thurber displays his characteristic fascination and agility with words, along with a probing sense of language's limitations. He demonstrates the wide range of confusion possible in trying to deal with common grammatical problems (he is once again finding laughter in the utterly familiar) and, implicitly, makes the comment that the English language, and perhaps all language, is absurd.[20] "Unfortunately, it is only in rare cases that 'where' can be used in place of 'whom'. Nothing could be more flagrantly bad, for instance, than to say 'Where are you?' in demanding a person's identity. The only conceivable answer is, 'Here I am,' which would give no hint at all as to whom the person was."[21] Language, the only hope for intelligent communication, is often the very factor in eluding meaning.

Is Thurber, as some critics have assumed, himself confused? This conclusion ignores the careful manipulation of the problems and properties of the English language in works like the "Guide." Think of the close attention to language demanded by Thurber's parodies; or consider the perceptive comment implicit in the following apparently nonsensical statement, which shows Thurber's knowledge of the confusion resulting from latinate English: "It is better to use 'whom' when in doubt, and even better to reword the statement, and leave out all the relative pronouns, except ad, ante, con, in, inter, ob, post, prae, pro, sub, and super." Thurber's knowledge of language and his precise ear for English prose are also demonstrated richly in the "Guide's" parodic passages. These passages, like all "effortless" art, are deceptively simple. Notice, for example, what is packed into the following paragraph, where language is materialized, grammatical problems are confronted, and Hemingway's style is explicated:

> The young man who originally got into that sentence was never found. . . . The safest way to avoid such things is to follow the path of the American author, Ernest Hemingway. In his youth, he was trapped in a which-clause and barely escaped with his mind. . . . [He learned to skirt the morass by writing in this way]: 'He was afraid of one thing. This was the thing. He had been warned to fear such things.'[22]

Thurber's eventual personification of language, which makes concrete his identification of language with life, is but an expectable step from such a passage. Although heavily exaggerated, this passage is apt and especially humorous because it is only a distortion of two very real things: a distinctive prose style and the perplexity of a man confronting a difficult linguistic decision. And, I would suggest, it also represents one of the most succinct analyses of Hemingway's style.

Lest we miss the essential link between language and life, even the hilarity of the "Guide" relates language problems to social ones: "Word has somehow got around that a split infinitive is always wrong. This is of a piece with the sentimental and outworn notion that it is always wrong to strike a lady." This seemingly flippant statement, apposing language and life, is followed by a description of the ease with which a polite dinner party turns into a brawl.[23] In Thurber's view of human experience, the abyss of chaos awaits in the drawing room, in the sentence. Thus, the anatomist is not concerned solely with examining the intricacies of grammar or with playing verbal tricks on his reader. He is interested in curing "grammatical confusion," a confusion which is preeminent in human life because it can lead into a fatal which-clause, or precipitate the breakdown of a mind, a marriage, a social event, or a nation. As he worked with language during thirty years as a writer, this connection between language and life became more explicit and more profound for Thurber. And slowly, the full consequences of linguistic confusion were revealed in his writing, so that the essential playfulness of the very early works became tinged with terror in his pseudoautobiographical masterpiece, *My Life and Hard Times*.

Indeed, if his memoirs are any indication, Thurber's youth was defined by his experience with the language of confusion. He dwelt, not in the Columbus, Ohio, of legend, but, as he would admit later, in a "secret world of idiom."[24] In a very basic sense, it is language that precipitates the wild disarray of events which comprise Thurber's personal history. As I suggested earlier, by the time Thurber wrote *My Life,* there was a notable tension between the precision of his prose and the imprecise communication of the characters in his stories. Tightly constructed stories like "The Night the Bed Fell" and "The Day the Dam Broke" describe, in remarkably clear and mature prose, a most perplexing assortment of confusions. But these stories not only describe confusions, they are themselves misnomers: the bed did not fall and the dam did not break, although the events are always referred to in these terms.

From the confusion inside the Thurber household, we are pushed into the streets of sunny Columbus, on "The Day the Dam Broke." Hundreds of citizens rush by the Thurber house (itself a paradigm of reason, as we already know), in a wild panic, while the words "the dam has broken" wreak havoc. Even the presumably calming announcement that "'the dam has *not* broken'. . . tended only to add to the confusion and increase the panic, for many stampeders thought the soldiers were bellowing 'the dam has now broken!,' thus setting an official seal of authentication on the calamity." Only after repeated announcements does the crowd disperse.[25] Paradoxically, the very words that had confused the masses eventually quelled the stampede: language is both the cause and the cure of our confusion. Since no one is injured in the mad running, the panic remains classically comic, but the image of group chaos instigated by a simple slip of the tongue is one that Thurber returns to again and again. And, each time he portrays it, it becomes more deadly.

In all of *My Life*'s adventures into the land of meaninglessness, there is no confusion like the confusion in the narrator's mind on that balmy evening after he "had been trying all afternoon, in vain, to think of the name Perth Amboy." This is not simply a little boy trying to think of a word, or a piece of nonsensical humor; it is a consciousness trying to make sense from nonsense, exploring the meaning of meaning:

> I began to indulge in the wildest fancies as I lay there in
> the dark, such as that there was no such town, and even

that there was no such state as New Jersey. I fell to repeating the word "Jersey" over and over again, until it became idiotic and meaningless. . . . I got to thinking that there was nobody else in the world but me. . . . I began to suspect that one might lose one's mind over some such trivial mental tic as a futile search for terra firma Piggly Wiggly Gorgonzola Prester John Arc de Triomphe Holy Moses Lares and Penates.[26]

Although the tone of *My Life and Hard Times* is one of high spirits, brighter than many of the darkly humorous stories of the later Thurber, we must recognize the essential horror underlying this picture of his mind, echoing words and being menaced by sound and meaning. The scene is also quite funny, largely for two reasons. First, it fully exploits the principle of comic repetition; it is the long, involved obsession with the name "Perth Amboy" and its alternatives that makes us laugh. More subtly, it is funny because it violates, in another established technique of comedy, one of the "laws" of language. Auden has insisted, "words are man-made things which men use, not persons with a will and consciousness of their own."[27] Ah, that it were so simple!

Here, in the darkened room, words stalk the man in a scene both comical and frightening. In "Perth Amboy," humor and horror merge. Thurber always recognized the elements of pain and fear in laughter, his humor being a special blend of the funny, the sad, and the horrible. Those who say that Thurber revelled in confusion as a young man and was menaced by words and chaos only later in his life miss the point of near-hysteria in this description of this futile search for "Perth Amboy" and himself. Like the grammatical morass described in the "Guide" or the misfortunes of Mr. Monroe, *My Life and Hard Times* shows that language is a powerful demon. It appears as a possibility for reason and calm; language is the material with which a writer works, from which he constructs a pattern in the chaos. Even more surely, however, using language is the first step toward bedlam. And the stakes — universal pandemonium and personal nonexistence — become clearer to Thurber and his readers with time.

Communication problems become even more complex in Thurber's next book, *The Middle-Aged Man on the Flying Trapeze*. Since this distinguished collection has a greater diversity of subject matter and mood than the previous works, its linguistic pieces range from the flippant word games of "The State of Bontana" and the high burlesque of "Something to Say" to the eerily provocative "Black Magic of Barney Haller." It is interesting that Thurber liked "Barney Haller" the best of all these stories,[28] for in it, his fascination with language is balanced with even more menace than in the earlier battle against the words "Perth Amboy." I would like to take another look at "Barney Haller," since I believe it is one of Thurber's most successful pieces, and one that reveals much about his understanding of *Homo loquens.*

Thurber's description of how he (or, his assumed persona) reacted to Barney Haller illustrates his complex attitude toward language, confusion, and the nonrational aspects of life. Barney was the hired man who seemed to bring thunderstorms with him, as his Teutonic dialect triggered Thurber's wildest thoughts. This "traveller back from Oz" transported Thurber to the dark corners of his mind, and, through incantatory language, even transmogrified himself. "I had a notion that he was standing at the door barefooted, with a wreath of grape leaves around his head, and a wild animal's skin slung over his shoulder," Thurber remembers. All of these mental transformations are caused by what Barney says, what he mispronounces, and what these sounds seem to mean. Even the reasonable explanation of what it is, exactly, that Barney means does not diminish the efficacy of his oral black magic, however. Indicative of the ambiguities in the anatomist's art, Thurber admits that though he has at times deciphered Barney's language and found that it was describing "a commonplace, an utterly natural thing," he has never been able to forget it: "I should have dismissed it, but it had its effect on me."[29] The tonal shift in this last sentence reflects the necessary relationship between Thurber's style and his meaning, or, to put it another way, the essential link between his humorous voice and his serious intention.

The dilemma of Thurber and Haller is germane to an understanding of Thurber characters generally, since they seem continually to meet experience unprepared by reason or past experience, destined to make the same errors and fall into the same confusions as before. They are especially unable to use language reasonably. As little Jamie had thought that the physical presence of his body was weak proof of his existence when confronted with the insistent argument of the words "Perth Amboy," so here does the mature narrator, "Thurber," see Barney and the whole world transformed by language. What is real depends entirely upon what language reveals to us.

Since the narrator of "Barney Haller" is a writer, he uses the weapons of a literate man against this onslaught of verbal voodoo. He attempts to keep reading Proust while Barney drones on, but admits that "his words began to come between me and the words in the book." He then tries quoting Frost, which does not faze Barney, who could probably say, "I go to de voods—you come, too," without any smile of recognition. Only a rephrasing of Lewis Carroll makes some kind of crazy sense to the nonsense-speaker: "'Listen!' I barked suddenly. 'Did you know that even when it isn't brillig I can produce slithy toves? Did you happen to know that the mome rath never lived that could outgrabe me?'"[30] This is a marvelous climax to the story, exploding all the tension it has so carefully created between sense and nonsense. In this moment, sense and nonsense become one, or nonsense becomes the only way to sense. Thurber is again challenging the concept of language as an instrument of reason and as an objective reality in which constant meanings are established. In this world of endless permutations, we get sense from nonsense, only nonsense from sense. The choice of quotation is appropriate, of course, since Carroll used nonsense language to make much the same kind of statement.

Thurber demonstrates his understanding of Carroll's nonsense by adhering to the feigned syntax and parts of speech of the original. For example, Thurber knows that in English a mome rath could outgrabe anytime it wanted to, but we would not likely say, "Outgrabe brillig mome." Thus, does nonsense language both follow and break the rules of language at the same time, giving the reader a comical, bifocal vision of experience, a sense of the endless possibilities for meaning. The texture of "Barney Haller" also makes one think of the broader similarities between Thurber, the anatomist, who carefully dissects the world's confusion, and Carroll, the logician, who methodically takes apart common sense and exposes the madness that lurks just beneath its surface.[31] In both writers, the presumed rationality of language is shattered, so that the reader may see the fragile nature of sense and order in the world that language describes. Language is the key to human experience.

Thurber in some measure wins out over Barney Haller; his own

nonsensical incantations send Haller away forever. The artist transcends the language of confusion, and we cheer, secure once again
in the thought that experience is describable and, therefore, understandable. But the ambiguity of Thurber reappears in the last line
of the story where, with characteristic equivocation, he says of
Barney: "I am sure that he trafficked with the devil. But I am sorry
that I let him go."[32] The perplexities of life and language are
fascinating material for the imagination, irrevocably drawing the
writer to them, while another part of his nature fights for meaning,
tranquility, and order. The tension created by two such forces,
pulling against each other as they do in Thurber's work, imbues his
prose with great energy.

Thurber was never secure in his hope that the artist or literate
man could transform the world of Barney Haller into the world of
Proust's articulate sensibility. In "Something to Say," the astute
literary critic, James Thurber, makes fun of those would-be artists
who play at letters and at life. In this story, the elaborate joke of
language is exquisitely, outrageously developed. But here, the perpe-
trator of the "joke" is conscious (more or less) of what he is doing.
The story's hero, Elliot Vereker, does not waste much time on
finishing manuscripts, but, in the grand American tradition, concentrates instead on creating an "image" of himself, on huckstering to
willing victims. The essential irony of this typical Thurber title
(Vereker has, in fact, *nothing* to say) sets the tone of the story.

As a prototypical dilettante, Vereker has "an ordinate fondness
for echoes," which indicates that he has no capacity for real communication. And yet he speaks (and speaks!) and inexplicably finds
an audience: "Proust, I later discovered, he had never read, but he
made him seem more clear to me, and less important, than anybody
else ever has." (What a fine comment on much literary criticism
Thurber has slipped in here. It is a haunting line.) Vereker's banal
"insights" are effective, however, even when no one can physically
hear him: "Vereker always liked to have an electric fan going while
he talked and he would stick a folded newspaper into the fan so that
the revolving blades scuttered against it. . . . This exhilarated him
and exhilarated me, too, but I suppose that it exhilarated him more
than it did me."[33] On reflection, the superficial inanity of this
passage expands to a deeper meaning: it is the spellbinding nature
of even meaningless language that Thurber is again probing.

Language, presumably the instrument of meaning, can mesmerize a coterie or millions with gobbledygook. Precious as his language is, Elliot Vereker represents the defeat of communication by the specialist who is capable of speaking only to himself. As such, he is a representative figure from modern life, heir to the pseudoscientists of the early parodies and precursor of the mad specialists in the fairy tales. Thus, Thurber slays enough pretentious literary dragons to show that he is not even sure of the artist's grasp of measure and grace in this crazy world.

Two years after the *Middle-Aged Man on the Flying Trapeze*, Thurber attacked other specialists in *Let Your Mind Alone!* (see chapter 2). The reader who is familiar with *Is Sex Necessary?* immediately recognizes in these parodies Thurber's war against jargon. And, in a way, the short stories in the second part of the collection continue the portrayal of incoherent social relations begun in *The Owl in the Attic* and *My Life*.

As we noted in the discussion of Thurber's attack on science, the parodies of the first half of *Let Your Mind Alone!* reduce system formulators and confidence peddlers to absurdity. This is relatively easy to do, of course, because all the anatomist has to do is quote them: their language reveals their fundamental confusion. These are the authors of such successful banalities as "How to Worry Successfully," "Wake Up and Live!" and "Be Glad You're Neurotic."[34] (I will not pause over this last title. Many readers have found some sort of solace in it.) Inundated by mass culture, the problem is that people so easily believe and crave its slogans. Thus fed on a diet of linguistic garbage, the populace become unable to tolerate anything else. Or, as Orwell would later observe in "Politics and the English Language," the cliché obscures not only language but thought.[35] The cycle of language and life is always complete.

Thurber attacked pretentious and convoluted language in *Is Sex Necessary?*, and exposed the humor of repetitious and empty language in *My Life and Hard Times*. Now, he identifies the particular culprit in meaningless repetition: the cliché. The cliché becomes one of Thurber's perpetual targets, which reflects his movement toward language itself as a subject. Perhaps as a writer who found a voice with endless variety and flexibility, the very inelasticity of the cliché aesthetically offended Thurber. One can also connect the humor of such inelasticity with Bergson's notion that mechanized people become comic. The point is seriously comic, however, because the state of a culture is equivalent to the state of its language. Since the cliché is one of the most obvious dead limbs in English prose, anyone who would cure the ailing language (or the ailing culture) must skillfully excise it.

Science is also especially open to parody and ridicule because it concocts a specialized and often meaningless language (jargon), thus limiting communication and leading to confusion. This is particularly dangerous in the twentieth century, because people tend increasingly to look to the scientist for answers to their problems. An astounded Thurber notes that, for the modern person, the fear of a fear has come to be what the "psychologists call phobophobia (they really do). But now. . . the fear he had of being afraid. . . is. . . what I can only call phobophobophobia, and [he] is in deeper than he was before."[36] Thus, modern science often only exacerbates our problems by leaving us with a head full of empty language. Standing one step removed from the chaos under study, the anatomist watches the specialist watching human behavior. This vantage point provides both humor and insight, and infuses Thurber's prose with a peculiar combination of energy and calm.

Like the earlier works, *Let Your Mind Alone!* alternately castigates and celebrates the powers of language. In refuting Dr. James L. ("Streamline Your Mind") Murrell's attempt to force people to "get a precise and dogmatic meaning out of everything they read," Thurber writes: "There is no person whose spirit hasn't at one time or another been enriched by some cherished transfiguring of meanings. . . . [Consider] the youngster who thought the first line of the Lord's Prayer was 'Our Father, who are in Heaven, Halloween be thy name.'"[37] Unlike the pseudoscientists, the artistic consciousness permits much "disorderliness," so that experience itself is transformed endlessly by language. Since experience is the world revealed through language, life itself may emerge from such disorder.

For example, Thurber tells us that ever since his maid described a part of an old refrigerator as that "doom-shaped thing," his knowledge of reality, as well as his whole life, has been altered: "If I were a true guardian of the portal of my thought, I would have refused that expression admittance, because it is too provocative, too edgy, and too dark, for comfort, but then I would have missed the unique and remarkable experience that I had last Sunday, when, just as night was falling, I walked down a doom-shaped street under a doom-shaped sky."[38] Listen to the rhythm of the last half of this sentence, falling, along with the night, into a doom-shaped universe. Thurber is most in control of his art when he is thus delineating the language of confusion. By calling a dome that "doom-shaped thing," Thurber's maid reveals something more about the machine, and herself, and her relationship to the material world, than its proper name could.[39] She is also opening up Thurber's knowledge of reality. The new word has, in fact, forged a new shape for reality.

The thought of a doom-shaped universe may sometimes delight Thurber, but in *The Last Flower* he discovers humanity on the edge of the abyss, and the view is not delightful. This tale reveals the final results of confusion, and as much as anything, the parable is concerned with the role of communication in human life.

The Last Flower combines Thurber's primitive drawings and elegantly simple words with perhaps the most subtle interplay of his career. Neither the drawings, as bare suggestions of scenes, nor the words, radically simple and biblical in rhythm, can exist by themselves. The total effect of pictures and words working together is the verbal/visual equivalent of a finely executed concerto: the boy, the girl, and the flower are the soloists of hope, life, and love against an orchestrated background of hate, despair, and destruction.

Thurber chose pictures as well as words for his language, and unlike many cartoonists, he retained a high degree of suggestiveness even in pictorial language. Perhaps a result of his fantastic speed at drawing (*The Last Flower* was done after dinner one evening),[40] the pictures are composed generally of the fewest lines arranged in the most evocative manner. The nonspecificity of Thurber's figures is also thematic; they are barely there, only skeletons of life, but emblematic of a complete universe. The drawings are, indeed, but another aspect of the language of confusion. In them, Thurber freezes a moment of confusion that somehow represents the larger chaos of our world. Thus, ironically, he structures the chaos. It was perhaps this quality which led Dorothy Parker to conclude that Thurber's drawings deal "solely in culminations."[41]

As the anatomist draws an image to reveal the parts of an organism under study, Thurber's drawings cut through the body of human experience to reveal, at crucial junctures, telling images of confused and confusing human behavior. And, although most of his drawings were done as single frames, when they are rearranged into sequences in the collections or by the reader's mind, the individual figures take on another meaning as parts of the larger work, the anatomy of confusion. The most common image in this gallery is Thurber's depiction of *Homo loquens,* doing his uniquely human thing, often in the most remarkably incoherent way. How often, in fact, do the captions of Thurber's cartoons recall the muddled, inarticulate, and abrasive attempts made at communication by incomprehensible humanity.[42]

In *The Last Flower,* language pushes an incomprehensible humanity to its own destruction (and, paradoxically, to its own regeneration as well). Although it begins in a mute wasteland, the people of *The Last Flower* begin to speak after the young girl finds the flower. When she tells everyone that the last flower is dying, only one boy will listen, but their communication leads to a rebirth of human life. The silence of the world is broken, and people begin to laugh and speak again. That is, they become human again, engaging in those remarkably human activities of speech and laughter. Revolving in a cycle of irony, however, this regeneration inevitably leads to speakers without moral or genuine things to say. "Liberators" come along who speak to assembled sheepish masses and "set fire to the discontent,"[43] bringing about the world's second destruction. Language, the distinctively human activity, is the invaluable tool for digging through the rubble of civilization, but it is also the path to demagoguery, discontent, and destruction. Like so many modern writers, Thurber seems to have rediscovered the beast within the human being. And, since use of language is the defining quality of humankind, its powers are responsible most often for unleashing the beast inside.

In *The Last Flower* we see the culmination of much that Thurber had been working toward in the thirties, as well as the bridge to a series of new developments in his style, form, and understanding of language and life. Radically simple, *The Last Flower* makes frighteningly clear that "cloudier chaos" to which Thurber alluded in the preface to *My Life.* At last, it is all of civilization—not simply the Thurber persona, nor his household, his hometown, nor even his country alone—which suffers from the language of confusion and its concomitant social mayhem. This perception of universal chaos is not new since, even in *My Life,* Thurber admitted to a "twitchiness at once cosmic and mundane." Yet the focus is different. It is as though he can no longer escape brooding about all of the implications of eccentric human behavior and flawed human understanding.

Thurber's subtitle for *The Last Flower,* "A Parable in Pictures," in a way distills the change that his art was undergoing. Always interested in history and human nature, Thurber was developing new ways of dealing with his subject matter: the parable, the allegorical tale, the fable. These ancient forms allow a type of directness often impossible in conventional fiction. The forms make them both direct and indirect. They certainly were a change from the traditional *New Yorker* story which Thurber had been doing for a decade. Why should he choose a new direction at this time? Perhaps in a world reeling under fascism, or in a personal world darkening into blindness, such deftly effective, subtle analogies now appealed to Thurber. The imposition of these older, more rigid forms seems to enable the writer to speak more directly to his reader, after all. Perhaps, also, as a writer, Thurber now simply sensed the need to try new ways of saying what he had to say.

Always fascinated with the past, Thurber was also moving away from his heavy dependence upon personal, idiosyncratic memory, such as had informed *My Life and Hard Times,* toward more use of the cultural storehouse. Legends, myths, proverbs, and stock phrases generate much of his work now. And the shift in his forms and sources was accompanied by a shift, slowly emerging, away from preoccupation with individual character, toward what could be called the "typical."[44] Such a direction is expectable for the anatomist-humorist who, we must remember, studies eccentric cases only to be able to see the pattern in the chaos, to generalize one set of images from the many. From the beginning, Thurber's drawings show his basic interest in the typical. Thurber men, Thurber women, Thurber dogs, the Thurber living room—all are generalized images from American life. Indeed, since he was primarily a humorist, even Thurber's conventional fiction had always been concerned with types. But it seems that, by the end of the thirties, Thurber had established his set of types from the real or external world. Now, he turns from considering language as the key to human experience, with the emphasis on depicting the experience, to analyzing language itself as experience. This shift involves his trying to discern whether or not the actual and probable experience of confusion, which he knows from his study of human life, can be turned into a possible coherent life; whether the actuality of linguistic confusion can be overturned by language itself. Because this is so speculative, Thurber deals with the possibility of a coherent life only in the distant world of the fairy tales. The real twentieth-century world described in his stories and essays is always the hell of the early sketches—decadent, suffering, and inarticulate.

This shift toward the typical is manifested in the fables that Thurber wrote in the late thirties. As reworked Aesopian fables, these short, powerful pieces focus on the language with which we stumble through life. They attack especially the truisms, euphemisms, and clichés of our experience. Many of the fables' morals, in a modern ironic twist on Aesopian moralizing, question established values by rephrasing or punning axioms, proverbs, and clichés. Thurber's fables reveal experience through the language in which it is described. Perhaps the most pointed moral is the conclusion of the rewritten "Tortoise and the Hare." Thurber's tortoise loses to the hare in a ridiculous race inspired by the gullible tortoise's reading of the ancient fable. The moral: "A new broom may sweep clean, but never trust an old saw."[45] This moral typifies the thrust and tone of the entire collection. These are, Thurber announces, fables for our time. The implication is that the clichés of behavior and language must be rejected, not only because of their lack of artistic fire or elegance, but because they represent pervasive assumptions which are accepted too easily.

In the fables, as elsewhere, Thurber seems not only to be denying the validity of truisms or proverbial wisdom, although that motive is strong; he is also denying the conventional, assumed connections between language, or words, and the things or actions they represent. Nothing is constant, including meaning, in this world of endless permutations. This uncertainty leads us, as Thurber himself might say, to the remarkable case of the certain uncertainty, that fundamental paradox which his work reveals throughout human experience. The fables turn, therefore, on a necessary irony discovered by the anatomist, and are not merely verbal tricks played upon the reader.

Aptly titled, Thurber's next collection, *My World—and Welcome to It,* presents a cross section of his now widened world. The book includes once again both celebrations of language's power and cautions about its inherent limits. The collection begins with another invocation of Lewis Carroll in "What Do You Mean It 'Was' Brillig?"

Like Barney Haller before her, Thurber's maid sends his mind wandering by mispronouncing the word "wreath": "They are here with the reeves," she said rather calmly, instigating a trip through the semantic labyrinth. Unlike his battling with Barney, Thurber enjoys playing the game of language with Della. His own favorite garbling concerns Della's brother who, it seems, has just passed his "silver service eliminations. Della is delighted about that, but she is not half so delighted about it as I am." As part of their elaborate game, Thurber tells Della that he is from "Semantics, Ohio," and when she replies that there is one of those in Massachusetts, too, Thurber says, truthfully, that the one he means is "bigger and more confusing."[46] Della, and the reader, would agree, since the world is enlarged endlessly by language. The language of confusion, which permits the mistake of metaphor to open up the world anew, is presented here as a delight, for in this language one can go from Semantics, Ohio, to Proust's Combray, and back again, as easily as the slip of a letter.

From the joy of the scene with Della, Thurber, and a dictionary in "Brillig" to the blackness of "The Whip-Poor-Will" is not only a journey from one end of the Thurber temperament to the other; it is a trip from one pole of his language obsession to the other. Here, more completely than ever before, language stalks the man and wreaks total destruction. For the first time there is blood in the landscape of linguistic war: the nonsensical chirping of a whip-poor-will, coupled with Kinstrey's knowledge of the old saying that a whip-poor-will near the house means death, drives him to commit a triple murder and suicide. Inundated by the sounds, Kinstrey is horrified: "I suppose like the drops of water or the bright light in the third degree, this could drive you nuts," he says to himself. The "words" of the bird carry over into the rhythms and tones of all other words and actions; the phrases "nev-er have, nev-er have" and "nevermore nevermore" and "whip him now!" ring in Kinstrey's ears until he confronts the butler with the butcher knife and the simple question, "Who do you do first?"[47] In the Kafka nightmare of the modern world, Kinstrey's irrational but immediately comprehensible question is an easy garbling of such common, innocuous questions as "How do you do?" and "Who is first here?" He does them all in, driven to murder by the apparently trivial and meaningless repetition of a phrase.

Thurber not only recognized the ability of language to spellbind and confuse, but was acutely aware of the many psychological effects of hearing the spoken word. The world, or experience, is recreated through language each moment. In *My Life and Hard Times,* the excited crowd hears "*now* broken" instead of "*not* broken" because of a predisposition to hear that. But the crowd disperses, in the fortuitousness of comedy, without really suffering. In "The Whip-Poor Will," only Kinstrey is bothered by the bird, because his own distressed condition leads to a transformation of the words or sounds into horrifying shapes within his head. At last, however, the consequences become terrifyingly real and constitute the climax of the story. Even *The Last Flower* is less bloody and less real, distanced as it is from the middle-class kitchen of Kinstrey's nightmare. It is an indication of the depth and complexity of Thurber's ambivalence about confusion and order, sense and nonsense, clarity and suggestion, that he should include two such stories as "Brillig" and "The Whip-Poor-Will" in one collection.

As we have seen, "The Secret Life of Walter Mitty" also exposes the horror underlying the familiar world, and once again, this horror is revealed in language, or, more specifically, by Mitty's inability to communicate. Both the humor and the pathos of this story arise from the clash between the reality of Mitty and the clichés he accepts, or from the disparity between his experience and the words with which he describes it. This clash is both humorous and poignant, or in Thurber's terminology, tragicomic, because the distance between what a man is and what he thinks he is may excite laughter or tears. How the subject is treated makes the difference, of course, and in this story Thurber delicately manages to hold both Mitty's comicality and his sorrowfulness before us. Mitty is, in a sense, John Monroe pushed to the edge.

Like the debunking of proverbial wisdom in the fables and of slogans in *Let Your Mind Alone!*, "Walter Mitty" is partially an attempt to explain and destroy the cliché. This story is so provocative and so successful because it allows us into Mitty's cliché-ridden mind — a mind filled with the debris of a canned culture — where we actually hear the hackneyed phrases echo and reecho. In presenting Mitty's muddied stream of consciousness, this story is even more complex than the fables in its use of language. Much of its humor hinges on Mitty's absurdly inappropriate use of technical vocabulary; he is the victim not only of language, but of the specialists who continue to bastardize it. The free-association habit of Mitty's perplexed mind generates complicated and nonsensical lists, such as "toothpaste, toothbrush, bicarbonate, carborundum, initiative, and referendum."[48] In obvious emotional difficulty, Mitty's language shows that he is only a few steps beyond the state that young Thurber was in when he had tried, in vain, to remember the words "Perth Amboy." As unknowing wanderers in an alien world, Thurber people continually glide between sense and nonsense, understanding and confusion, as easily as saying "Perth Amboy" or turning into the wrong "which" clause.

Mitty is distinguished by an almost complete inability to communicate, partially because of his audience (Mrs. Mitty, the mechanic) and implicitly because of his own nature. The only intelligent thing Mitty says is the provocative, edgy statement to his wife that "Things close in." But, because she cannot listen, she ignores this distress signal.

Who in Babel does better than these two, interrupting each other's silences with unintelligible ejaculations, crisscrossing the other's space like the radio static that gives all reality a faraway, indistinct quality? And, what but the truth sounds so crazy in an insane world? The Mittys' language mirrors the emptiness, sterility, and confusion of their brittle existence. Walter Mitty has succumbed so completely to the emptiness of the cliché and has confused it so totally with reality because his life itself is unreal, filled as it is with the inhuman and the inarticulate. His use of the cliché further precludes experiencing reality, in a spiralling, self-destructive course. In fact, if we can say that Thurber saw language as the creator of experience, the Mittys are themselves dead because they have succumbed to the cliché.

Just as Thurber was developing an interest in new forms, "Walter Mitty" reveals him at the height of his powers as a short-story writer. We need to depart slightly from the chronology of this chapter for a final note on "The Catbird Seat," which can be regarded as a companion piece to "Walter Mitty." Indeed, some of their mutual characteristics may suggest why Thurber was turning away from conventional fiction.

Much of Thurber's work to this date had been concerned with the hostility between the sexes, a hostility caused largely by the inability of men and women to communicate with each other. Although Thurber would always return to this subject, he did so with less frequency after the early forties, and thereafter usually reflected on the situation in casual essays and conversation pieces rather than in stories. But "Walter Mitty" and "The Catbird Seat" show Thurber at the apex of his interest in the incoherent battle of the sexes. In "The Catbird Seat," perpetrating linguistic atrocities is reason enough to be murdered. Mr. Martin concludes that Mrs. Ulgine (ugly engine) Barrows has wrought confusion at their office by her incessant, inane repetition of such clichés as "tearing up the pea patch" and "sitting in the catbird seat." For this she must be "executed." Neither Martin nor Barrows transcends the language of confusion, however. Since Martin himself is victimized by language, he plans her murder with ridiculous adherence to the terminology and formulae of pulp detective fiction. He even hides in the euphemism, pretending that the term "rubbed out" makes the murder less nasty. Since the story focuses on Martin's actions, and not on the suffering of his victim, it remains humorous, but the humor has a bitter edge. Like the irony that informs the fables, the plot and humor of this story turn on the inversion of "positions" in the world: she who had imagined herself safely ensconced in the catbird seat of a trite world is roundly unseated, becoming the unluckiest person in the story.

Martin is really Mitty's second cousin, acting out the fantasies of Hollywood films that Mitty had only dreamed about. Taken together, these two stories represent the height of Thurber's powers as a short-story writer and the end of his preoccupation with individual character. Without stretching this too far, let me suggest that, in "Walter Mitty," the little man of Thurber's early period is perfected and simultaneously killed off (his last daydream is of his own execution); and, in "The Catbird Seat," his abrasive partner, the grotesque woman of the cartoons and early sketches, is also destroyed.

Thurber never abandoned fiction, of course, since he continued to do short stories until the end of his life, and the tales and fables are fiction of a sort. But conventional fiction, the preoccupation and glory of his early career, becomes progressively less important in Thurber's canon after 1940. The supreme achievements of the last half of his creative life were the fables, the fairy tales, the serious essays, and, in a limited but special way, the new kind of parody he developed. The only sustained narratives he was ever to complete were the last three fairy tales, which approximate novellas. Perhaps he had to break completely with *The New Yorker* casual-story format in order to do longer works and develop as a writer. Perhaps, also, he sensed that he had mined the subject of inarticulate man and woman as much as he could, and turned to a consideration of the possibility of constructing a new order from the old chaos. If, indeed, he now wished to reform the human condition and not simply to reveal it, he certainly chose forms with a long history of such purpose: the parable, the fable, and the allegory.

Thurber's only play, *The Male Animal* (1940), is not particularly involved with the subject of language, and it limits itself to the language of the middle–class living room. (And, in *The Male Animal,* that means a rather ordinary living room, not the surrealistic stage of Thurber's Columbus boyhood.) The fairy tales are quite a different matter. From *Many Moons* to *The Wonderful O,* this old literary form is reinterpreted by Thurber and all five books bear the inimitable Thurber stamp. If the fables show Thurber turning conventional wisdom upside down, allowing it to crush itself in the process, the fairy tales, as variations on ancient plots, show Thurber moving beyond a simple denial of the past (and its wisdom and sayings), as he slowly takes the tradition and makes it his own. The shift is, in a sense, away from a preoccupation with destroying the old, decayed world of clichés and conventional wisdom, toward emphasis on constructing a new world from the remnants. Therefore, Thurber is like so many modern artists (Eliot, Joyce, and Faulkner come to mind) in that his greatest inventiveness is reached, ironically, through his confronting and using the past: its myth, history, and art. As he developed variations on old forms, Thurber's language became more and more flexible, and ultimately, more complex, getting further away all the time from the relatively straightforward style of his early period. It is almost as if the departure from the traditional short story into the fable and fairy tale permitted him the fullest exploration of the power of language.

All of the tales make language itself an important element of the story. In *The Wonderful O,* language is both the subject and the hero of the action. The tales, in a way, show the fruition of all of Thurber's investigation of *Homo loquens.* They are the books he was getting ready to write all along, narratives that dramatize the resolution of verbal as well as social confusion.

We have already seen that the fairy tales represent a fictional ending of the war between men and women. In them Thurber also finally envisions the articulate speaker. If his early work was preoccupied with delineating the full range of linguistic confusion in the existing world of twentieth-century America, these tales signal his attempt to create a place where language and life would be genuine. Always alienated from society, always its only hope — the articulate voice of the poet now rises above time and place, shattering the lies, bombast, and cacophony of lesser mortals. This clear voice is now a character in the action, not simply the narrator of the story. He is an embattled figure, poised against a confused and inarticulate world, which is the Babel of the early stories transported to fairyland. But his victories are shining. They spell an end, however fragile and temporary, to the language of confusion.

In the simplest and earliest of these tales, *Many Moons,* Thurber writes in a particularly clear style, one that would be understandable to an audience of children. The language is deceptively simple even here, however. For example, the description of how little Princess Lenore "fell ill of a surfeit of raspberry tarts"[49] appears to be a formula phrase to elicit sympathy for the poor child. But a surfeit of raspberry tarts is hardly a calamity. The humorist is at his subtle work, even in fairyland.

The king in *Many Moons* is surrounded by a group of advisors so well schooled in legal and political jargon that they open wide the gates to confusion; they are as perplexed and perplexing as the psychologists of *Let Your Mind Alone!* When one of these advisors reminds the king of past favors, Thurber has his usual fun with dissonant collocation as a symptom of mental confusion: "I have got ivory, apes, and peacocks, rubies, opals, and emeralds, black orchids, pink elephants, and blue poodles...troubadors, minstrels, and dancing women, a pound of butter, two dozen eggs, and a sack of sugar — sorry, my wife wrote that in there." When the king objects that he does not remember any blue poodles, the bureaucrat replies nonsensically, "It says blue poodles right here on the list, and they are checked off with a little check mark....so there must have been blue poodles." And yet, such nonsense makes its own truest sense. The words "blue poodle" call up a visual image and, in so doing, create a new reality. We also hear that the Wizard believes that he has given the king "the golden touch, and a cloak of invisibility"; the Royal Mathematician takes credit for calculating "the distance between the horns of the dilemma....how far is Up, how long it takes to get Away, and what becomes of Gone." Thus, these unwise men make hackneyed phrases and ill-gathered data sound serious and accurate by couching them in language that is familiar enough to be convincing and involved enough to be meaningless. The important point is that, talk as they may, these men can do nothing.

When the mathematician argues that he has calculated "how far is Up, how long it takes to get Away, and what becomes of Gone," the humor progresses beyond criticism of the specious precision of statisticians or the jargon-mongering of science and government, however. What Thurber is doing here is calling attention to the metaphorical nature of all language. He does this by taking the metaphor literally, but he is not simply playing for a laugh. Like a poet, Thurber sees not only the metaphoric (or abstract) in the actual, but also the literal in the metaphor. Implicitly, his fiction thus raises important questions about art, reality, language, and knowledge. Piercing through the veil of words by anatomizing language, Thurber forces words to pose metaphysical questions. The bumbling characters that fill his stories suggest that, important as such questions may be, most human beings are unable to answer them. Especially unable to define meaning or forestall confusion are the very ones who claim this clarification as their "area": the specialists of the modern world. Only the Court Jester (or poet) speaks with any sense at all, which establishes a pattern in the fairy tales.

The Great Quillow further explores the confusing language of power and government. Much of its action occurs in the fertile territory of a town meeting in "a far country," which seems strikingly like any town, anywhere. The council indulges in the banalities of a comfortable, insular people: they discuss "the number of stars in the sky . . . the wonderful transparency of glass, and . . . the blueness of violets and the whiteness of snow."[50] Into this situation of institutionalized verbosity comes a giant who speaks simple, direct commands. And the council is dumbfounded. It is only through the simplicity and invention of Quillow, the quiet toymaker who becomes a teller of tales, that the city is saved.

Perhaps emblematic of the movement of the humorist, Thurber, into more directly didactic or "useful" forms, the toymaker, Quillow, goes from being merely a maker of amusement to functioning as a teller of tales with a moral vision; that is, from delighting alone to enlightening through the magic of his voice. We know that Quillow is able to make this change because he is a toymaker, but we also sense that it is because he is something more. This is not to suggest that Thurber's early work is inferior to these tales. But, it is almost as if he were now urgently announcing to the world, "You must listen to me, because I have seen things you must see."

Like the Jester in *Many Moons,* Quillow is the only character in the tale who is not a prisoner of language. His name identifies him as a writer, and he is able to mold words for his own purposes. He turns language into magic, contriving a story that convinces the giant that, when all words sound like "woddly" to him, his mind will be gone forever. This sounds so ridiculous to the giant that he is sure that it will never happen, and so, of course, it promptly does. Quillow cleverly chants the word (or nonword) "woddly" to the giant until he believes that he is deranged and drowns himself in the sea. The giant succumbs to the word and the town is saved by the story-teller. Gracefully, the tale warns complacent humanity to consider the fate of the giant, who thought that language could never be so mangled. Quillow, the poet, the maker, is one of the happy few who understand language, who can make it serve human beings caught in a generally chaotic and ineffectual existence.

The third tale, *The White Deer,* continues in the wasteland of confusion where *Quillow* was set. As our earlier discussions have shown, this is a densely rich, ambitious fairy tale for adults. One of Thurber's finest works, *The White Deer* reveals the extent of his linguistic virtuosity by this time. The texture of the story, which depends on much complexity of language and allusion, is partially the result of Thurber's verbal experimentation in "The Secret Life of Walter Mitty." The dreams of Mitty's mind become the surreal landscape of the Enchanted Forest. As in the earlier tales, the King is surrounded by a group of legalistic dunces who are totally divorced from reality. And, again, their inability to communicate is the chief symptom of their illness. The Royal Physician, like Elliot Vereker, talks only to himself; the Royal Wizard, equally deluded, attempts to discover the identity of the lost Princess by making up imaginary kings.[51]

Only Prince Jorn, the poet, can make sense out of the nonsense of this illusory world. His brothers, confused by the upside-down world of the Enchanted Forest, cannot understand Jorn's riddle, which states succinctly the theme of *The White Deer:*

What's black is white,
What's red is blue,
What's dark is light,
What's true is true.[52]

Even in this crazy world of endless permutations and confused language, the truth remains true, but only the poet can recognize it and name it. After debunking traditional thinking for over a decade, Thurber now seems to sense the urgency of reconstructing a new world from the old. This new world is envisioned in the order established at the end of *The White Deer*, *The 13 Clocks*, and *The Wonderful O*.

In fact, the real value of *The White Deer* is not in its condemnation of legal and political jargon, nor in its debunking of the romantic tradition, though it is highly effective at both. *The White Deer* is a great, enduring work because in it Thurber fashions something completely new from the old and the chaotic—an independent, living work of art. *The White Deer* is pure Thurber, and in a very real sense, its language is the tale.

The product of a thoroughly logocentric writer, even Thurber's earlier, more conventional fiction is peculiarly bound to the precise, written word for its impact. As a result, it is impossible to summarize a Thurber scene without destroying it. This is probably also the reason that Thurber's fiction, even though it is packed with visual imagery, has not translated well into film. Although it can be said that every truly talented writer creates a world of words, for Thurber this metaphor is literally true. The linguistic virtuosity of *The White Deer* justifies our looking at sections of it again, this time to see how it uses the language of confusion.

Marked by paradox and alliteration throughout, *The White Deer* is a magic web, drawing the reader into its sway with incantations of a trip in which:

Twenty hoofs thundered hotly through a haunted hollow
of spectral sycamores hung with lighted lanterns and past
a turquoise tarn and along an avenue of asphodel that
turned and twisted down a dark descent which led at last
to a pale and perilous plain."[53]

Pause over this remarkable passage; it is a most illustrative example of Thurber's consistent preference for alliterative language, a preference that becomes a passion around this time. It also demonstrates his developing gift of onomatopoeia. In this tale, we know that we have a poet working with language.

The White Deer is a linguistic extravaganza that delights partially because of the elaborate verbal tricks it plays on the reader. These tricks are both clever and profound, as the following discussion should show. The tale is generated by inversions and paradox, for its reader must travel through a world that is like a gigantic jigsaw puzzle with minute and seemingly ill-fitting pieces.

In constructing this puzzle, Thurber is at his anagrammatic and allusive best. Prince Gallow, for instance, is told that he has to find the Seven-Headed Dragon of Dragore "the Hard Way . . . down and down, round and round, through the moaning Grove of Artanis." To translate this from Thurber language into more prosaic English, the passage alludes to the lines from "Old Black Magic": "Down and down I go, round and round I go, / In a spin, love is the spin I'm in, / Under that old black magic called love." Gallow, his head spinning madly in an impossible quest for love, is told that he must go through the moaning Grove of Artanis, or the banal (Coconut?) Grove of S-i-n-a-t-r-a, to find it. If going through the Grove of Artanis were not perplexing enough for Gallow (and the reader), he is also advised to fear not "the dreadful Tarcomed" nor "the surly Nacilbuper" (try spelling these proper nouns backwards); and to turn "to the right and follow a little white light," presumably, to find the "paradise" of the Top Forty: "My Blue Heaven."[54] As his private world is darkening into blindness, Thurber is anatomizing bits of dialogue, pieces of lyrics and poems, even words themselves, trying to discover reality.

Amidst all the clever wordplay Thurber is, in fact, inquiring ever more deeply into the nature of reality. Prince Thag's journey is no easier to follow than Gallow's, but it is more frightening. He rides through a surrealistic landscape in which birds chirp, "verti verti verti go," while all language is hopelessly garbled. When Thag asks "What type is it?" a voice answers, "It's sick and thirsty . . . or half past hate or a quarter to fight." This is the revealing, horrifying language of dreams. Thag is directed out of the labyrinth by nonsensical guides (like the King's advisors in *Many Moons*) who say to "ride by the Bye" and "pass the Time of Day."[55] The need for direction and meaning in a directionless, incoherent world is a strong undercurrent in Thurber's work, often surfacing in *The White Deer*.

The poet Jorn is the hero of this tale because, like Quillow, he is a creator who is able to surmount the language of confusion and resist the clichés of existence. He is coherent man. After the King and his advisors have enumerated, in rather fancy language, the traditional ways to recognize a Princess ("I knew her . . . by the manner of her speech and the carriage of her head"), Prince Jorn says simply, "I knew her by the singing in my heart." He is, in fact, the only one in the tale who makes the right choice. Jorn has seen the real reality in a world of falsity and flux and can sing of it in a clear voice. *The White Deer* is a rich, rewarding experience, repaying in full the demands of its reading, largely because we delight in Thurber's having discovered and revealed such a voice in it. It is a book written by a man in love with the sound of the human voice, or with the sound of the human voice as it could be. This same man had been so bent on ridiculing the failures of human speech because, knowing its potential for glory, the awful reality of the language of confusion must have been painfully funny to him. As he aged, Thurber became more and more preoccupied with making the possibility of articulate speech an actuality, and this is partially the purpose of *The White Deer*.

At the end of *The White Deer*, Thurber uses for the first time the conventional ending of ancient comedy: a wedding feast. In the far world of fairy land, Thurber proposes that man and woman can communicate and live together. With this ending Thurber captures the very spirit of comedy. The reintegration of the hero, Jorn, into his world signals the triumph of order over chaos, of life over death.[56] And yet, the irony persists: this is Thurber's most modern, most Thurberian work to date. To understand what is new and old about the tale one need only remember that, instead of using the "pleasant place" of medieval romance, Thurber sets his story in the nightmare world of the Enchanted Forest, and his victorious questor is not a soldier, but a poet.[57]

The 13 Clocks also presents a poet who must journey through the labyrinth of this world to win his lady's hand. Everyone in this book speaks in frightening riddles, neologisms, and nonsense, except Prince Zorn, the wandering minstrel, who is menaced by nonsensical yet immediately comprehensible threats. "He will slit you from your guggle to your zatch" and "the Todal looks like a blob of glup," he is warned. The horror of Zorn's existence is recreated in the language of the tale, much in the same way that language constitutes the experience of *The White Deer.* Thus, incantations whirl around Zorn on his long and difficult quest, confusing him by saying that "The way is dark, and getting darker. The hut is high, and even higher. I wish you luck. There is none."[58]

Like the quests of the princes in *The White Deer,* Zorn's quest is described poetically in powerfully alliterative and assonant evocations of horror. The powerful imagery of the tale calls to mind the travellers of Bunyan, Spenser, and Hawthorne: "The brambles and the thorns grew thick and thicker in a ticking thicket of bickering crickets. Farther along and stronger, bonged the gongs of a throng of frogs, green and vivid on their lily pads. . . . the pilgrims leaped over a bleating sheep creeping knee-deep in a sleepy stream, in which swift and slippery snakes slid and slithered silkily, whispering sinful secrets."[59] The onomatopoeic quality of this passage demonstrates Thurber's identification of language with life, or of words with things. Although it is impossible to determine the exact relationship between Thurber's blindness and his later style, it is obvious that the works after 1945 show an increased awareness of sound. In another writer blindness could have other effects, but for Thurber, like Joyce, the encroachment of blindness intensified his interest in words themselves. It is almost as though, no longer able to see the little dramas of everyday life which are so easily transformed into fiction, Thurber turned even more to probing language as experience. Language and the experience it describes are completely under the control of a writer who can make the reader see the indescribable. With characteristic understatement, Thurber dares to write that ultimately evocative phrase, describing the friendly Golux: "He wore an indescribable hat."[60]

Thus, in considering the four fairy tales written between 1943 and 1950, we can discern a growing complexity in Thurber's style, along with an intensified interest in words and in the sound of the English language. But we also need to ascertain other patterns in Thurber's work around this time. It was not until 1948 that he brought out a new collection to add to his repertoire of story-drawing-essay anthologies, since his blindness had severely limited his work during this period. It should be helpful to note some similarities and some differences between *The Beast in Me* and Thurber's previous collections, in order to grasp more fully the direction that his art was taking. Some similarities are immediately clear. For example, a reader who knows the early scientific parodies will recognize the slant of several pieces in *The Beast in Me,* especially "A Call on Mrs. Forrester" and "The Beast in the Dingle." But now the parody is of a richer sort. I would like to look at "The Beast in the Dingle" in some detail because it, and Thurber's comments about it, exemplify some changes that had occurred in his work since the early 1930s.

Thurber worked for a number of years on "The Beast in the Dingle," which he said was not, in fact, a parody (in his earlier, denigrating sense), but a "literary pastiche," imitating how Henry James would have written the story.[61] Thurber was, in a sense, trying to be James in this piece, which is to say that he was trying to recapture something palpable and living from the past, so as to make it live again. This is parody as understood by the mature author of *The White Deer.*

A closer look at the story's language should help explain how this remarkably allusive, parodic piece works. One cannot get beyond the title without recognizing the story's humor. Any reader familiar with James reads the word "dingle" for "jungle" and smiles at the incongruity of the sound of the word "dingle" (what it seems to mean) and James's monumentally serious and involved story. "The Beast in the Jungle" is the story of John Marcher, a man to whom nothing ever happened (a fertile subject for humor). The humor is not quite so simple, however. Dingle is not a nonsensical substitute for the word jungle, after all, but a genuine Anglo-Saxon word meaning shady dell. The choice is both humorous and appropriate, or more complexly comical.

On first reading, it appears that Thurber is interested only in mimicking the involved Jamesian language, and he has done an excellent job of parodying the late style of the master.[62] Absurdly exaggerated, yet close to the rhythms and syntax of their model, the sentences written by Henry James Thurber (as the author might now be known) would delight any reader who both knows and likes the later James. Thurber himself was such a reader, of course.

"The Beast in the Dingle" is more than a parody of "The Beast in the Jungle," however; it recalls much of James's later work, especially the subjects of *The Golden Bowl* and the imagery of *The Wings of the Dove,* with allusions to "The Turn of the Screw," and to the poetry of T. S. Eliot. Most of Thurber's work requests a reader of relatively high verbal and literary sophistication because of his often complex irony and subtle allusions, but this story demands such a reader, since the allusions are the entire point. This is increasingly true of Thurber's work from the mid-forties until the end of his life.

Thus, a reader who knows the complicated imagery of *The Wings of the Dove* more fully enjoys Thurber's repetition of elaborate metaphors in the story. And the reader who knows something of James's artistic method better understands those particularly happy and hilarious lines of Grantham to Amy Lighter (better names could not be chosen, but James would do as well): "'Incident! Incident!' he had softly cried, and when, at this, his poor bewildered confidant could only give back a halting 'What?' he had found for his abject surrender a plainer form: 'Dramatize! Dramatize!' he had then implored her."[63] Add to the Jamesian references the involved echoes of "Prufrock" in the last part of the story and the reader's task becomes even more complex. Although humorous, "The Beast in the Dingle" also delicately manages to be serious about James. Students of his fiction would do well to study this lesson on the master, anatomized and made clear, parodied and made new, by his truly sympathetic reader, James Thurber.

Like the wordplay of *The White Deer*, the allusions in "The Beast in the Dingle" are not simply part of an esoteric joke. Thurber always admired James; that he saw the humor in James's seriousness does not diminish this fact. But the language of "The Beast in the Dingle" is also carefully chosen to make a statement about James and the modern world. In a melange of references to the refined sensibility of James's characters and the nervous hypersensitivity of Prufrock's "question," Thurber denies the possibility of high seriousness in the twentieth century. When Grantham imagines "making a step," that is, taking action toward heroism, he says he fears that, unlike Marcher's beast in the jungle, he would only have "answer to my challenge, on veritable tippy-toe, the most comical of beasts." So Grantham's beast in the dingle is out: as the prototypical modern man, he has only a "kitty cat for a tiger!"[64] Even his defeat lacks significance because of the paltry size of the stakes and the enemy. This story is both funny and serious, or profoundly comic, and its complex humor is the result of the rich, many-layered language and style in which it is written. Like the fiction of Henry James, the story's meaning is largely in its language; its form is its content.

Balanced against the confusion of human experience in *The*

A Trochee (left) encountering a Spondee.

Beast in Me are the animals, real and unreal, of Thurber's increasingly complex and new world. "A New Natural History" playfully depicts imaginary animals which are literal portrayals of words or what words suggest. The title of this section is interesting; it is as though Thurber knew that his new version of experience, his new history of the world was linked inextricably to his developing passion for words themselves. Rather than a new history of an existing world, this is the history of a new world: we see a trochee encountering a spondee (the trochee has a slanted back, the spondee a straight one, in case you did not know); a preposterous but threatening bird called "a garble with an utter in its claws"; and an animal with six feet, which is, of course, a hexameter.[65]

There are even drawings completely unrelated to the denotative meanings of their captions, images derived from the slightest evocation of a word or name. We see scones and crumpets, peering; a Great Gatsy butterfly, preening; and a Tantamount, doing what a tantamount does.[66] In his natural history, Thurber is able to visualize and materialize words and phrases. He has only to move to a single letter as actor in the human comedy and his journey will be complete. This is just what happens, in *The Wonderful O,* a decade later.

In comparison to earlier collections, *The Beast in Me* has fewer conventional short stories and more straight (that is, nonhumorous) essays. This is a change in degree, not kind, for Thurber always wrote essays. In fact, *The New Yorker* "casual," although often involving fictionalized settings, is a sort of compromise between the short story and the informal essay. After the early forties, however, Thurber was less inclined to write conventional fiction and more likely to develop his ideas in fables, tales, essays, and that disguised dialogue which he called "the conversation piece."

The collections published during his last decade reveal this shift. In 1952, when Thurber looked back on the Columbus of *My Life and Hard Times,* he did so as a researcher and essayist rather than as a storyteller. *The Thurber Album* presents these historical pieces, which are obviously colored by the passage of time and the preferences and judgments of the "historian." But they do not consciously invent characters and scenes, as the earlier stories had frankly done. It is clear, also, that Thurber's long obsession with language has taken on the connotations of a religious and patriotic duty. Whereas "The

Day the Dam Broke" had focused on the uproarious language of confusion spoken in the streets of turn-of-the-century Ohio, Thurber now
chooses to praise those teachers at Ohio State who had taught him
"the good writer's dissatisfaction with imperfect statement," those
who had "fought the good fight against Slur."[67] His earlier works
had been the record of the daily assaults on language, but *The
Thurber Album* is partially a tribute to those engaged in the perpetual
war against linguistic confusion, the prophets who would make way
for the poet that Thurber envisions in the future articulate world.

Thurber Country (1953) is also largely comprised of essays,
conversation pieces, and memoirs, and here again, the linguistic
battlefield receives much of Thurber's attention. In Thurber's country
we meet Aunt Wilma, whose stubbornness prevents her from com-
municating with anyone; a room full of pseudointellectuals who say
that they know that Eliot's *Cocktail Party* is not really about a
cocktail party; and the remarkable Chanda Bell, who both titillates
and infuriates with her "fondness for surrogate words with ambiguous
meanings, like words in dreams: 'rupture' for 'rapture,' 'centaur' for
'sender.'"[68] This is the cacophonous world revealed in the short
stories of the thirties, but now it is often discussed without the veil
of fiction.

In the 1957 retrospective collection, *Alarms and Diversions*, the
shift from conventional fiction is most apparent. Unlike the retrospective *Carnival*, which was published in 1945, *Alarms* has no new
short stories. Indeed, the majority of the pieces in the collection are
nonfiction pieces and drawings. If Thurber's form changed per-
ceptibly, however, his subjects were consistent. His interest in language only intensified through the years. In *Alarms and Diversions*
we see the anatomist-*cum*-pathologist present a treatise designed to
cure "the carcinomenclature of our time." This is the purpose of "The
Psychosemanticist Will See You Now, Mr. Thurber," Thurber's
penetrating analysis of a dead and dying language. He is so successful
in this piece because, like his earliest parodies, the essay uses the language of obfuscation itself to expose the cancerous state of language,
reason, and society.[69]

Even Thurber's last completed book, *Lanterns & Lances*, explores the state of the American language in more detail. In one
conversation piece in the collection, Thurber angrily decries the
"crippled or wingless words that escape, all distorted, the careless

human lips of our jittery time."[70] (Note the characteristic deftness with which even our slovenliness is described by the anatomist of language.) This defender of the English language has never been more serious or more adept.

Lanterns & Lances is, in fact, preoccupied with the subject of language. "The Last Clock, A Fable for the Time, Such as It Is, of Man" presents a horrific picture of a country "the other side of tomorrow," where life has ended because its people had not known that life should be more than "mummum." The fable implies that, where all words are "woddly," life is only "mummum." Thurber also discusses Henry James in a serious essay, considering him chiefly as an architect of language: "He can set so many metaphors and implications dancing at the same time on the point of his pen that it is hard to make out the pattern in the fluttering of all the winged words." But as "The Wings of Henry James" makes clear, the pattern is there. Only the artist can achieve such a pattern, because "the pure artist [is] less susceptible than almost any other to the unreasoned impulse." This is the message, of course, of all of Thurber's fairy tales, and indeed of his work generally. As the title indicates, the writer of *Lanterns & Lances* wants to enlighten and cure his constantly degenerating, "diseased" audience, the speakers of the language of confusion. It has become increasingly obvious, he writes, that "something central and essential in the mechanism of meaning began losing its symmetry long ago." Recalling familiar subjects, Thurber once again identifies the agents of this loss: the mass media, advertising, popular culture, cliché and jargon mongerers in every faction of society, and ultimately, human nature itself.[71] Like the world of Chanda Bell, human existence is "all carnival and bedlam," with only the coherent voice of the artist to bring order out of chaos.

Near the end of his life, sparring with nonsense and chaos in a now completely verbal universe, Thurber is pursued by words, phrases, even letters of the alphabet. His work is filled with lines, famous and obscure, and with titles of works, slogans, garbled quotations, puns, malapropisms, mispronunciations, and barbarisms of every sort. These words and phrases ricochet throughout his prose, as they do through modern life, while he tries to fight the good fight for meaning. His style is so complex during the late period that whole paragraphs are the result of layer upon layer of allusion, wordplay, and irony.[72] This growing complexity is, in part, the result of his movement away from personal, individual memory, which had been so prominent in the early work, toward using and reusing more bits and pieces of the cultural store or universal memory as the generator of his fictions and essays. It is almost as though the vivid memory and attention to detail which Thurber had used in depicting particular people in particular settings in the early fiction is now directed toward remembering in minute detail the morphology of a word or phrase, the schematism of a work of art. Given Thurber's linguistic propensity, this change in his style is an expectable accompaniment to his adoption of older forms during this period, but it is a shift in degree, not kind. Thurber's work was always a mixture of the simple and complex, the timely and the timeless.

As I have been stressing, the general pattern of Thurber's work, which always focused on delineating the language of confusion, moved toward the typical and the universal at the end of the thirties. His first collection of fables, published in 1940, in a way heralded this shift. In 1956, Thurber returned to the fable form, with a collection called *Further Fables for Our Time*. Perhaps it would be useful to say how these two collections of fables are similar and how they are different. First, the later fables parallel the earlier ones in their questioning of proverbs and clichés, usually by rephrasing them in morals: "Let us ponder this fact about the human: Ahead of every man, not behind him, is a woman"; "Nowadays, most men lead lives of noisy desperation"; and "It is not always more blessed to give than to receive, but it is frequently more rewarding."[73]

This second collection of fables is not, however, content simply to reject or invert traditional wisdom, as the earlier ones had done. Grown more inventive as a result, in a sense, of having lost himself in older and more rigid forms, Thurber is making something really new from the old, not simply destroying the old logic. He is constructing new fables on the form of ancient ones, even writing several versions of the same fable (see the first and last fables in the collection, which, I suggest, only Thurber could have written, and the series called "Variations on a Theme"). Consider also the two versions of "The City Mouse and the Country Mouse" as told in the two collections of Thurber's fables.

In the early version, called "The Mouse Who Went to the

Country," Thurber completely inverts the message of the Aesopian original. In Thurber's fable, the city mouse is the knowing mouse, and his life, by implication, is the better life. He goes out to the country for a visit, but is unable to find the "great good place." In direct opposition to conventional wisdom, the mouse returns to the city because, the moral urges, that is where he should have stayed anyway. The second version of this fable, called "The Mouse and the Money," is consciously much closer to the story of the original, and perhaps even to its meaning. Here, the city mouse also goes to the country, but in this fable he is revealed as a boor and a snob, a greedy parasite on the country. The fable ends with his punishment for these "sins": the city mouse dies in the wall of a country house, where he has become too fat from having eaten hidden money to escape. Much like ancient versions of the fable, Thurber's punning moral attacks the mouse's greed: "This is the posture of fortune's slave: one foot in the gravy, one foot in the grave."[74]

What distinguishes these later fables is the complexity and density of their language and style. Although the early collection of fables had used puns in their morals—these puns were, in fact, Thurber's chief way of upsetting conventional wisdom—the later fables are laced with all kinds of wordplay from beginning to end. They are linguistically much more complex than the early fables, and if language creates the world, then the world of the later fables is denser, richer, even more ambiguous than the one revealed in the first collection. In the second version of "The City Mouse, Country Mouse" fable, Thurber's mouse is "living. . .on the fat of the lath," belching out witticisms such as "Legal tender is the night" and "Money makes the nightmare go." He is so smug because, like the American for whom Thurber writes this fable, he has fantasized a noble past: he believes, for example, that the phrase, "*mise de chateau*" on a bottle of imported wine refers to his ancestors, who were "castle mice."[75] The complex language of this fable thus allows Thurber to satirize much more than conventional wisdom or human weakness: through involved wordplay, he subtly attacks many aspects of American culture, as well as humanity's basic misunderstanding of itself and the world.

Consider the richness, ambiguity, and beauty created through wordplay in the following characteristic passage from one of these later fables:

"There is nothing in the wood, I think, but horned owls in hollow oaks," the dove declared, "and violets by mossy stones."

"Violence by mossy stones is what I crave!" the fountain cried. . . .

"I have nothing to remember and nothing to forget," sighed the rose. "I waste my sweetness on the verdant air."

Even the brilliance of the first collection of fables, startling as it is, seems a bit brittle next to the mellow wit of lines such as these from the later works: "O why should the spirit of mortal be proud, in this little voyage from swaddle to shroud?"; or "*Tout,* as the French say, in a philosophy older than ours and an idiom often more succinct, *passé*"; or "Oh, why should the shattermyth have to be a crumplehope and a dampenglee?"[76]

Thurber, of course, knew by this time that a shattermyth did not have to be a dampenglee, and his own work is one man's courageous attempt to enlighten through delighting. This last moral demonstrates the kind of originality that Thurber developed through using old sources and forms, for what is more unusual in the twentieth century than the Old English kenning? Thurber's diction here is so old that it is fresh. As the later parodies show Thurber learning from James in order to be able to depart from him and reconstruct his world anew, so, too, do these last fables reveal a writer creating, through manipulation of an ancient form and language, some of his most original, most modern work. Thurber was able to mine the storehouse of human culture—its truisms, clichés, forms, plots, commonplaces, and histories—to discover, at its foundation, his own voice. Neither "original" nor "derivative" explains these richly allusive, ironic, dense, and inventive later works.

Perhaps the most original of these fables is the last one in the collection. It imagines, as one of Thurber's most perceptive readers noted, the end of human life as only Thurber could have envisioned it: in "The Shore and the Sea," all of humankind is destroyed because of verbal confusion.[77] Life and language are one. Similar in its confusion to "The Day the Dam Broke," in this fable someone inexplicably cries, "Fire!" and others run screaming after him, shouting also inexplicably, "the world's coming to an end," as they all run down to the sea to drown themselves. In the mad running, someone's comment that "It's a pleasure jaunt" is transformed into "It's a treasure hunt," until finally "there were almost as many alarms as there were fugitives."[78] So ends the time of *Homo loquens* on earth.

The irrationality of running away from nothing but toward disaster; the inability of language to communicate any intelligent idea, in fact, its hinderance of reason and truth; and the apparently spontaneous nature of the action — all place this fable very close to the meaning of "The Day the Dam Broke." Nothing demonstrates better the continuity and consistency of Thurber's understanding of both language and life than these parallels. But, because language has by this time become completely identified with life for Thurber, "The Shore and the Sea" ends not only in verbal confusion, but in mass death. Perhaps this is because, as Thurber matured, the ultimate result of such confusion became clearer to him, and here the whole world collapses.

At the end of this fable, the lone scholarly lemming watches the mass of lemmings drown themselves, just as the artistic consciousness had looked back on the chaos of other moments for the stories in *My Life and Hard Times;* in fact, just as the anatomist had watched the lemming-like human creature for three decades. Notice, however, that Thurber (or his persona) is closer to his subject now. Standing on the very edge of destruction, the lemming-watcher was so distressed that he "tore up what he had written through the years about his species, and started his studies all over again."[79]

Like Thurber's continuing work in the face of civilization's collapse, he is first disgusted and defeated, but then rallies to fight and study again. Ambiguously, this fable is about life's continuance as well as its end. This is the essence of the comic spirit, like the fine thread of hope that is woven through *The Last Flower.* The only shred of hope left here is the remaining literate creature, the writer, who will perhaps be better able to interpret experience the next time. In Thurber's world this understanding remains only a hope for which to strive. The few who approach it are the poets, the artists, the writers, those who not only see the confusion of their species but attempt to interpret it, and thereby to surmount it. Perhaps, too, the goal of a fable is to so transform the understanding of its readers that such a change will also take place in them. Thurber is able to imagine coherent life only in his fairy tales, which brings us to the plot of his remarkable last tale.

Written shortly after completing the last collection of fables, *The Wonderful O* is both Thurber's most ambitious linguistic effort and the work in which the relationship between language and life becomes concrete. It is also, in a way, the book that he had been working toward all of his career. Here, language is not only his subject and his medium; it is also his plot, action, character, and theme. Since language is now equal to life for Thurber, a development which has been slowly emerging in his writing for thirty years, the world of this story is peopled with words and letters, and they — not actual people — are the focus of the story. At the end of the tale, we do not cheer the poets who save language as much as we proclaim the wonders of language itself. It is "The Wonderful O" that claims our hearts. For the first time in Thurber's fairy tales, in fact, the eccentric, individual characters are not the most interesting part of the tale. The role of language in human life is what interests us here, and by the end of the tale, the chanting to "The Wonderful O" reveals that the human voice was made so that it could sing in beautiful, coherent language.

Although the fairy tales were always poetic in language and style, in *The Wonderful O* Thurber's prose actually sings in the reader's ear. Listen to the internal and end rhymes, the fine rhythms, and the extended assonance and alliteration in the passages that follow. They show that Thurber has become more "poetic" in two senses of that word: first, in that he is using conventional poetic devices more often; and second, in the density and explosive compression of his language, which now has infinite power for connotation and suggestion. To borrow from Emily Dickinson, when I read Thurber's last tale, I feel as if I have had the top of my head taken off — and I know this is poetry.

The Wonderful O dramatizes the linguistic and social predicament of the island of Ooroo, thrown into confusion, or "cnfusin," by the banning of the letter "O." Ooroo thus becomes "R," or one-fifth of itself, and all things and ideas that have "O" in them are destroyed. Think of it: here we have no books, no love, no freedom, no hope. "The crew set about their new task with a will, and before they were through they had torn down colleges and destroyed many a book and tome and volume, and globe and blackboard and pointer and banished professors, assistant professors, scholars, tutors, and instructors. There was no one left to translate English into English.

Babies made as much sense as their fathers." It is a grim scene, this world in which language has been destroyed. We dwell, Thurber suggests, in a land where English must be translated into English; where dogma, hatred, fear, and barbarism crush the flowers of civilization: the books, the poems, the words and things themselves. Here, we are both delighted and frightened to hear, Goldilocks sounds only "like a key jiggled in a lck," and Ophelia Oliver's name sounds so horrid that she identified herself as "Phelia Liver" but once and then vanished.[80] To the trite question, "What's in a name?" Thurber answers—everything.

Ooroo is also where poetry died, because without their "O's," a poet and his dog became one thing: "pets." Eventually, the whole world became, in Thurber's provocative term, "chatic," that is, a cross between chaos and static. Here, everything dies at the slip of a letter. In this world of slippery language and equally slippery thought and reality, there are no constant distinctions:

'When coat is cat and boat is bat and goatherd looks like gathered, and booth is both, since both are bth, the reader's eye is bothered.'

'And power is pwer, and zero zer, and worst of all, a hero's her,' the old man sighed as he said it.

'Anon is ann, and moan is man,' Andrea smiled as she said it.

'And shoe,' Andreus said, 'is she.'

'Ah, woe,' the old man said, 'is we.'[81]

When the reader watches words and things slide away in this remarkable passage, constantly turning into something else, and thereby disappearing, he literally experiences Thurber's point about the fragility of reality, order, and sense in a world of multiple confusions. This is the world that "Barney Haller" had implied, now completely realized. Rather than becoming more abstract as he has generalized his images of confusion, therefore, Thurber has discovered a concrete principle to dramatize his thesis. *His subject and form are one.* As the anatomist sees one movement away from symmetry change the shape of the entire human figure being drawn, so Thurber sees a change in language, even one slip of the letter, affect the state of the whole organism under his scrutiny: human life.

It is once again a poet, Andreus, who decides that something must be done, "or we shall never know what we are saying," for without coherent language, "They are swing chas. What is slid? What is left that's slace? We are begne and webegne. Life is bring and brish. Even schling is flish."[82] This is English made into gibberish by the cruel decrees of a tyrant. It is also, of course, the world thrown into general chaos by language.

Andreus concludes that the answer must lie in the past, in what has been written. Although most of the books have been destroyed, a woman named Andrea finds one. Her name identifies her with Andreus, and in this, Thurber's most original fairy tale, she and the poet work together to save their ailing culture. The quest in *The Wonderful O,* unlike those in the earlier tales, is not for a princess's hand, but for human freedom; and the reinstatement of that freedom is the real celebration which ends the book, not the traditional marriage feast, which seems almost a footnote here.

It is difficult to arouse the people of "R" to overthrow the tyrant, however, because they have fallen prey to conformity:

> 'O-lessness is now a kind of cult in certain quarters,' Hyde observed, 'a messy-lessness, whose meaninglessness none-theless attracts the few, first one or two, then three or four, then more and more. People often have respect for what they cannot comprehend, since some men cannot always tell their crosses from their blessings, their laurels from their thorns. . . . O-lessism may become the ism of the future.'[83]

Even here, in never-never-land, where national, cultural, historical, and sexual distinctions are blurred, Thurber's text subtly connects with the real (or monstrously unreal) world of America in the 1950s, an America of blacklists and witch-hunts. Pertinent as *The Wonderful O* was to its time, however, the book now rings with the sound of prophecy. Could it be that we are edging more into "messy-lessness" all the time?

Finally, the repetition of the word "hope" by Andrea and a few followers calls the soldiers for this holy war out of long-forgotten stories where they had been waiting all along. They come to end, in a pun both witty and wise, the "law of the letter." "Lancelot and Ivanhoe, Athos, Porthos, Cyrano, Roland, Rob Roy, Romeo, Donaldbane of Burnham Wood, Robinson Crusoe and Robin Hood; the Moody

Doones of *Lorna Doone,* Davy Crockett and Daniel Boone; out of near and ancient tomes, Banquo's ghost and Sherlock Holmes."[85] All come to the aid of the poet. In this passage the anatomist of language is as attentive to sound as any poet. The scene is delightful, mixing as it does the peculiar humor, seriousness, poignancy, and beauty of Thurber's writing. Who else could have seen this image?

At the eleventh hour, the only clock that was not destroyed by Black's henchmen (the internal clock, "the clock that strikes in conscience") chimes. It is, therefore, through memory — both individual and cultural, particular and universal — that the people find their salvation. And, what can human beings remember but words?

> They then heard the ringing of a distant bell, sounding near and sounding nearer, ringing clear and ringing clearer, till all the sky was filled with music as by magic.
>
> 'Freedom!' Andreus cried, naming the gleaming word the men had found, the word that glowed and glittered.
>
> 'Freedom!' Andrea echoed after him, and the sound of the greatest word turned the vandals pale and made them tremble.
>
> 'I knew that the word could not be doom,' the old man said, 'or sorrow. I was afraid that it might be tomorrow.'[85]

This is a vision attained in none but the rarest of comedies, the vision of man transcending himself and time, endlessly reborn. It is a special ending for Thurber, which he severely qualifies by having it happen "nowhere," so to speak, in the distant world of fairyland. It is, however, the vision that he had worked toward through many darker places in the human experience. If most of his work portrays the anti-utopia of a chaotic world reeling under the language of confusion, *The Wonderful O* at least suggests the possibility of Thurber's utopia: a place where people would speak clearly and directly, without fear or superstition, in full possession of both words and the things they name, fully conscious, fully living. This is how *Homo loquens* was meant to be.

At the end of this tale, the people are reminded of the "O's" they must never lose: those in love, hope, valor, and freedom. Language has become so identified with life for Thurber that the name of the thing is the thing; without the word "freedom," we have no freedom.

This is his curious, provocative inversion of the understanding of language by cultural anthropologists, who assume that naming occurs after a thing exists.

As the bell chimes in the "O's," along with freedom and life, at the end of *The Wonderful O,* society moves into the palpable, vibrant present. Thus, the sound of this bell is much like the ringing of the bells on the Third Christmas of *In Memoriam,* or like the resounding bell of memory invoked in the last pages of *The Past Recaptured.* In all three cases, the work of art has been the vehicle by which the writer has recaptured, through language, not only the past, but the timeless change that is life itself.

As indicated earlier, the essays and stories in *Lanterns & Lances* and even the posthumous *Credos and Curios* demonstrate an obsession with the decay of language, viewing it as an index to the poor quality of life on "this misfit globe." Many of these last essays are fine, written in the mature and assured style of a man who no longer uses the humorous edge in all of his prose. There are even a few good stories written this late.[86] But the essential Thurber, the purest Thurber, is in *The Wonderful O.* This work is his fulfillment. Everything else is but footnote and embellishment.

I have attempted to note something of the range and fineness of Thurber's language, while demonstrating that his interest in language is consistent with his world view. His own expression, precise, subtle, and evocative, is always at odds with the language spoken by most of his characters, the language of confusion. It is a language that alternately delighted and frightened him, one that always perplexed and intrigued him. He must often have felt, along with King Clode of *The White Deer,* that he blew his horn in wasteland, as he reported on a dying language leading an unwitting humanity to meaninglessness and death. But blow the horn he did, clearly and with more insistence as the years passed: for Thurber was really much closer to Prince Jorn, who knew that "What's true is true." His quest was to discover timeless truth in a mutable, illusory world. And it is language that reveals whatever truth can be known and brings the inchoate world to life.

Language is thus not only the cause but the cure of the human disease, and Thurber's later works show him examining the possibility of turning the chaos of the modern world into a coherent actuality. His creation of order from disorder is perhaps what is most satisfying for his readers. Knowing Thurber means both to see the awful reality of our world and to experience that which is most humane in it—language. Both pain and joy, frustration and fulfillment, Thurber's world is as rich as human experience itself. His prose is variously simple and complex, understated and extravagant, and the convergence of these characteristics lends energy to his writing. The tension between indulgence and restraint results in a superior and distinctive style which has freshness and vigor as well as symmetry.[87] A bit like Twain, much more like James, something like Carroll, or E. B. White, there is but one word for this style and it is—"Thurber."

Always fascinated with *Homo loquens,* or man the talking animal, language became identified increasingly with life for Thurber. Finally, *The Wonderful O* describes the quintessential Thurber predicament: a society in chaos because its language is dead. And, since language was life for Thurber, as he grew and developed his style became increasingly complex. Thus, the anatomy of confusion fuels itself; for, as its subjects and the language in which they are expressed become more complex and diverse, the drive toward order and sense becomes more intense and urgent. Even in a world of disorder and destruction, what Malcolm Cowley called the "well-built wall" of Thurber's prose[88] stands as a monument to the war against nonsense and confusion. From the top of this edifice, Thurber saw more clearly and more completely the carnival of human life on all sides.

He walks that high wall yet: taking his steps gingerly, carefully, even dubiously, his only balance bar being the words and syntax of that dangerous tongue, the English language. Walking thus precariously balanced, Thurber's hard-worn victories over the imminent slip of a letter or wrong turn of a phrase make a joyous spectacle for those lesser speakers below—those who can only applaud his enduring triumph over the language of confusion.

5 A Bright and Melancholy Spectacle
The Anatomist in a World of Time and Death

After this brief light, the unending dark.
— *The White Deer*

Though Thurber's prose stands as a well-built wall of enduring strength, the world that it describes is a delicate organism — ever changeful, ironic, elusive — always on the brink of collapse or dissolution. This mutable world, ruled by the twin tyrants of time and death, is both the subject of and the reason for the anatomy of confusion. Only in such a finite, changeful world is the art of anatomy needed at all. Since Thurber envisioned a world of perpetual chaos and defined his artistic purpose as anatomizing that chaos, he was plagued by the specter of time, change and extinction. For it is time that causes human life to revolve in confusion. Thurber's preoccupation with time's passage and his perception of the chaotic human predicament are, thus, concomitant: taken together, they explain why the humorist-anatomist works, as well as the deep strain of melancholy running throughout his humor. We therefore end our investigation of Thurber's work by considering the role of time and death in his art.

Thurber's friend and collaborator, E. B. White, seems to have been the first to discern the thread of melancholy in the fabric of Thurber's humor. In his 1931 introduction to *The Owl in the Attic,* White recalled: "I finally met Thurber in New York. I see him now, slinking around the streets, trailing a thin melancholy and leading a terrier bitch."[1] Thurber continued the half-somber yet mocking characterization in his preface to *My Life and Hard Times:* "To call such persons [as himself] 'humorists,' a loose-fitting and ugly word, is to miss the nature of their dilemma and the dilemma of their nature. The little wheels of their invention are set in motion by the damp hand of melancholy."[2] Thurber's critics have usually either ignored the melancholy basis of his work ("the nature of his dilemma"), or have explained his poignancy as a "counterbalance" to his humorous inclination.[3] Yet I would argue that Thurber's melancholy results from the same source as his humor: from his painful perception of imperfect, finite human nature in a chaotic, destructive world. Both are related to a strong and persistent sense of the inevitability of time, change, and extinction, a sense that necessarily accompanies any anatomist's work. Perhaps the melancholy sense of time pervading Thurber's humor is the legendary thread that unravels the whole. At any rate, students of Thurber's anatomy must examine this thread in order to appreciate fully the pattern of his art.

Thurber's suggestion that the essence of humor is "that hysterical laugh that people sometimes get in the face of the Awful" may surprise at first glance, because the reader does not often experience such hysterical laughter in reading Thurber's high comedy.[4] There is, however, a feeling of near-hysteria about many of his characters, situations, and themes, and glimpses of "the Awful"—the frightening, the decadent, and the evil—fill his anatomy. The most common of these glimpses is of the specter of mutability, aging, and death, and the general chaos resulting from this perception of our mortality. As death is the consummate awful reality that we all must face, Thurber's humor provides us with a helpful release from our common fear, as well as a healthy recognition of our fate. Indeed, Thurber's tragicomic humor is based more in what he calls a "kind of mellowed self-pity" than in the feeling of cool superiority stressed by many comic theorists.[5] Since everyone is subject to time and confusion, an art that acknowledges them should necessarily effect self-recognition and pity. It is, to say the least, an unsettling and transforming art for a reader of sensibility.

A roughly chronological survey of Thurber's references to time should illuminate its function in his anatomy, as well as suggest the significance of this motif in Western art generally. All works resonate in a context of other works, and the world of Thurber's creation has wide resonance indeed.

Although Thurber was just past thirty when he began to publish, his characters have a remarkably aged feeling about them, even in the early work. Like his contemporaries, Eliot and Fitzgerald, Thurber seems to have enjoyed "aging" both himself (as narrator) and his characters far beyond their actual ages. Eliot was, in fact, quite young when he wrote "The Love Song of J. Alfred Prufrock," and Fitzgerald managed to make the passage of Nick Carraway's thirtieth birthday suggest the coming of age of the Western world.[6] Thurber's fiction, it seems, plays directly to the laughter that such self-consciousness causes upon reflection.

In one early work, *The Owl in the Attic,* the narrator admits that Mr. and Mrs. Monroe are "quite young," but their behavior places this prototypical Thurber couple among those vaguely middle-aged creatures of his drawings: John Monroe forgets things, they sleep in separate bedrooms, and they seem to have suffered life together for a long, long time. This is most evident in "The Middle Years," the neo-Jamesian story in which John Monroe is portrayed as too tired even for an appealing indiscretion. John Monroe, impotent, tired, and bored, is Hemingway's Jake Barnes, but seen from Thurber's ironic side-glance. Monroe's self-image recalls sardonically both Prufrock and his antithesis, Sweeney: "It struck him as he glimpsed himself in a long glass, that a tall thin man looks like an ass in socks and garters."[7] The bittersweet laughter evoked by such a line flows from that "mellowed self-pity" experienced by a finite creature when facing his finitude.

The preface to *My Life and Hard Times* continues in this vein, but this time the rapidly aging character is the narrator "Thurber." Admitting that he is not yet forty (the age recommended by Cellini for writing one's autobiography), Thurber declares that "the grim date moves toward me apace; my legs are beginning to go, things blur before my eyes, and the faces of the rose-lipped maids I knew in my twenties are misty as dreams." Thurber's descent into blindness just a few years after he wrote these lines makes them particularly poignant, it is true, but the essential terror lurks beneath the surface. The plight of men like Thurber is made worse, we are told, by the knowledge that age has not brought them much; for "in the House of Life they have the feeling that they have never taken off their overcoats." Like Prufrock, these loosely-defined humorists have seen Death, the eternal Footman, hold their coats and snicker. And, in short, they were afraid. The preface ends with Thurber's peculiar synthesis of humor, sadness, and fear. Whatever happens, he says in a deceptively light and simple line, "the claw of the sea-puss gets us all in the end."[8] With this comical metaphor for the inevitability of death, Thurber incongruously begins the high hilarity of his famous reminiscences.

My Life and Hard Times, Thurber's humorous masterpiece, is a collection of memories—the creation of a time-bound animal—sandwiched between ruminations (in the "Preface" and the "Note at the End") on the meaning of life, from which we all suffer, and death, the only thing to which we all look forward.

In the fictional memoirs, "University Days" and "Draftboard Nights," it is time moving swiftly past Thurber that makes the narratives both funny and sad. In the first story, Thurber remembers having to retake botany and military drill each year during college because he continually failed both. In his last year he was trapped in time as the only senior at Ohio State still in uniform, a uniform he had outgrown. Even worse, "Draftboard Nights" dramatizes the bureaucratic mix-up that repeatedly "drafted" Thurber during the First World War. Each week, after marking precious time in the maze of befuddled examiners, Thurber failed the physical because of poor eyesight. (This had been, of course, the cause of his failing botany.) The end of this story demonstrates powerfully the inevitability of fate and time's caprice: "Late one morning, shortly after my last examination, I was awakened by the sounds of bells ringing and whistles blowing. It grew louder and more insistent and wilder. It was the Armistice."[9] If at college Thurber had missed being *au courant,* he went on to miss history.

Four years after *My Life and Hard Times, Let Your Mind Alone!* was published. It included two stories, which were discussed in the section on men and women in Chapter 2, about married couples whose trivial lives seem especially poignant when played out against the background of passing time. In "The Breaking Up of the Winships," a once-happy couple get into an absurd argument that ends in profound loneliness and alienation, that is, in a type of death. As in so many Thurber stories, the reader of "Winships" is reminded of universal confusion by insistent references to clocks: "It started innocently enough, amiably even, with laughter from both of them, laughter that froze finally as the clock ran out and their words came out sharp and flat and stinging."[10] This sentence suggests not only the ease with which human beings move from amiability to malice or from laughter to tears, but the similarly simple step from life to death; as one hears the laughter dying out in this line, one is impressed with the fragility of human lives so engrossed in trivial action. This is the tragicomic vision. "Winships" uses many extended metaphors for time that remind the reader of the texture of the later fiction of Henry James, and often Thurber characters seem to be "missing their own lives," like the Strethers and Marchers of James's final stories.[11]

"A Couple of Hamburgers" shows another man and woman creeping in a mysteriously ailing automobile down a highway (a metaphor for life in Thurber's urban world), while they bitterly argue and misunderstand each other. The wife threatens, knowingly if enigmatically, that her husband will understand only "when it is too late," and the narrator describes the whole oppressive scene in terms of time's passage: "It had been raining for a long time, a slow cold rain falling out of iron-colored clouds. They had been driving since morning and they still had a hundred and thirty miles to go."[12] This is a picture of dying animals, creeping inevitably toward death. The fundamental unhappiness of these Thurber people is especially moving because of the narrator's repeated reminders that time is running out for them.

In an even more somber tone, "After the Steppe Cat, What?" looks at the general ravages of time on planet Earth. This essay, which recalls *The Waste Land* as well as Shelley's "Ozymandias," concludes that rodents will soon take over the modern world. Because time and change are the only constants in this world, Thurber argues that the inevitable doom of a decadent civilization is foretold in our awful knowledge of history, in the past: "where Carthage once stood in her glory and pride there rises a cluster of modern villas, forming a suburb of the modern city of Tunis. Thus has the greatness of a sovereign power diminished. To what new kind of metropolis may Tunis someday become a suburb?"[13] With this chilling question, Thurber deftly implies the cycles of time moving relentlessly on, as both individuals and cultures reel in unending confusion and decay.

After *Let Your Mind Alone!*, Thurber published a collection whose very title indicates his obsession with aging and its incongruities, *The Middle-Aged Man on the Flying Trapeze*. This collection appropriately presents a host of sad, lonely, vaguely middle-aged characters who are being overcome by time.[14] For example, the unnamed main character of "The Evening's at Seven," another impotent modern man out of the Jamesian mold, watches the clock as he sleep-walks through life and experiences only "the mingled thoughts clocks gave him." Similarly, Mr. Kirk of "One Is a

Wanderer" marks time drinking, wandering in and out of a hotel lobby, looking for messages that do not come, and singing the ruefully nostalgic lines of "Bye, Bye, Blackbird," as the clock ticks on:

> "George," he said, when the waiter walked over for his empty glass, "I will be forty-one next November." "But that's not old, sir, and that's a long way off," said George. "No, it isn't," he said. "It's almost here. So is forty-two and forty-three and fifty, and here I am trying to be—do you know what I'm trying to be, George? I'm trying to be happy.... But you see, George, I am an analyzer. I am also a rememberer. I have a pocketful of old used years. You put all those things together and they sit in a lobby getting silly and old."

There is the Thurber coupling: silly and old. In Thurber's tragicomic view of the human carnival, it is not a daring young man, but a middle-aged and frightened one, who performs on the flying trapeze. And no one moves through this cosmos with the greatest of ease— not when the narrator and the characters alike sense their finite nature and death's paradoxically eternal presence. This is the sepia-toned world of memory and regret, a world where even reading of Proust's conquering time through art cannot stave off the devilish presence of Barney Haller, with his incantations of death and destruction.[15]

Holding before us the glimmer of brightness in a largely melancholy world, *The Last Flower* dramatizes with great economy humankind's tenuous hold on life: even though change, confusion, and destruction are ubiquitous on earth, *The Last Flower* asserts paradoxically that there yet remains a creative human desire to rebuild. Life and death, creation and destruction, as thus linked inextricably in the chain of human experience. A book neither humorous nor comical yet essentially comic in its guarded affirmation of life, *The Last Flower* demonstrates, as well as any of his work, Thurber's ambiguous view of life.

Following *The Last Flower*, Thurber's fairy tales portray time as the great enemy. *Many Moons*, the earliest of the tales, has a King and royal advisors who work against time as they attempt to secure the moon for the little Princess before it rises again in the sky. In *The Great Quillow*, the townspeople work through the night to satisfy the demands of a destructive giant, but many still cannot finish their tasks on time. The three princes in *The White Deer* ride against time in quest of a lady's hand; and in *The 13 Clocks,* the Prince has only ninety-nine hours to achieve a goal that should take ninety-nine days. Finally, in *The Wonderful O,* the blighted people of Ooroo, who seem doomed to a world without a sense of either history or personal time, race against an unseen clock and only at the eleventh hour manage to end the chaotic reign of tyrants.

In each of these tales, people must work against time—that time which necessarily limits and defines human experience. In *The White Deer* the quests are manipulated by a woods wizard, so that the princes all arrive triumphantly at the same moment. No matter what the odds or effort, it seems, we all come to the same end. Time is the great equalizer. The tale's truthteller, the blind clockmaker, Tocko, who must be identified with the now-blind Thurber, carves foreboding but wise legends on sundials, those oldest of timekeepers: "After this brief light, the unending dark"; "It is darker than you think"; and "This little light and then the night."[16] These repeated light and dark images used as metaphors for death suggest that Thurber's encroaching blindness during this period only intensified his feeling about the swiftness of time and the harsh relentlessness of change. In a way, the sundials' legends distill into haunting, simple phrases Thurber's view of this mutable human world.

Time is an invincible enemy. In the early stories, Thurber characters suffer from time as pathetic victims of their own lives. In the fairy tales, however, the Thurber villain emerges; he is the one who tries to "kill time," to make the metaphoric cliché dreadfully literal. *The 13 Clocks,* for example, is about the wasteland created by an evil duke who mistakenly thinks he can conquer time: "The clocks were dead, and in the end, brooding on it, the Duke decided he had murdered time, slain it with his sword, and wiped his bloody blade upon its beard and left it lying there, bleeding hours and minutes." Like Macbeth, who in murdering Duncan and the social order also murdered sleep, the Duke of Coffin Castle had thrown his kingdom into utter confusion by his arrogant attempts to rule time. By the end of the tale, however, the Duke succumbs, as everyone must, to time. When the thirteen frozen clocks are finally started, we know that the unnatural order of the Duke is about to be replaced by pulsating, human life: "No mortal man can murder time. . . . and even if he could, there's something else: a clockwork in a maiden's heart, that strikes the hours of youth and love."[17] Time is the inevitable medium of human life, and more: it is part of our essence. With this acceptance of time's necessity, Thurber is ready for the mature vision of his final tale, *The Wonderful O*.

The Wonderful O paradoxically admits both a fear of time and a resignation to it. As we have seen, a profound sense of urgency, of fighting against insurmountable odds before time runs out, pervades all of Thurber's fairy tales. But nowhere is the battle won with such definitive glory as in *The Wonderful O*. At the beginning of this tale, Thurber sets the tone with this somber and beautiful opening sentence: "Somewhere a ponderous clock slowly dropped a dozen strokes into the gloom." This is the sound of doom. Thurber's fairyland, which is the decadent modern world, is a world marked by quick changes in the face of reality, ever on the brink of collapse, where life seems all too easily snuffed out:

> "We live in peril and in danger," Andreus told the people, "and in a little time may have left few things that we can say. Already there is little we can play. I have a piece that I shall read. It indicates the quandary we're in." And then he read it:
> 'They are swing chas. What is slid? What is left that's slace? We are begne and webegne.'[18]

We are, indeed, "webegne" in a world where language is so mangled and people are subjected to such a death-in-life existence.

By the end of the story, however, irony inverts the tale. Time returns as an unseen clock strikes at the last possible minute, not only ringing in inevitable time, but ending the deathly reign of the tyrant, Black, who would kill both language and life. Black, too, must race against time, but he loses the battle. ("No mortal man can murder time.") When an unseen clock finally strikes and the freedom bell rings out unexpectedly, the tension felt throughout the book turns into joy in the final beautiful image, which stresses our necessary reliance upon time: "'I knew the word could not be doom,' the old man said, 'or sorrow. I was afraid that it might be tomorrow.'" In Thurber's world, then, time is as necessary as death, while language is the generator of life. Overturning laws and truisms to allow the paradox of life to reveal itself, the action of *The Wonderful O* turns the enemy into the savior, the victim into the victor. The people of Ooroo have learned, with Thurber, that since time defines human experience, human beings must learn to live life on its own unrelenting terms, that is, in the difficult, ambiguous present. Like the Duke in *13 Clocks,* the villainous Black erroneously thought that he had murdered time: "'I destroyed all clocks,' he cried, as the last clock chimed. 'All clocks save one,' said Andreus, 'the clock that strikes in conscience.'"[19] This enigmatic image suggests that Thurber has come to understand that people carry time within them, as part of their very nature; along with a natural sadness about and fear of time, therefore, a human being must come to accept it. This movement toward an acceptance of time is possibly a movement that comes, paradoxically, with aging.

Just before beginning to write fairy tales, Thurber published his first collection of *Fables for Our Time,* which are distinguished by the fact that the majority of them end in death, sometimes in mass slaughter. Typical of Thurber's deathly fables, "The Green Isle in the Sea" describes ironically an old gentleman's being destroyed systematically in a painfully recognizable modern landscape under a "living" sun: "The blood-dimmed tide is loosed, and everywhere / The ceremony of innocence is drowned,"[20] these fables seem to argue. (See also "The Birds and the Foxes," "The Owl Who Was God," and "The Hen and the Heavens," for bitterly ironic fables that depict mass death.)

Because of their emphasis on the fragility of life, Thurber's fables usually cause a wince or a sigh, rather than a lighthearted laugh. Like Mark Twain, the source of Thurber's art is pain and disappointment. And, even though Twain's broad comicality often elicits the belly laugh, his motivation is the same. Think, for example, of that hilarious tale, *The Adventures of Huckleberry Finn*—a tale which is strewn with corpses and would-be corpses, a tale in which life and death on the Mississippi are as closely linked as the river and the shore. Twain's novel is, in fact, inundated with references to death and dying, and all of this in a story of innocence and initiation, a story of youth.[21] Perhaps it is just this ironic juxtaposition that we should expect in an American masterpiece, for our writers seem particularly charged with illuminating the ambiguous connections between life and death, triumph and defeat, desire and fulfillment. In a country so committed to youth, progress, and the future, these juxtapositions are especially striking and significant.

Written during the same period as the early fables, that quintessential Thurber story, "The Secret Life on Walter Mitty," also depends heavily upon images of aging and death for its impact. The story ends, in fact, with Mitty's imagined death, a death that fittingly culminates his death-in-life existence. Throughout the narrative, the reader senses the pressing in of time on the Mittys, as they are locked into a sterile life while time moves swiftly and unknowingly past them. Mitty tries to acknowledge this in his statement that "things close in," but Mrs. Mitty, the unconscious destroyer, is oblivious to their fate.[22] The essential sadness of this story resides as much in its sense of time's passage as in the impossibility of Mitty's dreams. In fact, Mitty's daydreams could be understood as his attempts to deal with the fear of death, which closes in all too easily. Like the physical anatomist, who operates on the dead, Thurber's anatomy dissects again and again the "Walter Mitty type": a passive, enervated, and decadent specimen of modern man.

The 1956 collection of *Further Fables* is as deathly and time-ridden as the earlier fables; just a perusal of their morals shows the persistence of Thurber's melancholy sense of time. These profoundly serious morals are expressed in the lightly ironic, fragile tone that characterizes Thurber's style: "*Tout,* as the French say, in a philosophy older than ours and an idiom often more succinct, *passé*"; "O why should the spirit of mortal be proud, in this little voyage from swaddle to shroud"; "Ashes to ashes, clay to clay, if the enemy doesn't get you, your own folks may"; and "This is the posture of fortune's slave: one foot in the gravy, one foot in the grave."[23] This is verbal wit of the highest order, coupling witticism and wisdom in graceful, quickfire delivery.

That we come to know ourselves better and to face our fate more fully was really Thurber's aim, regardless of our inability to conquer time, avoid death, or transcend confusion. The results of our attempts at awareness, made permanent in arts and letters, are ironically our only form of immortality. The human paradox thus revolves endlessly, periodically illuminating the darkened world. The illuminating quest for self-knowledge was fittingly the theme of Thurber's last completed collection, *Lanterns & Lances,* as he says in its preface: "We all know that, as the old adage has it, 'It is later than you think.' I touch on that theme myself, as every writer who can think must, but I also say occasionally: 'It is lighter than you think.' In this light, let's not look back in anger, or forward in fear, but around in awareness." That is, we must not surrender either to the past of memory or to the future of dreams, but rather confront the present bravely, thus living on the only terms that human life allows. Always tinged with terror, this growing awareness is the only solace offered by Thurber's work. What comfort can we find in hearing Thurber decide half-seriously to "mourn the swift mortality of Man that will prevent him from reading *The Decline and Fall of Man,* by Professor B. N. Dolphin"?[24] In his consistently apocalyptic vision, Thurber declines, the West declines, Man declines.

"The Last Clock" tells of yet another despot who has made havoc with human life by attempting to murder time. This clock-ogre has, in fact, destroyed life on earth because language and communication have died along with time: in a savage parody of Longfellow, Thurber portrays the end of human civilization as consisting of only "mummum in the sands of time."[25] A people without history and language simply evaporate, the fabulist warns.

By 1960, the world's perpetual sickness seemed even more severe and intolerable to Thurber, as he was nearing his own death. The severity of the general malaise was reflected in a bitterly appropriate pun that was eventually published post-humously in *Credos and Curios:* "The greatest truth of our time is both simple and awful— total war means annihilation, and the Brink of War has become the Brink of Was."[26] History during Thurber's lifetime had sadly and eerily proven correct his earliest warnings about human nature. The humorist was driven finally to ask, most emphatically, "After the peculiar horrors of the Twentieth Century, what?"

Thurber became less detached from his subjects, and therefore less humorous, during the last few years of his life. In his early definitions of humor he had recognized the necessity for such detachment (viewing chaos in retrospect implies detachment), but it seems that toward the end of his life, as age, blindness, and illness closed in, Thurber began to address his themes more directly, with less laughter and more urgency than ever before. It is perhaps unfair to judge him on the basis of *Credos and Curios* (1962), which Mrs. Thurber put together from the work left after his death in 1961. When much of this was written he was already suffering from a series of minor strokes which, although undiagnosed at the time, undoubtedly affected his behavior and thinking.

In looking at *Credos* it is obvious that Thurber sensed his own time was running out and that his obsession with the universal ravages of time and disorder was more intense than ever. In one poignant line he says that he remembers turn-of-the-century Columbus, Ohio, "as fondly and sharply as a man on a sinking ship might remember his prairie home." In another piece, recalling an old Thurber theme, he warns that the collapse of civilization is just around the corner. The anxious, ambivalent title of a representative piece from the collection, "The Future, if Any, of Comedy, or Where Do We Non-Go from Here?" reveals his overwhelming fear that laughter and awareness are not enough. This is the darkest version of Thurber's consistent distrust of human nature, filled with more anger, bitterness, and frustration than ever before. He finally questions whether there is any future at all for humanity, a fear that probably grew as much out of the debilitating problems of the Atomic Age as out of his own illness. Accompanying this dark conversation piece about the imminent collapse of civilization is a drawing originally published in *Men, Women, and Dogs* (1942) with the caption "Destinations."[27] It is a stark, ironic picture of an unwitting mass of people scurrying feverishly about their business, unaware that they are all the while passing a large and imposing cemetery — their final "destination." On viewing this drawing, with its glimpse of "the Awful," one experiences that inaudible, enduring, and perhaps somewhat painful laugh that is the essence of Thurber's peculiar brand of humor.

Is it fitting for a humorist to be so obsessed with time and death? Is not comedy, at least in its classical form, concerned with the survival of life rather than with death? One could say that Thurber's tragicomedy is a way out of this dilemma, since his humor blends the comic and the tragic attitudes toward life. More importantly, however, as a humorist-anatomist, Thurber must deal with "the dead." His art is one that is practiced on the dead, as he analyzes the structures that move too quickly for comprehension when "alive," in order to discover the reality beneath the tricky surfaces of the world. If human life were immutable and eternal, there would presumably be no need for the art of anatomy at all, but this study of structure and system has particular relevance for a dying animal like *Homo sapiens*. Indeed, sometimes the anatomist becomes a pathologist, seeking in the *corpus* an explanation for its demise.

As the humorist-anatomist dissects the human carnival, he is

DESTINATIONS

able, like all students of anatomy, to discern the parts of the whole and their interrelation. Finally, he is able to draw an image which generalizes from the observed data (from the "body" of information under study), to make an image of the structure disguised as chaos. This image is the telling cut, the defining shape of reality as the anatomist understands it after all of his surgery and reconstruction. Ironically, only a "dead" society — the decadent *corpus mundi* — need suffer such dissection, but through the art of anatomy, this body may live again. It is reborn in the eternal image constructed by the artist. Like great poetry, Thurber's anatomy seeks to capture mutable life for a moment and thus make it timeless: "So long as men can breathe, or eyes can see, / So long lives this, and this gives life to thee."[28]

To deepen the paradox even further, the death and consequent dissection of the *corpus* make possible the lessons of anatomy, which in turn, help the living. Thurber's anatomy of confusion, therefore, is not only necessarily driven by death-consciousness, but is also life-affirming and transcendent. Mingling the vision of tragedy — the dense images of time, death, and extinction — with the spirit of comedy, this humor is as complex and ambiguous as life itself.

Even the characteristically allusive and parodic quality of Thurber's prose is related to his consciousness of time. By so acknowledging literary tradition and attempting to extend and transform it, his work deftly makes a connection between past, present, and future. Or rather, it renders such distinctions inadequate. The work of art exists essentially outside of time, endlessly recreating experience and being recreated by it. Thurber's fables, for example, could not have been written by La Fontaine, but they also could not have been written without the work of earlier fabulists. When we read them, we delight in their bringing to life an old form, a form renewed and redefined by use. This is the delight we feel when confronting permanence in a mutable world.

If most of Thurber's characters are dead or dying, the life that survives in his time-ridden world is the life of the artist. The survival of the artist's consciousness, superimposed above a dead and dying land, is what makes Thurber's anatomy of the human carnvial life-affirming. Struggling in a world of time and death, this artist is balanced tenuously, always on the brink of extinction, but gamely plodding on: he is the comic hero.

Thurber manages to find humor in the grimmest of situations and subjects: the decline of the West, the imperfection of human nature, the unending chaos and disappointment of human experience. In fact, his complex comicality is rooted in his painful perception of these phenomena. He is not always humorous, but he always works with a steady hand and a keen eye to analyze the confusion in which humankind revolves. In a sense, then, Thurber's art freezes for a moment the endless revolutions of an erratic universe. Working in the glimmer of that brief light called human life, the anatomist constructs a timeless structure against the certain encroachment of unending dark: his anatomy of a bright and melancholy spectacle, our fleeting time on earth.

Epilogue

Humor is a feathered thing that perches in the soul.
—Lanterns & Lances

Thurber himself warned that "the Anatomy of Confusion is a large subject," as it has indeed proven to be. We have watched the anatomist cut through the many layers of human experience to discover the essence of confusion—from the *corpus mundi,* inward to the *corpus mentis,* and finally, to the very stuff of thought—language. Whether Thurber writes about societies in chaos, marriages in dissolution, or communication breaking down, he is always studying images of confusion for his anatomy. And, although he never completed the novel that he wanted to write, the compilation of all his short works actually constitutes his magnum opus: *The Anatomy of Confusion.*

Perhaps in America, where bigger so often masquerades as better, it is especially difficult for us to recognize the greatness of writers who work only in the tightly structured forms—the short story, the fable, the essay, the lyric. If so, this is highly ironic, since America has spawned some of the great talents in each of these forms. The writers of short, economical pieces are also difficult to discuss for another reason; they present the would-be critic with many parts and no ostensible whole. The student of Thurber, for example, must work to find the pattern running through a large and complex carpet that is composed of diverse, often conflicting elements. But the pattern is there, and if its challenge is great, the rewards are rich. In contemplating Thurber's achievement, we must attempt to find this pattern, and must ask what kind of mind would create such a complicated gallery—a gallery that includes Ulgine Barrows and Princess Rosanore, Walter Mitty and the Thurber dog, dolphins and declensions—all presented in a variety of forms and styles ranging from conventional short stories to Aesopian fables, from fairy tales to satiric essays, from nonsense humor to serious investigations of history, culture, and literature. We must discover the means by which Thurber's individual works may be regarded as parts of the whole, and derive the principle by which they are integrated into one vision of experience.

Our exploration of the anatomy of confusion shows us that, by dissecting the confusions of language and reason, of governments and households, of threatening machines and perplexing systems, of dogs and their masters, Thurber is able to outline the central figure in the human carnival and to sketch the pattern of the *corpus mundi*. When we, his readers, stand back from the canvas of Thurber's carnival, we are able to see the humorist drawing this figure, or to watch the artist watching human experience. From this vantage point, we are both delighted and enlightened by the human tragicomedy, by life playing itself out on the enormous field of experience. It is as though the anatomist's dissection reveals at last a new nerve in the body of human experience, the nexus of laughter and tears, hope and disillusionment, pleasure and pain. In discovering this tragicomic nerve at the heart of human existence, Thurber reveals why the anatomist of confusion works: he attempts endlessly to recreate life in a world scarred by time and death. The resulting work of art, or the anatomy of confusion, is his only chance for meaning, order, and permanence in a world suffering from change and extinction. The artist grasps meaning from the dark chaos only at the moment of poetry—that fleeting moment of life and consciousness in a generally dead and unknowing existence. For Thurber, this is the moment when we contemplate the human skull, frozen into a timeless, enigmatic grin that is neither happy nor sad—the moment when we glimpse our common destination and emit a nervous snicker of recognition.

Thurber's stories are most often about the small events of everyday, but we must not miss his essential profundity. He focuses upon the moment because "moment" provides the better part of the momentous, as well as the chief force in momentum. The moment is both the essence and the energy of life. Thurber's real subjects are not automobiles and cocktail parties and marital arguments, for these are but particular symptoms of the general disease of confusion. The anatomist actually addresses timeless subjects—freedom, justice, hope, fear, love, hate, life, and death—and is able to raise the fundamental questions of human experience without either embarrassment or banality. His works subtly and gracefully dare to ask: "What does it mean to be a human being?" "What is the end of human activity?" "How can a human being survive in a chaotic, destructive world?" The high seriousness of Thurber's mind and art dictates raising these questions in spite of his knowledge that answers will not be forthcoming. He seems to believe that human beings were given language so that they could ask such questions, and the sound of the human voice is our imprint upon the universe.

The world of Thurber's creation is made of words, words that embody his great, resounding cry for order and meaning. His voice is unlike any other, a clear and unique sound above the babble. The world that it creates is a spectacle both bright and melancholy, the paradoxical creation of an individual, significant, and enduring vision of human life. Like Emily Dickinson's hope, Thurber's "Humor is a feathered thing that perches in the soul."[1] It is the life-spirit that persists even in the face of death, denial, and destruction—doggedly creating life from death, order from chaos, and art from nothing at all. Thurber's humor is the supreme balancing act of a humorist who was really a poet, of an artist who attempted to see life steadily and whole while the universe was turning madly about him. I like to think of his creation still perching at the center of this dismal and difficult universe, sonorously singing its timeless song and always just ready to soar.

Notes

1 Introduction

1. See Edwin T. Bowden, *James Thurber: A Bibliography* (Columbus: Ohio State University Press, 1968), for a detailed description of Thurber's publishing history, including collections and adaptations. Also, Richard Tobias, *The Art of James Thurber* (Athens: Ohio University Press, 1969), 7; and Lewis Gannett, "James Thurber: Pre-Intentionalist," *New York Herald Tribune Book Review,* 12 Nov. 1954, 5, enumerates the occurrence of Thurber references and quotations in different countries; Peter DeVries, "James Thurber: The Comic Prufrock," *Poetry* 63 (Dec. 1943): 150, describes several experiences in terms of "feeling like a Thurber cartoon."

2. Some of the more notable ones are: Malcolm Cowley, *The Literary Situation* (New York: Viking Press, 1954), 193; W. H. Auden, "The Icon and the Portrait," *The Nation* 150 (13 Jan. 1940): 48; Edmund Wilson, "Book," *New Yorker* 21 (27 Oct. 1945): 91–94; and Dorothy Parker, Introduction to James Thurber, *Men, Women, and Dogs* (New York: Harcourt, Brace, and Company, 1943), vii–x.

3. T. S. Eliot, quoted in "Priceless Gift of Laughter," *Time* 58 (9 July 1951): 88; Harvey Breit, "Talk with James Thurber," *New York Times Book Review,* 29 June 1952, 19.

4. The DeVries article cited in note 1 is the first and perhaps still the best of these. Additional studies include: Otto Friedrich, "James Thurber: A Critical Study," *Discovery* 5 (Jan. 1955): 166; Robert E. Morsberger, "The Predicaments and Perplexities of James Thurber" (Ph.D. diss., University of Iowa, 1956); Stephen Black, *James Thurber: His Masquerades* (The Hague: Mouton, 1970; Alice B. Baldwin, "Congruous Laughter: The Linguistic Form of Humor in James Thurber's Casual Essays" (Ph.D. diss., University of Massachusetts, 1970); and a collection of essays, largely reprinted from journals, entitled *Thurber: A Collection of Critical Essays,* ed. Charles Holmes (Englewood Cliffs: Prentice-Hall, 1974).

5. Robert Morsberger, *James Thurber* (New York: Twayne, 1964); Tobias, *James Thurber;* Charles Holmes, *The Clocks of Columbus* (New York: Atheneum, 1972); see also Burton Bernstein, *Thurber: A Biography* (New York: Dodd, Mead, 1975).

6. "Thurber, an Old Hand at Humor with Two Hits on Hand," *Life* 48 (14 March 1960): 108.

7. Samuel Bernard Baker, "James Thurber: The Columbus Years" (M. A. thesis, Ohio State University, 1962), 67.

8. "James Thurber in Conversation with Alistair Cooke," *The Atlantic* 198 (August 1956): 39.

9. Quoted in Max Eastman, *Enjoyment of Laughter* (New York: Simon and Schuster, 1936), 342.

10. Wylie Sypher, ed., *Comedy: An Essay on Comedy by George Meredith & Laughter by Henri Bergson* (Garden City, New York: Doubleday and Company, 1956), 193–94. I am indebted to Sypher's discussion of comedy.

11. James Thurber, *The Thurber Album* (New York: Simon and Schuster, 1952), 137.

12. "Obituary," *New York Times*, 3 Nov. 1961, 35.

13. James Thurber, *Thurber's Dogs* (New York: Simon and Schuster, 1955), 152.

14. James Thurber, *Thurber Country* (New York: Simon and Schuster, 1953), 103.

15. Thurber uses the word confusion and other forms of "to confuse" repeatedly in his work; often, the word is even capitalized, or it is repeated throughout a piece, to emphasize its importance. Thurber also frequently uses as synonyms for confusion such terms as chaos, bedlam, and mix-up.

16. James Thurber, *Lanterns & Lances* (New York: Harper and Row, 1961), 143. Throughout my discussion, I will be using the word tragicomic with the meaning Thurber ascribes to it in this passage. Tragicomedy, in this context, does not mean a distinct literary form, as the word signifies in late Renaissance drama. In fact, what makes most of Thurber's work tragicomic is not that it combines parts that are, variously, comic and tragic, but that the dominant actions and images are, paradoxically, both tragic and comic at the same time.

17. Susanne Langer, "The Comic Rhythm" in Robert W. Corrigan, ed., *Comedy: Meaning and Form* (San Francisco, 1965), 119–40. This term is the culmination of Langer's probing analysis of the distinct nature of the comic vision; readers familiar with her work will note its great influence on my understanding of comedy.

18. James Thurber, *Further Fables for Our Time* (New York: Simon and Schuster, 1956), 174; and *Fables for Our Time* (New York: Harper and Row, 1940), 30.

19. Could not Uncle Vanya have been Thurber's creation? For a discussion of Thurber's similarities with Henry James, see Chapter 3. Thurber's fables remind the reader of Shavian inversion, especially as it informs Shaw's prefaces and the discussion scenes in plays like *Major Barbara* and *Saint Joan*. And regarding Wilde, I am, of course, referring to his subtitle for *The Importance of Being Earnest*.

20. Thurber, *Lanterns*, 142.

21. Henry Fielding, *The Adventures of Joseph Andrews*, author's preface (Boston: Houghton Mifflin, 1961), 7.

22. I use the term comicality to mean humorous or evocative of laughter, as opposed to comic, which refers to the form itself and how its plot is resolved. Langer also uses the word comicality to mean funny. This dis-

tinction is very important, especially since many readers still confuse humorousness with comedy and seriousness with tragedy.

23. James Thurber, *Credos and Curios* (New York: Harper and Row, 1962), 166.

2. *Corpus Mundi*

1. James Thurber, *My Life and Hard Times* (New York: Bantam Books, 1971), 10.

2. Thurber, *Thurber Country*, 156.

3. James Thurber, *The Seal in the Bedroom* (New York: Harper and Row, 1932), unpaginated; in the Introduction by Dorothy Parker.

4. James Thurber, *The Years with Ross* (Boston: Little, Brown, and Company, 1959), 125. Tobias understands the character of Ross in direct opposition to this interpretation; see *Art of James Thurber*, 154–62.

5. James Thurber, "Statement," in *I Believe*, ed. Clifton Fadiman (New York: Simon and Schuster, 1939), 295–300.

6. See *Men, Women, and Dogs*, 79, 153, 47; and *Seal in the Bedroom*, unpaginated, for some of the quintessential Thurber depictions of chaos: "And *this* is my *father*, Mr. Williams—home from the wars or something"; "He hates people"; "One of us ought to be a Boswell, taking this all down"; "Stop me!"; "Will You Be Good Enough to Dance This Outside?"; and "They say he has no weakness."

7. Thurber, *Credos*, 86.

8. E. B. White, *A Subtreasury of American Humor* (New York: Modern Library, 1948), xvi.

9. James Thurber, "Statement," in Eastman, *Enjoyment of Laughter*, 342, 43.

10. Thurber, *Lanterns*, 142, 143.

11. Constance Rourke, *American Humor* (New York: Harcourt, Brace, and Company, 1931), 257.

12. Thurber, *My Life*, 12.

13. Ibid., 13.

14. Ibid., 42, 45.

15. Thurber, *Credos*, 89.

16. Thurber, *My Life*, 17–26.

17. Ibid., 52.

18. Ibid., 96.

19. Ibid., 94, 96, 107.

20. James Thurber, *The Middle-Aged Man on the Flying Trapeze* (New York: Harper and Brothers, 1935), 204–14. "The Greatest Man in the World" should also be compared to Fitzgerald's scathing criticism of modern America and the American Dream in *The Great Gatsby* (New York: Charles Scribner's, 1925).

21. James Thurber, *The Last Flower* (New York: Harper and Row, 1939), unpaginated.

22. Thurber, *Fables,* 99.

23. Ibid., 96.

24. Ibid., 46.

25. James Thurber, *My World—And Welcome to It* (New York: Harbrace Paperbound Library, 1969), 83.

26. Kenneth Burke, "Thurber Perfects Mind Cure," in *The Critic as Artist* (New York: Liverright, 1972), 305.

27. Thurber, *Men, Women, and Dogs,* 143, 30, 39, 44, and 58.

28. Ibid., 119, 67.

29. James Thurber, *The White Deer* (New York: Harcourt, 1963). The sophisticated language and style of this book mark it as a fairy tale for adults and not a book for children. Richard Tobias also regards the book in this light. Mrs. Thurber confirms that, of all his fairy tales, Thurber intended only *The Great Quillow* to be equally suited to children and adults (Interview with author, 2 Dec. 1973).

30. Thurber, *White Deer,* 5, 45, and 111.

31. Ibid., 63 and 71.

32. Morsberger (*James Thurber*) discusses Thurber's "little man" in his historical context, especially regarding Benchley's influence. I am suggesting Thurber's place in an even broader cultural tradition, however. Think, for example, of Hawthorne's indictment of "science" in the character of Holgrave (*The House of Seven Gables*) and in "The Birthmark"; of Thoreau's retreat from "progress" in *Walden.* Tobias also briefly refers to what he calls Thurber's "comedy of the two cultures" (*Art of James Thurber,* 170).

33. See Chapter 3 for a fuller discussion of this subject.

34. I am dealing here primarily with the first section of this collection. The second half is comprised mainly of short stories that I will not discuss here because they do not relate to Thurber's criticism of science.

35. James Thurber, *Let Your Mind Alone!* (New York: Grosset and Dunlap, 1960), 3.

36. Ibid., 11, 18.

37. Friedrich, "James Thurber": 167.

38. Thurber, *Let Your Mind Alone!,* 41, 42.

39. Ibid., 43, 44.

40. Ibid., 67, 68.

41. Ibid., 159–62.

42. Walter Blair, *Horse Sense in American Humor* (Chicago: University of Chicago Press, 1942), 289–93.

43. Thurber, *Let Your Mind Alone!,* 223–34.

44. Thurber, *My World,* 11, 115–16.

45. Thurber, *Let Your Mind Alone!,* 28.

46. In Thurber, *The Beast in Me and Other Animals* (New York: Harcourt, 1948), 173–88. See also Thurber, "Statement," in *I Believe,* ed. Fadiman, 295–300; "The Human Being and the Dinosaur" and "The Sea and the Shore," in *Further Fables; Beast in Me,* passim; and "After the Steppe Cat, What?," in *Let Your Mind Alone!*

47. *Selected Letters of James Thurber,* ed. Helen Thurber and Edward Weeks (Boston: Little, Brown, 1981), 11.

48. Thurber, *White Deer,* 44, 45.

49. Thurber, "Statement," in *I Believe,* ed. Fadiman, 295–300.

50. Thurber, *Further Fables,* 103.

51. Thurber, *Lanterns,* 53.

52. Thurber, *Years with Ross,* 7, 8.

53. This marvelous put-down is from the Monroe stories in *The Owl in the Attic & Other Perplexities* (New York: Harper and Brothers, 1931), 30. See also, "The Car We Had to Push," in *My Life;* "Mr. Pendly and the Poindexter" and "Smashup," in *Middle-Aged Man;* and "The Secret Life of Walter Mitty," in *My World.*

54. Thurber, *My Life,* 31.

55. Thurber, *My Life,* 33.

56. Katherine Kent Child Walker, "The Total Depravity of Inanimate Things," in *Mark Twain's Library of Humor* (New York: Charles L. Webster Company, 1888), 435–46.

57. Morsberger, *James Thurber,* 22. This point was also made earlier by Walter Blair in *Horse Sense.*

58. Mrs. Thurber confirms the reader's suspicions on this, saying that this aspect of Thurber's created world was closely connected to his actual difficulty with anything mechanical. (Interview with author, 2 Dec. 1973). See also *Selected Letters of James Thurber,* 31–33.

59. Thurber, *My Life,* 27–36.

60. Tommy Trinway and Mr. Pendly from *Middle-Aged Man* and, of course, Walter Mitty in *My World.*

61. Thurber, *Let Your Mind Alone!,* 57–65.

62. Ibid., 57, 58.

63. Thurber, *Further Fables,* 94.

64. Thurber, *My World,* 72–82.

65. See "I come from haunts of coot and hern!" and "ooooo, guesties!" in *Men, Women, and Dogs;* this most comprehensive of Thurber's cartoon collections is filled with drawings of aggressive and active women.

66. Thurber, *My World,* 80.

67. See Holmes, *Clocks of Columbus,* 131.

68. Interview with author, 2 Dec. 1973.

69. Thurber, *Men, Women, and Dogs,* 61, 65, 113, 121.

70. Ibid., 21, 31, 62, 66, 70, 87, 93, 107, 123, 125, 127.

71. Thurber, "The Race of Life," in *Seal in the Bedroom,* unpaginated.

72. Thurber, *Men, Women, and Dogs,* 118; reproduced on the cover of *Thurber Carnival.*

73. Thurber, *Owl in the Attic,* 19, 22, 64, 35.

74. Morsberger, *James Thurber,* 68; W. H. Auden, *The Dyer's Hand and Other Essays* (New York: Random House, 1962), 377.

75. See especially *Owl in the Attic's* Monroe stories.

76. Henry James, *The Portrait of a Lady* (Boston: Houghton Mifflin,

1956), 356. Isabel Archer is one of James's strong, likeable women. I am not suggesting that she or her "type" in the Jamesian novel is the basis for Thurber's scathing portrait. Rather, the Thurber woman seems a cousin of those crass female characters against whom Archer is measured.

77. Thurber, *Let Your Mind Alone!*, 83, 87, 89.

78. Ibid., 112–17.

79. Thurber, *The Thurber Carnival* (New York: Dell, 1963), 36, 38.

80. Thurber, *Is Sex Necessary? or, Why You Feel the Way You Do* (Delta Book edition of 1929 text; New York: Dell, 1963), 36, 38.

81. James Thurber and Elliott Nugent, *The Male Animal* (New York: Random House, 1940).

82. See Thurber, *Years with Ross*, 189. Thurber enjoyed remembering that Ross thought a happy marriage to Helen Wismer would ruin Thurber's fiction. The link between biography and art is always an ambiguous one, of course, but Thurber's personal life, as well as the life of the world, during these years must have had an effect on his work.

83. I am using this term with caution, since Thurber is close to the classical comic plot only in his fairy tales.

84. Thurber, *White Deer*, 101, 111, 113, 115.

85. Thurber, *13 Clocks* (New York: Simon and Schuster, 1950), 17.

86. Ibid., 118.

87. Thurber, *The Wonderful O* (New York: Simon and Schuster, 1957), 31, 32.

88. Cf. T. S. Eliot, "Ash Wednesday": "Because I cannot hope to turn again / Consequently I rejoice, having to construct something/ Upon which to rejoice," in *Complete Poems and Plays*.

89. Thurber, *Lanterns*, 61.

90. Thurber, *The Thurber Album* (New York: Simon and Schuster, 1952), 140, 137, 86, 96, 102.

91. Thurber, *Let Your Mind Alone!*, 230. Tobias understands Thurber's meaning very differently (*Art of James Thurber*, 232).

92. Thurber, *Further Fables*, 2, 3.

93. Thurber, *Lanterns*, 19.

94. James Thurber, *Thurber on Humor* (Cleveland: World Publishing Company, n.d.), 10.

95. See Morsberger, *James Thurber*, 89; Holmes, *Clocks of Columbus*, 140; and Tobias, *Art of James Thurber*, 46, for characteristic comments.

96. Thurber, *Thurber's Dogs*, 9.

97. *Thurber's Dogs* should be consulted for a thorough survey of Thurber's pieces about the species.

98. Thurber, *Thurber's Dogs*, 205.

99. Holmes, *Clocks of Columbus*, 140.

100. Thurber, *Thurber's Dogs*, 122.

101. Ibid., 223.

102. James Thurber, Interview with Harvey Breit, *New York Times Magazine*, 4 Dec. 1949, 79.

103. Thurber, *Let Your Mind Alone!*, 84.

104. Thurber, *Men, Women, and Dogs*, 105, 96, 194.
105. In Thurber, *Seal in the Bedroom*, unpaginated.
106. Thurber, *Men, Women, and Dogs*, 36. This drawing was reused several times, most notably on the title page of *Middle-Aged Man*.
107. Thurber, Interview with Harvey Breit, 4 Dec. 1949, 78.
108. Thurber, *Lanterns*, 204, 206, 207.
109. Thurber, *Last Flower*, unpaginated.
110. Thurber, *13 Clocks*, 17, 18, 110.
111. Thurber, *Let Your Mind Alone!*, 235, 239. I read Thurber's portrayal of urban America differently than many of his critics, including Walter Blair (see *Horse Sense*, passim).
112. Thurber, *Lanterns*, 149–52.
113. Thurber, *Fables*, 9, 10.
114. Thurber, *Further Fables*, 65–69.
115. Thurber, *Beast in Me*, ix.

3. Corpus Mentis

1. *Letters of James Thurber*, 11.
2. Kenneth MacLean, "Imagination of James Thurber," *Canadian Forum* 33 (Dec. 1953): 201; De Vries, "James Thurber: The Comic Prufrock," 156.
3. Morsberger, *James Thurber*, 44–66; Tobias, *Art of James Thurber*, 131–33.
4. Wordsworth defined poetry as "the spontaneous overflow of power-ful feelings: it takes its origin from emotion recollected in tranquility," in "Preface" to *Lyrical Ballads*, in Walter J. Bate, *Criticism: The Major Texts* (New York: Harcourt, Brace, Jovanovich, 1952), 344. Holmes, *Clocks of Columbus*, 330.
5. See "Introduction" to *Owl in the Attic*. White seems to have been the first to notice Thurber's similarity to Henry James. Mrs. Thurber has confirmed the extent and seriousness of Thurber's interest in James, including his regular rereading of James's novels, (interview with author, 2 Dec. 1973).
6. Henry James, *The Future of the Novel*, edited by Leon Edel (New York: Vintage Books, 1956), 12.
7. Ibid., 50, 12.
8. These characteristic Jamesian "centers" are in, respectively, *The Portrait of a Lady* and *The Ambassadors*.
9. Francis Downing, "Thurber," *Commonweal* 41 (9 Mar. 1945): 518.
10. Henri Bergson, "Laughter," in Sypher, *Comedy*, ed. 71, 77.
11. Thurber, *My Life*, 112.
12. Ibid., 17, 25.
13. Ibid., 16, 20; italics mine.
14. Ibid., 21.
15. Ibid.
16. Ibid., 21, 23, 24, 26; italics mine.
17. Ibid., 26; italics mine.
18. Ibid.

19. Ibid. It is interesting that the story itself fits Thurber's metaphor for comprehending crazy events; it is constructed like a jigsaw puzzle, of disparate and incomprehensible parts presented to the reader.

20. Ibid., 31, 34, 51, 50.

21. Ibid., 43.

22. See Ibid., 38–47, for a similar dramatization of the clash between expectation and reality in "The Day the Dam Broke."

23. Ibid., 64. Thurber uses this term in a different context here, referring to his linguistic confusion as a "trivial mental tic," but the term seems remarkably appropriate to all the quirks displayed by characters in *My Life*.

24. Thurber, *Fables*, 43.

25. Ibid.

26. Ibid.

27. Ibid.

28. Timing and the manipulation of tension in this fable help to create the half wince, half laugh that is the characteristic response to Thurber's work.

29. Thurber, *My Life*, 115.

30. Thurber, *Fables for Our Time*, 65, 66.

31. Ibid.

32. Ibid.

33. Ibid., 63.

34. Ibid., 13.

35. Thurber, *Further Fables*, 15–17.

36. This is not to claim, of course, that Thurber's fables are equivalent to this long and complex novel, but only to say that, in their extreme economy, these fables are able to create one of the novel's effects. Thurber's deft manipulation of point of view must have been learned at least partially from Henry James.

37. Thurber, *Further Fables*, 17.

38. Ibid., 74–78.

39. Ibid., 4–8.

40. Thurber, *The White Deer*, 25, 27, 33.

41. Ibid., 85.

42. Thurber, *Let Your Mind Alone!*, 230.

43. See Morsberger, *James Thurber*, chapter on "The Romantic Imagination," for a good discussion of this aspect of Thurber's art.

44. Thurber, *Let Your Mind Alone!*, 22, 23. See also Chapter 2, "Grisly Gadgets and Systemless Systems," for a discussion of this subject.

45. Thurber, *Let Your Mind Alone!*, 242, 243, 241.

46. Leo Tolstoy, *The Death of Ivan Ilych* (New York: New American Library, 1960), 104: "Ivan Ilych's life had been most simple and most ordinary and therefore most terrible."

47. Thurber, *My World*, 73.

48. F. O. Matthiessen, "Alienation of the Writer," in *Responsibilities of the Critic* (New York: Oxford University Press, 1952), 137.

49. See Thurber, *Let Your Mind Alone!*, 242, 243, 241.

50. Thurber, *Middle-Aged Man,* 75, 76, 77, 79.
51. "Our New Sense of the Comic," in Sypher, *Comedy,* 198.
52. James Thurber, *Many Moons* (New York: Harcourt, Brace, and World, 1943), unpaginated.
53. Thurber, *13 Clocks,* 34, 118, 123.
54. James, "The Art of Fiction," in *The Future of the Novel,* 12.
55. Morsberger, *James Thurber,* 64.
56. Thurber, *Thurber Carnival,* 33, 34.
57. Thurber, *Middle-Aged Man,* 160–61, 161–62. "The Black Magic of Barney Haller," one of Thurber's finest and most original short stories, was based upon an actual gardener employed by the Thurbers one summer (author's interview with Mrs. James Thurber, 2 Dec. 1973).
58. Thurber, *Middle-Aged Man,* 163.
59. Ibid., 161.
60. In Thurber, *Let Your Mind Alone!* and *The Beast in Me.*
61. Thurber, *Beast in Me,* 120–26.
62. Ibid., 126.
63. Sypher, *Comedy,* 213, 201.
64. Thurber, "Statement," in *I Believe,* 295.
65. William Shakespeare, *The Complete Works,* ed. Alfred Harbage (Baltimore: Penquin Books, 1969). These lines are from *The Tempest* (IV, i, 148–58).

4. The Language of Confusion

1. Walter Percy, *The Message in the Bottle* (New York: Farrar, Strauss & Giroux, 1977), 17. I am indebted to Percy not only for suggesting this appropriate term, but also for his generally insightful discussion of language in these essays.
2. Malcolm Cowley, "Lions and Lemmings, Toads and Tigers," *The Reporter* 15 (13 Dec. 1956): 43. Cowley's reviews were consistently among the most perceptive analyses of Thurber's work.
3. See Blair, *Horse Sense,* 284–85; and John Updike, "Indignation of a Senior Citizen," *New York Times Book Review,* 25 Nov. 1962, 5.
4. Thurber, interview with Harvey Breit, 4 Dec. 1949, 79.
5. James Thurber, *Alarms and Diversions* (New York: Harper and Brothers, 1957), 66.
6. Random comments about Thurber's style are scattered throughout his reviews. Only one sustained scholarly study of his language and style has been attempted, and that concerns a very limited range of his work: the nonfiction short piece known as the "casual." See Baldwin, *Congruous Laughter.* See also Michael Burnett, "Thurber's Style," in *Thurber: A Collection of Critical Essays,* ed. Charles Holmes (New York: Prentice-Hall, 1974), for a consideration of style in one of Thurber's works, *My Life.*
7. James Thurber, *My Life,* 17, 24. The qualifying pattern of those statements might remind the reader of Mark Twain, who was also using

qualification partially for comic timing. See *Huckleberry Finn*, in *The Portable Mark Twain*, ed. Bernard De Voto (New York: Viking, 1968), 193–94: "That book was made by Mr. Mark Twain and he told the truth, *mainly*. . . . [it] is mostly a true book, *with some stretchers*. (Italics mine.)

8. Thurber, *Thurber Country*, 103, 110.

9. There will be no attempt to ascertain Thurber's similarity to standard "*New Yorker* style." This is covered in Baldwin, *Congruous Laughter*.

10. Thurber and White are representatives of a tradition of experimentation in American humor. See Jesse Bier, *The Rise and Fall of American Humor* (Chicago: Holt, Rinehart, and Winston, 1968), 17.

11. Thurber shares this predilection for parody with other humorists, and comic writers generally. Pretension and bombast, as well as fuzziness of language and thought, led writers from Shakespeare and Fielding to Wilde and White to write parodies.

12. W. H. Auden, *Dyer's Hand*, 382.

13. James Thurber and E. B. White, *Is Sex Necessary?*, 49. Thurber wrote the preface and glossary, chapters 1, 3, 5, and 7, and did all of the drawings for this collaborative effort.

14. Baldwin, *Congruous Laughter*, 92.

15. Thurber, *Is Sex Necessary?*, xxiii.

16. Ibid., 183–87; see Northrup Frye, "The Mythos of Spring: Comedy," in *Comedy*, ed. Robert Corrigan, 147.

17. Thurber, *Is Sex Necessary?*, 118.

18. Thurber, *Owl in the Attic*, 12, 14, 20.

19. Ibid., 80.

20. Baldwin, "Congruous Laughter," 89.

21. Thurber, *Owl in the Attic*, 100–1.

22. Ibid., 102, 105–6.

23. Ibid., 111.

24. Thurber, *Thurber Carnival*, 33, 34.

25. Thurber, *My Life*, 45.

26. Ibid., 63, 64.

27. Auden, *Dyer's Hand*, 379. Although some critics have noticed the similarities between Joyce and Thurber after the onset of blindness, no one has acknowledged the Joycean handling of this passage. The point is not, of course, that they were both blind writers, but that blindness seems to have affected them in similar ways.

28. Holmes, *Clocks of Columbus*, 178.

29. Thurber, *Middle-Aged Man*, 160, 162, 160.

30. Ibid., 163.

31. See "A Mad Tea Party," in Lewis Carroll, *The Annotated Alice* (New York: New American Library, 1960).

32. Thurber, *Middle-Aged Man*, 164.

33. Ibid., 175.

34. Thurber, *Let Your Mind Alone!*, 41, 26, 19, 49.

35. George Orwell, *A Collection of Essays* (New York: Doubleday,

1964). Orwell said, "if thought corrupts language, language also corrupts thought," 174.

36. Thurber, *Let Your Mind Alone!*, 74.

37. Ibid., 75, 76.

38. Ibid., 149.

39. Percy, *The Message in the Bottle*, 64–82. Percy makes the point that language mistakes can be thus liberating.

40. Bernstein, *Thurber*, 318.

41. Dorothy Parker, "Introduction" to Thurber, *Seal in the Bedroom*, vii.

42. See Thurber, *Men, Women, and Dogs*, 67, 70, 81, 90, 122, 130.

43. Thurber, *Last Flower*, unpaginated.

44. This push toward the "typical" or the "social," in their purest senses, is evident in other twentieth-century writers. A writer very different from Thurber, Thomas Mann, reflected on this change in his own work by saying: "I had suffered in my own person, with whatever violent struggles, the compulsion of the times, which forced us out of the metaphysical and individual stage into the social." He also asserted that "these interests of today are not inappropriate tastes for a time of life that may legitimately begin to divorce itself from the peculiar and individual, and turn its gaze upon the typical—which is, after all, the mythical." *A Sketch of My Life* (New York: Knopf, 1970), 65, 67.

45. Thurber, *Fables*, 61.

46. Thurber, *My World*, 3, 5, 7.

47. Thurber, *My World*, 18–32.

48. See James Ellis, "The Allusions in 'The Secret Life of Walter Mitty,'" *English Journal* 54 (1965): 311–13; Thurber, *My World*, 72, 75.

49. Thurber, *Many Moons*, unpaginated.

50. James Thurber, *The Great Quillow* (New York: Harcourt, Brace, Jovanovich, 1944), 5.

51. Thurber, *White Deer*, 35.

52. Ibid., 15.

53. Ibid., 19.

54. Ibid., 45, 68, 69. Thurber persistently borrowed from popular culture (see "Tea for One," in *Further Fables*, for example.)

55. Ibid., 54, 55–56.

56. See Tobias, *Art of James Thurber*. Tobias has the fullest discussion of Thurber's use of classic comic rituals, although I think that he over-emphasizes this aspect of Thurber's art.

57. Thurber would seem to have much in common with the nineteenth-century writers he grew up reading. His view of the poet is quite close to Shelley's and Arnold's, for example.

58. Thurber, *13 Clocks*, 50, 24, 73.

59. Ibid., 73.

60. Ibid., 31.

61. Cowley, *The Literary Situation*, 92.

62. Cf. Thurber, *Beast in Me*, 128, 133, 146, 147; and Henry James,

Great Short Works of Henry James (New York: Harper and Row, 1966), 450. Thurber's work generally reflects some of the cadence of James's complex style.

63. Thurber, *Beast in Me,* 133.

64. Ibid., 146, 147.

65. Cf. Tenniel's drawing of "The Mock Turtle," a similar image in Carroll's *Alice;* and Thurber, *Beast in Me,* 151–68.

66. Thurber, *Beast in Me,* 151–58.

67. Thurber, *Thurber Album,* 179, 185–86.

68. Thurber, *Thurber Country,* 11, 152.

69. Thurber, *Alarms,* 18–25.

70. Thurber, *Lanterns,* 40.

71. Thurber, *Lanterns,* 59, 110, 60.

72. See Ibid., 127, 167–81.

73. Thurber, *Further Fables,* 3, 94, 158.

74. Ibid., 112.

75. Ibid., 110.

76. Ibid., 77, 59, 17, 143.

77. Cowley, "Lions and Lemmings," 44.

78. Thurber, *Further Fables,* 172–74.

79. Thurber, *Further Fables,* 174.

80. Thurber, *Wonderful O,* 30, 26.

81. Ibid., 50.

82. Ibid., 28, 29.

83. Ibid., 46.

84. Ibid., 60–61.

85. Ibid., 65.

86. See Thurber, "My Senegalese Birds and Siamese Cats," in *Lanterns;* and "The Other Room," in *Credos.*

87. Thurber seems to combine the two characteristics of American humor identified by Constance Rourke in her *American Humor,* 134. She considers these to be the ebullience of Western humor and the classic economy of Yankee speech. If what Rourke concludes about the tradition is true, it would seem that Thurber is our quintessential humorist.

88. Cowley, "Lions and Lemmings," 43.

5. A Bright and Melancholy Spectacle

1. E. B. White, "Introduction," in Thurber, *Owl in the Attic,* xiii.

2. Thurber, *My Life,* 11.

3. See Tobias, *Art of James Thurber,* for a discussion of Thurber focusing on a traditional "comic" interpretation of his work; and Holmes, *Clocks of Columbus,* 330.

4. By "high comedy" I simply mean a rather urbane comedy, relying heavily on verbal wit and irony for its impact and meaning.

5. Eastman, *Enjoyment of Laughter*, 343. I am contrasting Thurber's understanding of humor with Bergson's theory of the comic, for example. Thurber's definition of "tragicomedy" is rather loose; his term does not imply any special characteristics of form, but rather describes work which causes both laughter and tears, or joy and sadness, in the reader.

6. See Fitzgerald, *Gatsby*, 136, 179.

7. Thurber, *Owl in the Attic*, 4, 64, 65, 71.

8. Thurber, *My Life*, 9, 10, 13.

9. Ibid., 88, 98, 111.

10. Thurber, *Let Your Mind Alone!*, 83.

11. In *The Ambassadors* and "The Beast in the Jungle."

12. Thurber, *Let Your Mind Alone!*, 192.

13. Ibid., 229.

14. See especially "One is a Wanderer" and "The Evening's at Seven," in Thurber, *Middle-Aged*.

15. Ibid., 191, 221; see also "The Black Magic of Barney Haller."

16. Thurber, *White Deer*, 26.

17. Thurber, *13 Clocks*, 20, 110.

18. Thurber, *Wonderful O*, 1, 28.

19. Ibid., 65, 64.

20. William Butler Yeats, "The Second Coming," lines 3–4, in *The Collected Poems of W. B. Yeats* (New York: Macmillan), 956.

21. See especially Chapters 9, 17, and 19 in Twain, *Huckleberry Finn*.

22. Thurber, *My World*, 80.

23. Thurber, *Further Fables*, 197, 59, 86, 112.

24. Thurber, *Lanterns*, xv, 150.

25. Ibid., 58, 59.

26. Thurber, *Credos*, 90.

27. Thurber, *Credos*, 57, 97, 86.

28. William Shakespeare, Sonnet 18. One might also think of Keats's "Ode on a Grecian Urn."

Epilogue

1. Thurber, *Lanterns*, 148.

Bibliography

Primary Sources

BOOKS

THURBER, JAMES. *Alarms and Diversions*. New York: Harper and Brothers, 1957.

_____. *The Beast in Me and Other Animals*. New York: Harcourt, Brace and World, Inc., 1948.

_____. *Credos and Curios*. New York: Harper and Row, 1962.

_____. *Fables for Our Time and Famous Poems Illustrated*. New York: Harper and Row, 1974.

_____. *Further Fables for Our Time*. Illustrated by the author. New York: Simon and Schuster, 1956.

_____. *The Great Quillow*. Illustrated by Doris Lee. New York: Harcourt, Brace, Jovanovich, 1944.

_____. *Is Sex Necessary? or, Why You Feel the Way You Do*. (With E. B. White) Delta Book edition of 1929 text. New York: Dell Publishing Company, 1963.

_____. *Lanterns & Lances*. New York: Harper and Row, 1961.

_____. *The Last Flower*. New York: Harper and Row, 1939.

_____. *Let Your Mind Alone!* Universal Library Paperbound printing from 1937 edition. New York: Grosset and Dunlap, 1960.

_____. *Many Moons*. Illustrated by Louis Slobodkin. New York: Harcourt, Brace, and World, 1943.

_____. *Men, Women, and Dogs*. New York: Harcourt, Brace, and Company, 1943.

_____. *The Middle-Aged Man on the Flying Trapeze*. New York: Harper and Brothers, 1935.

_____. *My Life and Hard Times*. Bantam Paperback edition of 1933 text. New York: Bantam Books, 1971.

_____. *My World—and Welcome to It*. New York: Harbrace Paperbound Library printing from 1942 edition, 1969.

_____. *The Owl in the Attic & Other Perplexities.* New York: Harper and Brothers, 1931.

_____. *The Seal in the Bedroom.* New York: Harper and Row, 1932.

_____. *Selected Letters of James Thurber.* Edited by Helen Thurber and Edward Weeks. Boston: Little, Brown, 1981.

_____. *The 13 Clocks.* Illustrated by Marc Simont. New York: Simon and Schuster, 1950.

_____. *The Thurber Album.* A Touchstone Book. New York: Simon and Schuster, 1952.

_____. *The Thurber Carnival.* A Delta Book printing from the 1945 edition. New York: Dell Publishing, 1964.

_____. *Thurber and Company.* With an Introduction by Helen Thurber. New York: Harper and Row, 1966.

_____. *Thurber Country.* New York: Simon and Schuster, 1953.

_____. *Thurber's Dogs.* A Touchstone Book. New York: Simon and Schuster, 1955.

_____. *Thurber on Humor.* Cleveland: World Publishing Co., n.d.

_____. *The White Deer.* With Drawings by the Author. Harbrace Paperbound Library edition of 1945 text. New York: Harcourt, Brace, and World, Inc., 1963.

_____. *The Wonderful O.* Illustrated by Marc Simont. New York: Simon and Schuster, 1957.

_____. *The Years With Ross.* With Drawings by the Author. Boston: Little, Brown, and Company, 1959.

PLAYS

_____. *The Male Animal.* (With Elliott Nugent) New York: Random House, 1940.

_____. *A Thurber Carnival.* (Revue) New York: Samuel French, Inc., 1962.

UNCOLLECTED PERIODICAL ARTICLES AND STORIES

_____. "Advice from a Blind Writer." *Newsweek,* 1 Feb. 1960, 55.

_____. "Books I Have Liked." *New York Herald Tribune Book Review Section,* 1 Dec. 1957, 8.

_____. "The Character of Catastrophe." *New Yorker,* 28 May 1938, 17–18.

_____. "Essay on Dignity." *New Yorker,* 4 Jan. 1936, 19–20.

_____. "The Future of Psychoanalysis (More or Less in the Manner of the Science Itself)." *New Yorker,* 19 July 1930, 16–17.

_____. "If You Ask Me." *PM,* 24 Feb. 1941, 19.

_____. "If You Want to be a Writer." *Writer's Digest,* Sept. 1961, 78.

_____. "James Thurber." *New York Herald Tribune Book Review Section,* 8 Oct. 1950, 4.

_____. "James Thurber on the Perplexities of Educating a Daughter." *Chicago Tribune Magazine,* 26 May 1963, 16, 18, 20, 22, 24–25.

_____. "Notes for a Proletarian Novel." *New Yorker,* 9 June 1934, 15–16.

_____. "The Quality of Mirth." *New York Times,* 21 Feb. 1960, sec. 2, pp. 1, 4.

_____. "Recollections of Henry James." *New Yorker,* 17 June 1933, 11–13.

_____. "Self-Portraits and Self-Appraisals." *Harper's,* August 1966, 44–45.

_____. "Some Notes on the Married Life of Birds." *New Yorker,* 27 June 1931, 13–14.

_____. "State of Humor in States." *New York Times,* 4 Sept. 1960, sec. 3, p. 3.

_____. "Taps at Assembly." *New Republic,* 9 Feb. 1942, 106, 211–12.

_____. "The Threefold Problem of World Economic Cooperation (By Six or Eight Writers for the "Times" Magazine section, All Writing at Once)." *New Yorker,* 5 August 1933, 19–20.

_____. "Tom the Young Kidnapper; or Pay Up and Live: A Kind of Horatio Alger Story." *New Yorker,* 10 June 1933, 14–16.

_____. "What Price Conquest?" *New Republic,* 16 Mar. 1942, 370.

_____. "Wizard of Chitenango." *New Republic,* 12 Dec. 1934, 14.

INTERVIEWS

Interview with Harvey Breit. "Mr. Thurber Observes a Serene Birthday." *New York Times Magazine,* 4 Dec. 1949, 79.

Interview with R. T. Allen. "Women Have No Sense of Humor, But They Don't Seem to Know It." *MacLean's Magazine,* 1 June 1951, 18, 19.

Interview with Harvey Breit. "Talk with James Thurber." *New York Times Book Review,* 29 June 1952, 19.

Interview, "Says Superwoman Will Force Peace." *AP News,* 22 Aug. 1953. Reprinted in *Columbus Dispatch,* 23 Aug. 1953, 7.

Interview with George Plimpton and Max Steele. "The Art of Fiction." *Paris Review,* 10 (Fall 1955): 35–49.

"James Thurber in Conversation with Alistair Cooke." *The Atlantic* 198 (Aug. 1956): 36–40.

Interview with Maurice Dolbier. "A Sunday Afternoon with Mr. Thurber." *New York Herald Tribune Book Review,* 5 Nov. 1957, 2.

Interview with Henry Brandon. "Everybody is Getting Serious." *New Republic* 138 (26 May 1958): 37.

Interview with Arthur Gelb. "Thurber Intends to Relax Till '61." *New York Times,* 28 Mar. 1960, 35.

Interview with W. J. Weatherby. "A Man of Words." *The Manchester Guardian Weekly,* 9 Feb. 1961, 13.

Secondary Sources

BOOKS

Auden, W. H. *The Dyer's Hand and Other Essays.* New York: Random House, 1962.

Baker, Samuel Bernard. "James Thurber: The Columbus Years." M.A. thesis, Ohio State University, 1962.

Baldwin, Alice Breme. "Congruous Laughter: The Linguistic Form of Humor in James Thurber's Casual Essays." Ph.D. diss., University of Massachusetts, 1970.

Bate, Walter J., ed. *Criticism: The Major Texts.* New York: Harcourt, Brace, Jovanovich, 1970.

Benchley, Robert. *My Ten Years in a Quandary and How They Grew.* New York and London: Harper and Brothers, 1956.

Bernstein, Burton. *Thurber: A Biography.* New York: Dodd, Mead, 1975.

Bier, Jesse. *The Rise and Fall of American Humor.* Chicago: Holt, Rinehart and Winston, 1968.

Black, Stephen Ames. *James Thurber: His Masquerades.* The Hague: Mouton, 1970.

Blair, Walter. *Horse Sense in American Humor.* Chicago: University of Chicago Press, 1942.

_____. *Native American Humor.* New York: American Book Company, 1937.

Bohn, William E. *I Remember America.* New York: Macmillan Company, 1962.

Bowden, Edwin T. *James Thurber: A Bibliography.* Columbus: Ohio State University Press, 1968.

Comedy. "An Essay on Comedy," George Meredith. "Laughter," Henri Bergson. With an Introduction and Appendix by Wylie Sypher. Doubleday Anchor Books. Garden City, New York: Doubleday and Company, Inc., 1956.

Corrigan, Robert W., ed. *Comedy: Meaning and Form.* San Francisco: Chandler Publishing Company, 1965.

Cowley, Malcolm. *The Literary Situation.* New York: Viking Press, 1954.

Eastman, Max. *Enjoyment of Laughter.* New York: Simon and Schuster, 1936.

Eliot, T. S. *The Complete Poems and Plays 1909–1950.* New York: Harcourt, Brace, and World, Inc., 1952.

Enck, John J., and others, eds. *The Comic in Theory and Practice.* New York, 1960.

Fadiman, Clifton, ed. *I Believe.* New York: Simon and Schuster, 1939.

Fielding, Henry. *The Adventures of Joseph Andrews.* Boston: Houghton Mifflin, 1961.

Fitzgerald, F. Scott. *The Great Gatsby.* New York: Charles Scribner's, 1925.

Ford, Corey. *The Time of Laughter.* With a Forward by Frank Sullivan. Boston and Toronto: Little, Brown, and Company, 1967.

Hackett, Francis. *On Judging Books in General and Particular.* New York: John Day Company, 1947.

Harrison, Margaret Case. *The Vicious Circle: The Story of the Algonquin Round Table.* New York: Rinehart and Company, 1951.

Hauck, Richard Boyd. *A Cheerful Nihilism.* Bloomington, Ind.: Indiana University Press, 1971.

Holmes, Charles S. *The Clocks of Columbus: The Literary Career of James Thurber.* New York: Atheneum, 1972.

_____, ed. *Thurber: A Collection of Critical Essays.* Englewood Cliffs, New Jersey: Prentice-Hall, 1974.

James, Henry. *The Future of the Novel.* Edited by Leon Edel. New York: Vintage Books, 1956.

————. *Great Short Works of Henry James.* New York: Harper and Row, 1966.

————. *The Portrait of a Lady.* Riverside Edition. Boston: Houghton Mifflin Company, 1956.

Lauritsen, John Roland. "A Preface to Thurber: Mind and Morality in the Early Collected Works, 1929–1937." *Dissertation Abstracts International* 40: 4597A.

Mann, Thomas. *A Sketch of My Life.* New York: Knopf, 1970.

Morsberger, Robert E. *James Thurber.* Twayne's United States Authors Series No. 62. New York: Twayne, 1964.

————. "The Predicaments and Perplexities of James Thurber." Ph.D. diss., University of Iowa, 1956.

Murrell, William. *A History of American Graphic Humor.* 2 vols. New York: Whitney Museum of American Art, 1932.

Nitsaisook, Malee. "An Analysis of Certain Stylistic Features of Selected Literary Works and Their Relationship to Readability." *Dissertation Abstracts International* 40: 4453A.

Percy, Walker. *The Message in the Bottle.* New York: Farrar, Straus and Giroux, 1975.

Petrullo, Helen Batchelor. "Satire and Freedom: Sinclair Lewis, Nathaniel West, and James Thurber." Ph.D. diss., Syracuse University, 1967.

Rourke, Constance. *American Humor.* New York: Harcourt, Brace, and Company, 1931.

Ryberg, Charles Lewis. "Humor and Pathos in James Thurber's Short Stories." M.A. thesis, Southern Illinois University, 1959.

Segal, Lili Packman. "James Thurber Literary Humorist." M.A. thesis, University of Louisville, 1970.

Shakespeare, William. *The Complete Works.* Edited by Alfred Harbage. Baltimore: Penguin Books, 1969.

Spitzmiller, Olive Hershey. "The Little Man and the Unicorn: The Creative Imagination in James Thurber's Fiction." *Dissertation Abstracts International* 40: 4046A.

Stroud, Beverly Jean. "An Analysis and Production Book of *The Male Animal.*" M.A. thesis, Ohio State University, 1950.

Tobias, Richard C. *The Art of James Thurber.* Athens, Ohio: Ohio University Press, 1969.

Twain, Mark. *The Adventures of Huckleberry Finn,* in Bernard De Voto, ed., *The Portable Mark Twain.* New York: Viking, 1968.

———. *Mark Twain's Library of Humor.* New York: Charles L. Webster Company, 1888.

Van Doren, Mark. *The Autobiography of Mark Van Doren.* New York: Harcourt, Brace, and Company, 1958.

White, E. B. *The Second Tree from the Corner.* New York: Perennial Library, 1965.

———. *A Subtreasury of American Humor.* New York: Modern Library, 1948.

Yates, Norris. *The American Humorist Conscience of the Twentieth Century.* Ames, Iowa: Iowa State University Press, 1964.

———. *Robert Benchley.* Twayne's United States Authors Series No. 138. New York: Twayne, 1968.

SERIALS AND PAMPHLETS

Acosta, E. C. "James Thurber, I Love You." *Saturday Evening Post,* 20 May 1967, 88–89.

Albertini, Virgil R. "James Thurber and the Short Story." *Northwest Missouri State College Studies* 28 (1 Aug. 1964).

———. "A Study of James Thurber's Fables." *Northwest Missouri State College Studies* 30 (1 May 1966).

Arnold, Olga. "James Thurber, Humorist." *Amerika* 7 (4 Dec. 1956): 1–8.

Auden, W. H. "The Icon and the Portrait." *The Nation* 150 (13 Jan. 1940): 48.

Baldwin, Alice. "James Thurber's Compounds." *Language and Style* 3 (1970): 185–96.

Benchley, Nathaniel. "If There Is No Human Comedy, It Will Be Necessary to Create One." *New York Herald Tribune Book Review,* 25 Nov. 1962, 3.

Benet, Stephen Vincent and Rosemary. "Thurber: As Unmistakable as a Kangaroo." *New York Herald Tribune Book Review,* 29 Dec. 1940, 6.

Benet, William Rose. "Carnival with Spectres." *The Saturday Review of Literature* 28 (3 Feb. 1945): 9.

Bigda-Peyton, Frances, and Gary Alan Fine. "The Hephaestus Complex: Power Themes in the Life of James Thurber." *Biography* 1, no. 2 (1978): 37–60.

Black, Stephen A. "The Claw of the Sea-Puss: James Thurber's Sense of Experience." *Wisconsin Studies in Contemporary Literature* 5 (1964): 222–36.

————. "Thurber's Education for Hard Times." *University Review* 32 (1966): 257–67.

Booth, T. Y. "The Cliché: A Working Bibliography." *Bulletin of Bibliography* 33 (1960): 61–63.

Brady, Charles A. "What Thurber Saw." *Commonweal* 75 (1961): 274–76.

Brandon, Henry. "A Conversation with James Thurber." *New Republic,* 26 May 1958, 11–16, 57–58.

————. "Thurber Used Humor to Camouflage His Exasperations with the Human Race." *Washington Post,* 5 Nov. 1961, sec. B, p. 4.

Branscomb, Lewis. "James Thurber and Oral History at Ohio State University." *Lost Generation Journal* 3 (1975): 16–19.

Braunlich, Phyllis. "Hot Times in the Catbird Seat." *Lost Generation Journal* 3 (1975): 10–11.

Budd, Nelson H. "Personal Reminiscences of James Thurber." *Ohio State University Monthly* 54 (Jan. 1962): 12–14.

Burke, Kenneth. "Thurber Perfects Mind Cure." in *The Critic as Artist.* New York: Liverright, 1972, 55–59.

Coates, Robert M. "Thurber, Inc." *Saturday Review of Literature* 21 (2 Dec. 1939): 110–14.

Cowley, Malcolm. "James Thurber's Dream Book." *New Republic* 112 (12 Mar. 1945): 362–63.

————. "Lions and Lemmings, Toads and Tigers." *The Reporter* 15 (13 Dec. 1956): 42–44.

————. "Salute to Thurber." *Saturday Review of Literature* 44 (25 Nov. 1961): 14–18, 63–64.

De Vries, Peter. "James Thurber: The Comic Prufrock." *Poetry* 63 (Dec. 1943): 150–59.

Dias, Earl J. "The Upside-Down World of Thurber's 'The Catbird Seat.'" *CEA Critic* 30 (Feb. 1968): 8–9.

Downing, Francis. "Thurber." *Commonweal* 41 (9 Mar. 1945): 518–19.

Elias, Robert H. "James Thurber: The Primitive, the Innocent, and the Individual." *American Scholar* 27 (Summer 1958): 355–63.

Ellis, James. "The Allusions in the 'Secret Life of Walter Mitty.'" *English Journal* 54 (1965): 310–13.

Englund, Ken. "The Secret Life of James Thurber: Fond Recollections of Thurber's Lost Dreams." *Point of View* 1 (Oct. 1963): 13–30.

Fadiman, Clifton. "Reading I've Liked." *Holiday,* March 1963, 56–57.

Feldges, Alfred. "James Thurber: 'The Secret Life of Walter Mitty,' Eine Interpretation." *Die Neueren Sprachen* 42 (1964): 433–40.

Fitzgerald, Gregory. "An Example of Associationism as an Organizational Technique from Thurber's 'Walter Mitty.'" *CEA Critic* 31 (11 Jan. 1969): 13–17.

Follmer, Henrietta. "Thurberism." *Mark Twain Quarterly* 8 (1949): 14–15.

Friedrich, Otto. "James Thurber: A Critical Study." *Discovery* 5 (Jan. 1955): 158–92.

Gannett, Lewis. "James Thurber: Pre-Intentionalist." *New York Herald Tribune Book Review,* 12 Nov. 1954, 5.

Gilder, Rosamund. "Brain and Brawn, Broadway in Review." *Theatre Arts* 24 (March 1940): 58–62.

"Glimpse into Thurber's World." *New York Times Magazine,* 6 Mar. 1960, 18.

Goldwyn, Sam, and James Thurber. "Goldwyn vs. Thurber." *Life,* 18 Aug. 1947, 19–20.

Holmes, Charles S. "James Thurber and the Art of Fantasy." *Yale Review* 55 (Autumn 1965): 17–33.

"James Thurber, Aphorist for an Anxious Age." *Time* 73 (10 Nov. 1961): 81.

"Jim." *Newsweek* 58 (13 Nov. 1961): 35–36.

Kane, Thomas S. "A Note on the Chronology of 'The Catbird Seat.'" *CEA Critic* 30 (April 1968): 8–9.

Klaw, B. "James Thurber, Doodler Extraordinary." *American Heritage* 16 (Feb. 1965): 56–57.

Krutch, Joseph Wood. "Review of the Male Animal." *Nation* 150 (20 Jan. 1940): 81–82.

MacLean, Kenneth. "Imagination of James Thurber." *Canadian Forum* 33 (Dec. 1953): 193, 200–1.

_____. "James Thurber—Portrait of the Dog Artist." *Acta Victorana* 68 (Spring 1944): 5–6.

McCord, David. "Anatomy of Confusion." *Saturday Review of Literature* 36 (5 Dec. 1953): 33.

May, Charles E. "Christian Parody in Thurber's 'You Could Look It Up.'" *Studies in Short Fiction* 15 (1978): 453–54.

"Men, Women, and Thurber." *Time* 42 (15 Nov. 1943): 38.

Morsberger, Robert E. "The World of Walter Mitty." *Utah Academy Proceedings* 38 (1960): 37–43.

Moynihan, Julian. "No Nonsense." *New Statesman* 64 (14 Dec. 1962): 872.

Nugent, Elliott. "James Thurber of Columbus." *Ohio Valley Folk Publications New Series,* no. 95 (April 1962).

———. "Notes on James Thurber, the Man or Men." *New York Times,* 25 Feb. 1940, sec. X, p. 3.

Numasawa, Koji. "Everyman/Schlemiel." *Eigo Seinen* 114 (1968): 516–17.

"Obituary." *The Columbus Dispatch,* 3 Nov. 1961, sec. 1, pp. 1, 6, 10B.

"Obituary." *The New York Times,* 3 Nov. 1961, sec. 1, p. 1.

Pollard, James E. "James Thurber." *Ohio Authors and Their Books.* Edited by William Coyle. Cleveland and New York: World Publishing Company, 1962.

"Portrait." *Vogue* 135 (1 Apr. 1960): 141.

"Priceless Gift of Laughter." *Time* 108 (9 July 1951): 88–90.

Ritchie, J. D. "The Thurber Tranquilizer." *Mark Twain Journal* 13 (1966): 4, 21.

Rutledge, Howard, and Peter Bart. "Urbanity, Inc." *Wiener Slawistisches Jahrbuch,* 30 June 1958.

Satterfield, Leon. "Thurber's 'The Secret Life of Walter Mitty.'" *Explicator* 27, item 57, 1969.

Schlamm, William S. "The Secret Lives of James Thurber." *Freeman* 2 (28 July 1952): 736–38.

School, Peter A. "Thurber's Walter Ego: The Little Man Hero." *Lost Generation Journal* 3 (1975): 8–9.

Sheed, Wilfred. "Thurber Carnival." *Horizon* 13 (Autumn 1971): 16–17.

Smith, Warren A. "Authors and Humanism." *Humanist* 11 (Oct. 1951): 204.

Soellner, Rolf. "James Thurber as a Shakespeare Critic." *Kansas Quarterly* 7, no. 4 (1975): 55–65.

Sundell, Carl. "The Architecture of Walter Mitty's Secret Life." *English Journal* 56 (1967): 1284–87.

Taylor, Wilfrid. "James Thurber." *Rothmill Quarterly,* Autumn-Winter 1958, 94–101.

"That Thurber Woman." *Newsweek* 22 (22 Nov. 1943): 84–86.

Thorpe, Willard. "American Humorists." *University of Minnesota Pamphlets on American Writers,* no. 42. Minneapolis: University of Minnesota Press, 1964.

Thurber, Helen. "Long Time No See." *Ladies Home Journal* 81 (July 1964): 50–51.

"Thurber." *Life* 48 (14 Mar. 1960): 103–8.

"Thurber Amuses People by Making Them Squirm." *Life* 28 (19 Feb. 1945): 12–14.

"Thurber and His Humor. . . . Up with the Chuckle, Down with the Yuk." *Newsweek* 51 (4 Feb. 1957): 52–56.

"Thurber, an Old Hand at Humor with Two Hits on Hand." *Life* 48 (14 Mar. 1960): 103–8.

Tobias, Richard C. "Thurber in Paris: 'Clocks Kept Different Time.'" *Lost Generation Journal* 3 (1975): 2–6.

Treisch, Manfred. "Men and Animals: James Thurber and the Conversion of a Literary Genre." *Shakespeare Studies* (Tokyo) 3 (Spring 1966): 307–13.

Updike, John. "Indignations of a Senior Citizen." *New York Times Book Review,* 25 Nov. 1962, 5.

Weales, Gerald. "The World in Thurber's Fables." *Commonweal* 65 (18 Jan. 1957): 409–11.

White, E. B. "James Thurber." *New Yorker* 37 (11 Nov. 1961): 247.

White, Ruth Y. "Early Thurber." *Life* 8 (22 Apr. 1940): 108–9.

Wilson, Edmund. "Book." *New Yorker* 21 (27 Oct. 1945): 91–94.

Yardley, Jonathan. "Cantankerous, Melancholy, Wild, Sane." *New Republic* 167 (21 Oct. 1972): 36–37.

INTERVIEW

Thurber, Mrs. James. Interview with author. New York, New York, 2 Dec. 1973.

Index